Human Diversity
A Guide for Understanding

Second Edition

Stuart E. Schwartz
University of Florida

Belinda Dunnick Karge
San Diego State University

Craig A. Conley, Managing Editor

McGraw-Hill, Inc.
College Custom Series

New York St. Louis San Francisco Auckland Bogotá
Caracas Lisbon London Madrid Mexico Milan Montreal
New Delhi Paris San Juan Singapore Sydney Tokyo Toronto

D1293980

Human Diversity
A Guide for Understanding

2 3 4 5 6 7 8 9 0 DOC DOC 9 0 9 8 7 6

ISBN 07-057259-3

Editor: Judy T. Ice
Design and Layout: Craig A. Conley
Photography: Kurt Lischka, Louis Mallory, Frank Conley
Sign Language Drawings: Robert Stiff
Cover Design: Pat Koch
Front Cover Photo: Bill Losh/FPG International
Back Cover Photo: Robert Reiff/FPG International
Printer/Binder: R. R. Donnelley and Sons Company

Dedication

In memory of Sylvia and Julius Schwartz

SES

In memory of Clairneil Wayne Dunnick

BDK

Acknowledgements

The development of this book would not have been possible without the support and assistance of many wonderful people. This is our attempt to thank our friends, students, and colleagues for their efforts. You all deserve a great deal of credit for your advice, contributions, and confidence.

Special thanks from SES to:

The many dedicated persons who have served as graduate and undergraduate teaching assistants in *Exceptional People*. You have been a constant inspiration and source of knowledge.

Robert Stiff for his excellent drawings of the sign language figures, and Eduardo Vidal for his contributions to the layout and design of the sign language section.

Ross Papish for kindly contributing information about stereotypes of diverse people.

Lisa Eaton for her valuable content review.

George Schaefer who has provided motivation and reinforcement for this project.

Special thanks from BDK to:

William Frazier, Jeannie Hart, Rocci Montesano, Jae Schmutz, Issac Singer, Michelle Wyman, and all of the Teaching Assistants from San Diego State University who devote their time to assuring *Disability and Society* is a fabulous course.

Michelle Tulenko and Irene Meadows for their research and editorial assistance.

Eric Douglas Karge for his editing and content suggestions and for his wonderful support throughout this project.

Dr. Patricia Cegelka, Dr. Ian Pumpian, Dr. Anne Graves, Dr. Rena Lewis, Ms. Caren Sax, and colleagues at San Diego State University for believing a class for non education majors was necessary and assisting during the past three years.

Special thanks from both:

To Ravic Ringlaben for his fine work on the Instructor's Activity Guide which accompanies this text.

Our sincerest thanks go to Judy Ice, our McGraw Hill Editor. She has served as a motivator, teacher, listener, manager, and friend. Judy is a true professional who knows how to guide the content, people, and business aspects of a book development project.

And finally, our highest praise goes to Craig Conley who lived, ate, and breathed this project. His writing and editing skills are unbeatable and his ability to handle many complex and varied tasks at once is incredible. We both recognize that this final project would have lacked its polish and cohesiveness if it weren't for his fine work. Thank you Craig.

SES & BDK

Preface

The writing of a textbook is not an easy task. However the recognition that this book may assist individuals in their understanding of human diversity and help improve their ability to interact with and respect others who are different from themselves is outstanding motivation. Both of us teach courses about human diversity at our universities and we have frequent opportunities to hear from our graduates. Letters from former students which inform us that they are now better able to cope with a child who has a disability, that they are comfortable with new friends who have a different sexual orientation, that they have been influential in the hiring of a diverse individual, or that they have chosen a career related to working with persons who are diverse are the true rewards of teaching our courses. This book extends our opportunity to be helpful to other students who, like our own students, have enrolled in a course in order to learn about diversity in society.

We suggest that you begin your study by becoming familiar with the components of the book. You'll find that the book is organized into three sections. In the first section we introduce you to general issues regarding persons who are diverse and provide you with an overview of the culture of diversity. In Section One you will also find a review of significant legislation which affects individuals who are diverse.

Section Two discusses specific categories of human diversity. Within each of the topics, which we recognize could easily by themselves be developed to such a level of depth that a book would be needed, we have given definitions, causes, terminology, and have suggested appropriate interactions. It is our hope that this information will assist you in reducing myths and misconceptions and give you suggestions for comfortable interactions with persons who are different from you.

Section Three starts with a discussion of issues relating to parents, siblings, and other family members and their interactions with those in the family who are different. Next we provide an overview of educational perspectives regarding diverse individuals. This discussion should assist you if you are a parent of a child who needs special education services or who may experience educational difficulties due to being different from typical classmates. It may also provide you with an introductory knowledge which is crucial if you are going into the field of special education or a related service. The final chapter is intended to challenge you to review your attitude, your level of respect for others, and your tolerance for disrespect toward diverse individuals by friends and colleagues.

Be sure to note that there are many components of the book which are designed to assist you. At the end of each chapter there are activities which we strongly encourage you to complete. A study guide with sample test questions (both essay and objective) is also provided at the end of the book. It is clear, from data collection and analysis, that students who have completed these activities have scored higher on course tests; we hope you will use these activities to your advantage.

An Instructor's Activity Guide, which we developed with a colleague, Ravic Ringlaben from the University of Arkansas, is available from McGraw Hill. The Guide offers many excellent suggestions, collected from college and university instructors across the United States, for group activities designed to enhance the study of human diversity. Your instructor may use some of those activities and we hope that you find them to be fun and beneficial.

Both of us want each of you to profit from your study of human diversity. If you started with some level of discomfort or misunderstanding about those who are different from you, that's perfectly understandable. All we want is for you to use this book and the course you are taking as an opportunity to assess your individual comfort level with those who are different. Recognize that each of us has some type of difference and we usually accept and respect those differences we are used to. Perhaps your study of human diversity will enable you to become used to other types of differences and therefore improve your comfort level in respect to others who are different.

We would love to hear from you. Your reactions and thoughts to your study of human diversity are very helpful and important to us. Please feel free to Email or write to either or both of us. Enjoy your study of human diversity!

Stuart E. Schwartz, Ed.D.
Box 117050
University of Florida
Gainesville FL 32611
(904) 392-0701 ext. 258
stuart_schwartz@qm.server.ufl.edu

Belinda D. Karge, Ph.D.
College of Education
San Diego State University
San Diego, CA 92182-1170
619-594-6627
bkarge@ucsvax.sdsu.edu

About the Authors

Stuart E. Schwartz

Stuart E. Schwartz joined the University of Florida special education faculty in 1974 after obtaining his doctoral degree from the University of Kansas in the area of transition for students with disabilities. He taught in the Philadelphia area, prior to his graduate studies, in middle school and high school special education and he coordinated a work study program for high school students with disabilities.

Dr. Schwartz has published numerous articles regarding research in transition and has developed five curriculum materials which are currently being used in high school special education programs. He is the author of *Coping with Crisis Situations in the Classroom* and has presented at many national conferences on the topics of human diversity, persons with disabilities, transition services, and sexual orientation.

Dr. Schwartz is currently the principal investigator of five state and federal projects dealing with transition and drop out issues. He regularly teaches a doctoral seminar on trends and issues in special education, a special education course on transition, and an undergraduate course, *Exceptional People,* for more than 2100 non education majors each year on the topic of human diversity. Dr. Schwartz has been selected as "Teacher of the Year" twice since 1985.

Belinda Dunnick Karge

Belinda D. Karge, a former teacher of diverse children and adolescents with various diabilities, was a professor at San Diego State University for six years and is currently Head of the Department of Special Education at California State University, Fullerton. She is the author of numerous instructional materials, journal articles, and monographs. She teaches theory and instructional methods courses for teachers in training as well as "Disability and Society," a course for non-education undergraduates. In 1994, she received the Department of Special Education Outstanding Faculty Award and the Faculty Member of the Year Award from the SDSU Panhellenic Association.

Dr. Karge received her doctorate from the Univerity of California, Riverside in Special Education, Educational Psychology, and Quantitative Research Methods in 1988. Current professional interests include effective teaching and instructional strategies, support and retention issues for beginning teachers and professional collaborations. Dr. Karge is one of three founding Co-Directors of the Center for the Study of Excellence in Teacher Preparation. She frequently consults with school districts across the country.

Contents

Chapter 1

Human Diversity

Introduction

We are surrounded by human diversity. Look around you and observe ten people. Using statistics from a 1994 Department of Education report, two of those people will be foreign born, two will have a speech problem, and one will be a member of a minority religious group. If your random sampling includes persons with children, two children will have learning disabilities, two will face future drug or alcohol abuse, one will be mentally retarded, and one will be homosexual.

Every individual is unique, but in our daily interactions with others we like to sub-divide sometimes, feeling that we belong in the same category as some, and not as others. We may tend to focus on the ways in which we are different because it makes us feel secure as part of a small group or societal designation, or because we feel uncomfortable or awkward with people who are different. Whenever our reactions to another are based on gender, race, physical or mental disability, sexual orientation, religion, economic class, or any other category, we are cheating ourselves of opportunities to benefit from that individual and we are cheating that person of his or her right to participate fully in the human community.

Most of us have found ourselves uncomfortable at one time or another in dealing with someone we perceive to be different. For example, we may feel unsure of how to talk to someone from another culture, we may have incorrect expectations regarding an individual with a different skin color, we may have difficulty having a relaxed conversation with a person of a different sexual orientation, or we may find ourselves staring at someone who looks different due to an injury or a disability. In order to enhance our interactions with others and to increase our self-understanding, we need to know what human differences are, examine some of their causes, and reduce our myths and misunderstandings about people who are diverse. Since every one of us fits into some category of diversity, we severely impoverish our lives if we limit our interaction through ignorance.

This book should help you to understand exactly how to define human differences and give you some guidance in regard to social interaction with various people. It includes helpful exercises and activities which will give you insights into other perspectives and will help you to develop sensitivity and self-awareness so that you can treat all people respectfully and fairly. Knowledge allows us to live and respond based on facts rather than myths.

Information is the key to interacting with others with tolerance and respect, which is a challenge most people want to meet.

In order to profit best from this course it is advisable to first acquaint yourself with this text. Each chapter provides insightful discussions for your consideration. The book explores the effects of being different both upon the person and upon his or her family. You will be introduced to the concept of diversity, learn a variety of terms, and review some myths and misconceptions about exceptional people.

What Constitutes Exceptionality?

Exceptional individuals—often called "persons who are diverse" or "persons who are different" thoughout this book—significantly differ, in one or more ways, from those who are considered to be average. This definition could, of course, apply to anyone, depending upon the group to which he or she is being compared. Historically, Caucasian, heterosexual, English speakers have not been considered exceptional in the United States. However, in some parts of our country now, Spanish is the predominant language, so English speakers are the ones who are different. In many communities Hispanic or African American families outnumber white families, so it is exceptional to be white there. In a group of mostly females, it is exceptional to be male.

The expectations that a certain population has upon members of its group for specific behaviors or group standards also affect whether the individual is considered different. A group of teens which expects its friends to dress in a specific style might consider anyone who dresses differently to be exceptional. Parents who have high academic expectations for their child might consider C's to be exceptional grades, while other parents might find those grades "average" and acceptable. How we are viewed and accepted depends largely upon the situation in which we find ourselves.

Some exceptional people have disabilities which inhibit or prevent their participation in some activities or interfere with their learning. Some have special gifts or talents which make them different. And some have both talents and disabilities. Although exceptional people differ from others in some major or minor way, they are individuals first. Their exceptionality is only one of their characteristics. They each have their own unique goals, dreams, hopes, and needs.

Many of us may think of disabilities as physical limitations. Indeed, a disability may be physical, but it may also be emotional, cognitive, or sensory. A disability may cause one to use a wheelchair, or it may be only a minor handicap or no handicap at all. For instance, most people with vision or hearing impairments can easily correct their conditions with eyeglasses or hearing aids. You can see that exceptional individuals function in every part of society every day.

In order to speak about human diversity with any real meaning, then, we would need to consider every possible difference from the norm, every possible norm, and every possible level of expectation as we examine the concept of exceptionality. That is clearly impractical if not impossible, but we can look at the most common types of diversity which you are likely to encounter in your school, your family, and your place of employment. These selected categories should enable you to have a thorough understanding of these areas of exceptionality and should help you to be a better friend, neighbor, family member, or employer of people who may, from time to time or from group to group, be considered different.

You yourself may now or in the future belong to a group which is characterized as exceptional because of your race, gender, sexual orientation, functional limitation, size, age, religion, or socio-economic class. An understanding of the fact that the perception of diversity shifts constantly depending upon time and place will help you to avoid the insensitivity that comes from ignorance. This book should help you, as well, to have a better understanding of yourself as an exceptional person in our complex society.

Historical Perspectives

Each category of diversity has, of course, had its own unique history. We can, however, speak in broad terms about some aspects of the acceptance and treatment of exceptional people in the past. For example, we know that the teachings of all the world's major religions include references to those who are sick, weak, unfortunate, or disadvantaged. Confucius, Buddha, Mohammed and Jesus all wrote or spoke about the need to show compassion. The sacred texts of the great religions all advocate humane and sympathetic treatment for every individual. However, in many cases and in all cultures, exceptionality was associated with sinfulness. It was looked upon as a kind of curse or punishment, either because of a lack of faith or because of some failure in the individual or in his or her parents. This mistaken attitude has fundamentally colored society's perception of differences, and even today the attitude has not entirely been dispelled.

Since earliest recorded history there have been instances of humane treatment of those who were different or disabled. In Athens, around 600 BC, a famous lawgiver named Solon designed a system for providing care for soldiers who had been disabled in war. However, Solon's attitude was uncommonly enlightened. In the Middle Ages, the lives of exceptional people were often full of suffering, and customarily they benefited from little or no support from society. Both Martin Luther and John Calvin, important Christian reformers in the sixteenth century, stated their belief that disabled individuals had no souls and that therefore society had no responsibility to them at all. Those who were deaf, mentally retarded, epileptic, and blind, as well as some especially gifted or talented individuals, were often

4

thought to be possessed by demons and sometimes were subjected to exorcisms to purge the "devils" from them.

The 18th and 19th centuries brought the beginning of efforts to educate and to care for exceptional people. There was more treatment for people who were mentally ill and mentally retarded, and programs were instituted to educate people who were deaf, mute, and blind. Special schools for special conditions—such as asylums for people who were blind—began to be established in the United States as well as in Europe. Programs within public schools in the United States were begun in the early 1900's, segregating exceptional children into special classes apart from the main student body. Since that time, programs for students with special needs have steadily grown and developed, with an emphasis on inclusion rather than exclusion.

While there have been flashes of enlightened attitudes and actions toward human diversity throughout history, in general our treatment of individuals with differences has been shameful. In every period of history so far, and in virtually all cultures, there has been a stigma attached to difference. Societies have neglected, persecuted, and sometimes exterminated those of its members who exhibited noticeable variation from the perceived norm. Since perception is always subject to change, and all of us fall into some category of exceptionality, it behooves us to continue to grow in humanity and in understanding. The best way to do that is to educate ourselves. Intolerance is the direct result of ignorance.

The on-going enactment of human rights legislation and the increasing awareness of the contributions of diverse people to our society gives hope that we may be entering a new century in which differences are not only recognized and tolerated but appreciated and honored. In the past two decades there has been phenomenal progress in the fields of medicine and technology. We must continually redefine exceptionality due to increased understanding of the causes of some categories of exceptionality, medical advances in the cure and treatment of some conditions, and new technology which enables people to function despite previously limiting handicaps. It is an exciting time to be studying the subject of human diversity.

Terms and Labels

The terms you use to describe or identify individuals who are different should be positive, current, and correct. The goal is not to expand the lexicon of political correctness. But it is important to think carefully about the words you choose to use. You can probably think of many inappropriate terms which have been used to identify people with diverse characteristics. The acceptability of terms changes with time, and a word may be the term of choice of one group or individual and be offensive to another. For example, some hearing impaired people prefer to be described as "hearing impaired," yet the National

Theater For The Deaf uses the term "deaf." The best way to be sure that you are not giving offense is to go to the expert. Ask a friend or acquaintance who is an exceptional person, or who has a close relationship with someone who is, what is most acceptable to them.

Labels serve an important purpose. They are the way we attempt to identify and describe people. They allow us to distinguish characteristics which may facilitate communication among professionals. For example, psychologists and educators may use labels to discuss the special needs of an individual or of a group of people. On the other hand, labeling may stigmatize a person, contribute to low self-esteem, and cause him or her to suffer discrimination. Once labels are applied to someone, particularly by an official evaluator such as a doctor, teacher, or psychologist, it may be difficult to remove the label. Consequently, we should carefully give consideration to the accuracy of those labels and to their potential effects.

In any culture, some labels are generally thought to be positive and others negative. Most of us would have a positive reaction to the label "intelligent," but we might have very different ideas what we mean by that label. Some of us say our dogs are intelligent if they can roll over, for instance. In our culture, "overweight" is usually a negative label, but a fashion model might be called overweight even though, by the standards of the society, she is thin. Words have different connotations, or meanings, for different groups, and the effect of labeling, as we have seen, can differ from person to person. The best guideline is to always remember that the person comes first and the label simply identifies a specific characteristic about that person. For instance, don't say "Moslems practice beautiful traditions," but rather "People of the Muslim faith practice beautiful traditions."

Attitudes

Consider your attitude toward people who are different. When you meet someone who is using a wheelchair or someone of a different race, how do you react? How do you feel? What about someone who speaks with a heavy accent or who uses gestures and sign language for communication? Or a street person? Or two men or two women dancing together? Are you uncomfortable? Do you try to avoid the person? The attitude that others display toward people who are exceptional is critical.

Attitudes are learned early in life when children interact with others and observe the human interactions of family members and friends. The child who hears his or her parents make negative remarks about diverse people, or who observes playmates ridicule and tease other children who are different, will probably be greatly influenced by these experiences. The child who grows up in an environment where individual differences are noted and treated with respect will more likely not have negative expectations, feelings of discomfort, or negative attitudes.

Can you improve the attitudes of children and adults toward exceptional individuals? You certainly can by being a good model and following these guidelines.

Always display your respect and comfort. It is important for you to set a good example. If you interact with exceptional individuals in a respectful manner and if it appears that you are comfortable in your interactions with those people, your friends, family members, fellow employees, and your children will follow your lead. Remember that others will copy your behaviors.

Don't worry about what other people may or may not be thinking. If you are heterosexual and are talking to someone who is openly gay, or if you are a Christian talking to a Hindu, don't worry what other people may or may not be thinking about you. Communicating with an exceptional person in no way compromises your identity. If other people react negatively to your association with an exceptional person, remind them that you were talking to the person, not to the label. If you are seen talking to an individual who is different, the only thing it says about you is that you are open, friendly, and non-judgmental.

Tell children about differences. Encourage children to ask questions as their curiosity is quite normal. If children are given correct information in a matter of fact manner, they will perceive that being different is not mysterious or something to fear. People tend to fear that which is unknown, so it is critically important to teach children about human diversity so that all possible fears about exceptionalities are eliminated.

Stop someone who is ridiculing or joking about people who are diverse. If someone begins to ridicule or joke about an exceptional individual, challenge that person to stop. If you sit there and laugh along with the crowd, you are just as guilty as the joke teller. By participating you are giving others the impression that you condone such negative behavior. It really takes guts to stop a friend or co-worker, but if you do so in a serious and positive manner, others will no doubt respect you for having the courage of your convictions. Comments such as, "Excuse me, but the racist joke you are telling is making me uncomfortable," or "If you don't mind I'd appreciate your saving any jokes about male-bashing for a time when I'm not around" will usually work. Another way to handle the situation would be to tell the group you are leaving because of the stereotypical jokes which are being told. Then walk away.

Expect normal behaviors and achievement from diverse individuals. If you think that a non-native speaker of English or an individual with a hearing impairment will be unable to get the job he or she is applying for, you will be hampering the employment success of that person. If you expect that a friend with mental retardation can never learn to ride a subway, you are setting a major roadblock in the way of that person's learning to use public transportation. The expectations of influential people, such as parents, teachers, and friends, have a strong effect on exceptional people's confidence level and motivation to achieve. The potential of people who are diverse is usually only limited by the opportunities to learn and the inappropriately low expectations of significant others.

Be yourself around those who are exceptional. If you are normally crabby, be crabby. If you are normally friendly, be friendly. Putting on an act around people who are different will be recognized as patronizing or demeaning behavior. It is not necessary for you to sprint ahead and open a door for someone in a wheelchair unless you usually do that for everyone. If you are taking a leisurely walk and normally say hello to people you meet, then by all means say hello to that person with a guide dog who is walking by. If you usually ignore people whom you don't know, and you don't know that person with an oxygen tank, then ignore him or her as well. Exceptional people want to be treated like everyone else and they can tell when you are acting. Therefore, be yourself and don't change your behaviors around those who are different.

Use your common, everyday vocabulary. The vocabulary you commonly use should be fine with anyone you come across. With people who are blind it is appropriate to say, "It's nice to see you," or "Isn't it a beautiful day?" It is able acceptable to say to a friend of yours who uses a wheelchair, "Let's take a walk to the park." People who are different use common, everyday language all the time, so don't feel the least bit awkward using your everyday vocabulary. If you stop to think about the "right" words to use, you will come across as uncomfortable and the substitute words you select will probably be wrong.

Suggest activities in which you are interested. Exceptional people often enjoy the same hobbies as you do. If you like tennis, ask your friend who has epilepsy to play. If you are going to a theme park, invite your friend who is a Buddhist to accompany you. If you want to go to an art museum, don't hesitate to invite your friend who is visually impaired along. Exceptional people should not be excluded from activities just because *you* think those activities would not be appropriate for them. Ask your friends who are diverse to participate. They are fully capable of selecting the activities which they will enjoy and which fit their interests.

Look at but never stare at someone who is different. It is fine to look, note any differences in your mind, and then go on with your interaction with an exceptional person in a normal fashion. Staring at someone who is dressed differently, or disfigured, or short statured is rude and will make that person feel uncomfortable. Some exceptional people will stare right back or will bluntly ask you why you are staring. It is very appropriate, however, to look in a normal fashion at people who appear different with whom you are interacting. Avoiding eye contact, or looking away, is just as rude as staring.

Talk to the person who is exceptional and not just to his or her companion. When interacting with an exceptional person who is with a family member or companion, be sure to address the person rather than the family member or companion. A person from another country can usually answer questions or respond appropriately in conversation without assistance. Likewise, if you are with a friend who has a disability, don't respond for the friend. When put in that situation, such as a waiter asking you what your exceptional companion would like to eat, don't respond for your friend. Politely suggest to the waiter that he or she should ask your friend. Although that situation may be a bit uncomfortable, it will be a good experience for that insensitive restaurant employee.

The guidelines suggested above should assist you in your efforts to improve your interactions with exceptional people, and they should serve as excellent examples for children and other adults who observe your behaviors. By interacting correctly and comfortably, you will greatly aid those people who are uncomfortable or afraid due to ignorance, myths, and misconceptions.

Summary

In this first chapter, you have had an opportunity to begin your exploration of the subject of people who are diverse. You have been introduced to some of the labels which have been applied to individuals who are considered different and to the effects those labels can have. You have learned correct terms, along with some guidelines for appropriate interactions, and you should have begun to consider the importance of positive attitudes. You can see that each of us, every day, falls into a category of being different at some time. As you learn more about how differences affect individuals, you will enjoy enhanced self-awareness and a keener sense of those around you.

References

U.S. Department of Education. (1994). *Schools in the United States: A statistical profile.* Washington, DC: Office of Educational Research and Improvement, National Center for Educational Statistics.

Suggested Readings

Angelou, M. (1989). *I know why the caged-bird sings.* New York: Literacy Volunteers of New York City.
This is the autobiography of an African-American woman, telling how she overcame the social biases of growing up poor and black to become a fully realized and successful person.

Brown, C. (1976). *The children of ham.* New York: Stein and Day.
This book offers personal accounts of African-American youth in the slums of Harlem and their proposed solution to their social ills.

Frank, A. (1956). *The diary of Anne Frank.* New York: Random House.
A young Jewish girl's spirit triumphs in the face of Nazi occupation, just before she and her family are exterminated on the basis of their race and religion.

Momaday, N. S. (1990). *The way to rainy mountain.* Albuquerque: University of New Mexico Press.
This is an account of the legends of the Kiowa Indians and how their ancient religion and culture were suddenly and brutally eradicated.

Monette, P. (1992). *Becoming a man: Half a life story.* New York: Harcourt Brace Jovanovich.
Provided in this autobiography are a gay man's poignant memories of growing up, coming out to his parents, and battling AIDS.

Neusner, J. (1994). *World religions in America.* Louisville, KY: John Knox.
This book examines the faiths of African-Americans, Hispanics, Native Americans, and all other major denominations. It also examines the subjects of women and religion, politics and religion, and society and religion.

Swift, J. (1960). *Gulliver's travels (1726)*. Boston: Houghton Mifflin.

This classic novel is about a man's adventures in four exotic nations of the world. The inhabitants he meets—some diminutive, some gigantic, some animalistic—are seldom what they seem at first. This book encourages us to look beyond the superficial.

Exploration

An exploration section is provided at the end of each chapter. The exploration activities should assist you as you consider the meaning and implications of the content of the chapter.

Individual Activities

1. You are an exceptional person! Every single person on earth has a unique talent. There are things you do much better than others, and there are some things you don't do as well. List eight things that make you a person who is different. Circle those which are extremely higher or lower than what you consider normal.

_____   _____
_____   _____
_____   _____
_____   _____

2. Now is the time to get rid of all the negative terms you can think of for describing exceptional people. You've probably heard many. List 20 of those terms. Then cross them out as a symbol of your decision never to use them again.

_____ _____ _____ _____
_____ _____ _____ _____
_____ _____ _____ _____
_____ _____ _____ _____
_____ _____ _____ _____

Group Activities

1. Get into a group of 4 or 5 people–people whom you don't know well. Have each person write down a list of 5 adjectives which are guesses about the skills and weaknesses of each person in the group. Now discuss what everyone in the group wrote. Were the people in your group right or wrong about you? Did you find out something about yourself you didn't already know? How correct were you about others? Welcome to the world of labels!

Reactions:

_____

_____

_____

_____

2. Stay in your group of 4-5 people. Review the guidelines presented in chapter one for interacting with exceptional people. Now, as a group, discuss and rank these guidelines from most to least important.

Reactions:

_____

_____

_____

_____

Reaction Paper 1.1

Imagine yourself as a person living in a world where everything is suited for people who are at least eight feet tall. How are you going to climb a flight of stairs, when each stair comes up to your waist? What would be easier to deal with—the stairs or the stares? Why?

Reaction Paper 1.2

When you were a child, didn't you hate being called names? Were you ever called a name or have a nickname that stuck with you for a while? What effects did that label have on you? On others? Relate your discussion to people who are diverse.

Notes

Chapter 2

The Culture of Diversity

Introduction

Our culture is made up of the ideas, customs, skills, arts, interests, and emotions of our people. We communicate and pass along these ideas and customs to succeeding generations, and thus our culture survives and prospers. Diversity strengthens our species and adds threads to the tapestry of our lives. It exponentially increases the possibilities for progress and positive change in the world because rather than seeing from only one point of view, it allows us to see from many. We would be sadly diminished if the music of the universe consisted of only one note. We would be even more sadly diminished if human beings were free of differences. Too often we speak of tolerating difference when we should always be celebrating it.

Sometimes science fiction films and books portray a world where diversity has been limited or eradicated. Without exception, those images are frightening in their sameness and colorlessness. We recoil from the prospect because we instinctively know that to destroy difference is to destroy our own individuality–the very thing which makes us feel human– our uniqueness. The lesson we must learn and never forget is that only by respecting and honoring the difference in others can we preserve our own. The English poet John Donne wrote, "Every man's death diminishes me." The corollary to that truth is that everyone's difference enhances me.

Aspects of Culture

We live in a dynamic, multifaceted, multicultural world. Cultural influences are pervasive. Inter-cultural communication skills are a necessity for everyone, not just for the culturally "deprived" or distinct, but for all people as cultural beings. All cultures have a history and a heritage which is carefully handed down. Cultures are identifiable because they share certain characteristics. People within the group have ways of telling who is and who is not a member. Members share a language through which cultural interactions take place, certain group values are shared, and various social and behavioral patterns are followed. Members follow special rules of etiquette when communicating with others, introducing themselves to strangers, getting someone's attention, and leave-taking, for example.

Members of each culture also have their own unique slang expressions and figures of speech. You can learn more about these codes of behavior and expression by asking what is appropriate in certain situations. However, some of these rules may not be meant for general public knowledge. Such cultural interactions are often kept private so that members of the specific community may identify outsiders easily (Bienvenu & Colonomos, 1993).

Defining Culture

The first contemporary effort to define culture was exerted by anthropologists, since culture is what their science is all about. There is a kaleidoscope of differing views on what constitutes culture. Three decades ago, in 1954, Kroeber and Kluckhohn analyzed 300 definitions of culture, yet they did not find a precise common denominator. Rather, culture emerged as a very broad concept embracing all aspects of human life. Culture has been described as a double-ended nexus with a person at one end and a social group at the other (Brooks, 1979).

In anthropology, important distinctions are made between "ideal" and "real" culture (Arvizu, Snyder, & Espinosa, 1980). Ideal culture refers to what people say they believe or how they think they should behave. Aspects of ideal culture frequently are expressed in proverbs, stories, myths, and jokes. These may contrast sharply with the real culture, which is how individuals actually behave in specific situations.

It is equally important to realize that some elements of culture operate at a conscious level of awareness, whereas others do not. Implicit (covert) culture includes elements hidden or taken for granted to the extent that they are not easily observable or consciously recognized by individuals. Attitudes, fears, values, religious beliefs, and assumptions are common elements of implicit culture. Explicit (overt) culture, on the other hand, is visible and can be described verbally. This includes speech, tools, styles of dress, and concrete behaviors.

Key Cultural Concepts

The following are concepts that need to be considered when thinking about culture and diversity:

Acculturation. This is the process by which the members of a society are taught the elements of that society's culture. Everyone goes through an acculturation process, immigrants and non-immigrants alike.

Cultural Pluralism. This refers to the belief that diverse groups coexist within American society and maintain a culturally distinct identity.

Ethnocentrism. This is the belief that one's cultural ways are not only valid and superior to other people's, but also universally applicable in evaluating and judging human behavior.

Heritage. This refers to something that belongs to a person by reason of his or her birth. A person may be born into one culture and later ignore or reject that cultural inheritance in favor of another.

Inter-cultural. This means "between" or "among" cultures. Inter-cultural interactions involve mutual or reciprocal exchanges.

Melting Pot. This refers to the concept that many cultures can blend into one. This concept has historically been a component of American culture. However, it no longer is widely accepted as a goal within our society.

Micro-culture. This implies a greater linkage with the larger culture, and emphasis is often put on the degree to which the micro-culture acts to interpret, express, and/or mediate the ideas, values, and institutions of the political community.

Multicultural. This refers to a number of diverse traditions, customs, arts, languages, values, and beliefs existing side-by-side.

Subculture. This is a term used frequently by sociologists to refer to a social group that shares characteristics that distinguish it in some way from the larger political society (usually called macro-culture) of which it is a part.

The Culture of Language

Imagine that you are taken to a non-English speaking country. Everything looks foreign to you–the land, the food, the homes, even people and their mannerisms. You begin to communicate by resorting to pointing, drawing, or gesturing. Gradually, you begin to pick up new words, sometimes substituting them for the ones you already know, sometimes mixing them in and forming word variations and chunks of meaning. Eventually, you have children and they begin to speak a little like you. Over time, this language is spoken in some form by an entire colony of your descendants who cling together through common language or because they have been purposely isolated by the original inhabitants.

The rest of society avoids this colony because its members are different.

This is a scenario somewhat similar to that which happened to Africans taken by force from their mother land and brought to America. However, the duration of their captivity was to be long lasting and its effects are still inhibiting, due in part to a visible difference–dark skin–which is a reminder of their lowly beginnings in this country. It matters not to some that Africa is the place of humankind's beginnings, or even that Africa had a highly developed civilization before contact with the outside world (Douroux, as cited in Bennett, 1986). Instead, attitudes predominate that were conjured up by social happenstance and its relationship to speakers of Black English.

Each culture has a similar language story. Be sensitive to language differences and development. To hear the word *chiren*, which is dialectically different from *children,* is not bad grammar, nor "lazy tongue," nor anything of a pathological significance. It is rather a learned pronunciation acquired over time. We all speak dialect of our native language.

Effective inter-cultural interactions are primarily a function of the success of the communication process between culturally different persons. Many times inter-cultural difficulties stem primarily from ignorance of cross-cultural communication. Knowledge and awareness are therefore the primary elements in inter-cultural competence (Hall, 1976).

Cultural Contrasts

Many people express strong commitment to and identification with their cultural groups. This is particularly true of people whose families are native to another country. Sometimes it becomes a challenge for diverse people to live in America and uphold the values traditional to the culture of their ancestors. For example, a colleague recently told of how a friend enjoys the freedom in the United States and the wonderful physical relationship she has with her three children. The children rough-house and talk with her in a playful manner, jump on her back, and give her hugs. However, when the children visit their Vietnamese grandparents, this behavior is not acceptable. Finding a happy median including both cultures can be challenging. The following statements provide several examples of American culture contrasted with traditional cultures from other areas of the world.

"American"/*Traditional Vietnamese*

A: Young children have a lot of freedom.
V: Children have to obey and respect parents and do not have much freedom.

A: Talking directly about the main subject is appropriate.
V: Talking around the subject and then returning to the main point.

A: Direct eye contact shows honesty and frankness.
V: Direct eye contact can show disrespect.
(Blafer, 1994)

"American"/*Traditional African American*

A: Uninterrupted monologue and presentations expected in classroom.
AA: Emphasis on general participation and spontaneity from audience during formal presentations.

A: Quiet listening shows respect for speaker.
AA: Equal verbal exchange and playful verbalizing should not
necessarily represent a challenge to speaker.

A: High value placed on verbal articulation.
AA: Body language, nonverbal communication, visual and dramatic expression frequently used as additional forms of expression.
(Ratleff, 1989)

"American"/*Traditional Filipino*

A: Cause and cure should be found for a disability.
F: Disability creates a sense of shame and guilt.

A: A tendency to turn to "outsiders" for help.
F: Family is first source for help.

A: High expectation for participatory, active student involvement.
F: Little tolerance for child's attempt to challenge teachers.
(Galang et. al., 1994)

"American"/*Traditional Native American*

A: Children are encouraged to be actively involved in learning.
NA: Children are encouraged to learn by silent observation.

A: Child rearing is the responsibility of the parent and/or guardian.
NA: Child rearing is the responsibility of several different relatives.

A: The focus is on self first, then to a higher being.
NA: Spirituality is pervasive in daily activities.
(Harris, 1993)

"American"/*Traditional Mexican-American*

A: School system dictates when various learning tasks are to be gained
MA: Adults believe that children will approach tasks when they are developmentally ready.

A: Very time oriented. When meeting is scheduled at 8:00 a.m. it begins on time.
MA: Members have a flexible sense of time.

A: During mother-child interaction, lots of verbal conversation is exchanged.
MA: During mother-child interaction, mother is often nonverbal; relies on tactile stimulation.
(Anderson & Battle, 1993)

Stereotypes of People not of the Majority

It is *not* true that people who are members of a minority group:

- Have had a disadvantaged background
- Need or want exceptions to get into school or a particular job
- Do not understand English
- Are in the U.S. illegally
- Are experts on their culture
- Spend all their money in their home country
- Have a chip on their shoulder
- Want special rights
- Have a large family

- Are wealthy or come from a wealthy family
- Are protected under the law for the same rights

Issues Culturally Diverse Individuals May Face

- Assimilation v. maintaining a cultural identity
- Being labeled as a foreigner or minority
- Perceived as stealing American jobs
- Homesickness
- Finding peer and cultural support
- Language issues
- Perceived as illegal immigrant
- Cultural differences
- Overcoming stereotypes
- Separation issues from family
- Inter-cultural relationships/marriage
- Valuing or celebrating of heritage
- Family origins
- Self-esteem and self-image issues
- Recognizing diversity within their community
- Feeling out of place
- Equal access or opportunity
- Prejudice or racism

Interactions

Respect all cultures. Culture is not just something that someone else has. All of us have a cultural, ethnic, and linguistic heritage that influences our current beliefs, values, and behaviors.

Celebrate similarities. One eight-year-old said, "My mom is Korean, my dad is Korean, and my sister is Korean. So I guess I must somehow be Korean. But I am just like the other kids." Why is it that sometimes it takes an eight year old to remind us that we are all similar? We all laugh, cry, love, and play, and in fundamental ways we are just like each other. We are all exceptional people.

Stop racial jokes. When friends or relatives tell racial jokes, ask them to tell it about people from their own culture, or have them use generic terms.

Choose friends by character, choose socks by color. This saying is on a chart hanging in the dorms at a local university. The sign further discusses that it wouldn't make sense to pick socks by character, nor friends by color.

Live by the "Creed for Citizens of a Diverse World." Griessman (1993) provides insight to appropriate interactions and ideas for respecting culture:

> I believe that diversity is a part of the natural order of things-as natural as the trillion shapes and shades of the flowers of spring or the leaves of autumn. I believe that diversity brings new solutions to an ever-changing environment, and that sameness is not only uninteresting but limiting. To deny diversity is to deny life- with all its richness and manifold opportunities. Thus I affirm my citizenship in a world of diversity, and with it the responsibility to:
> **Be tolerant.** *Live and let live. Understand that those who cause no harm should not be feared, ridiculed, or harmed-even if they are different.*
> **Look** *for the best in others.*
> **Be just** *in my dealing with poor and rich, weak and strong, and whenever possible, to defend the young, the old, the frail, the defenseless.*
> **Avoid** *needless conflicts and diversions, but always be willing to change for the better that which can be changed.*
> **Seek** *knowledge in order to know what can be changed, as well as, what cannot be changed.*
> **Forge** *alliances with others who love liberty and justice.*
> **Be kind,** *remembering how fragile the human spirit is.*
> **Be generous** *in thought, word, and purse.*
> **Live** *the examined life, subjecting my motives and actions to the scrutiny of mind and heart so to rise above prejudice and hatred.*
> **Care.**

Summary

Diversity enriches the lives of individuals and strengthens society as a whole. Diversity expands the possibilities for progress, evolution, and positive change in the world because it allows us to see from many different perspectives. If human beings were free of differences, the quality of our lives would be profoundly diminished. It is time to stop merely tolerating difference and start celebrating it.

References

Anderson, N. & Battle, D. (1993). Cultural diversity in the development of language. In D. Battle (Ed.), *Communication disorders in multicultural populations.* Boston: Andover Medical Publishers.

Arvizu, S. R., Snyder, W. A., & Espinosa, P. T. (1980, June). Demystifying the concept of culture: Theoretical and conceptual tools. *Bilingual Education Paper Series, 3*(11). Los Angeles: Evaluation, Dissemination and Assessment Center, California State University, Los Angeles.

Bennett, C. E. (1993). The black population in the United States. *Current Population Reports,* 20-471.

Bienvenu, M. J. & Colonomos, B. (1993). *An introduction to deaf culture: Rules of social interaction.* Burtonsville, MD: Sign Media.

Blafer, P. (1994). The ways of American through Vietnamese eyes. In *Assessment of Vietnamese speaking limited English proficient students with special needs.* Sacramento, CA: State Department of Education.

Brooks, N. (1979). Parameters of culture. In H.P. Baptiste, Jr. and M. L. Baptiste (Eds.), Developing the multicultural process in classroom instruction (pp. 42-47). Washington DC: University Press of America.

Galang, R., Rosenberg, L., & Lyn, S. (1994). *Assessment of Filipino speaking limited English proficient students with special needs.* Sacramento CA: Special Education Resource Network.

Greissman, B. E. (1992). *Diversity challenges and opportunities.* New York: Harper Collins.

Hall, E. (1976). *Beyond culture.* Garden City, NY: Anchor.

Harris, G. (1993). American Indian cultures: A lesson in diversity. In D. Battle (Ed.), *Communication disorders in multicultural populations.* Boston: Andover Medical Publishers.

Ratleff, J. E. (1989). *Instructional strategies for cross cultural students with special education needs.* Sacramento, CA: Resources in Special Education.

Suggested Readings

Commenger, H. S. (1970). Meet the U.S.A. Rev. ed. New York: Institute of International Education.
Historian Commenger wrote this book for foreign visitors to the United States.

Duval, L. (1994). Respecting our differences: A guide to getting along in a changing world. Minneapolis, MN: Free Spirit.
Discussions of accepting, respecting, and celebrating differences are provided in this guide.

Gold, S. & Kibria, N. (1993). Vietnamese refugees and blocked mobility. *Asian and Pacific Migration Journal, 2(1),* 27-56.
This journal examines data from published sources and ethnographic studies of the economic situation of Vietnamese refugees in the United States.

Kroeber, A. J. & Kluckhohn, C. (eds.). (1954). *Culture: A critical review of concepts and definitions.* New York: Random House.
This is an invaluable overview of cultural concepts and definitions.

Mindel, C. H. & Habenstein, R. W. (Eds.). (1988). Ethnic families in America: Patterns and variation (3rd ed.). New York: Elsevier Publications.
This book examines ethnic family strengths and needs as well as historical background and demographic characteristics.

Vedder, R & Gallaway, L. (1993). Declining black employment. *Society,* 30(5), 57-63.
This article explores income inequality during declining African-American employment, examines current welfare systems, and suggests ways to improve the economic disadvantages of minority groups.

Exploration

Individual Activities

1. This activity encourages you to examine the particular dialect you speak. If you are a native speaker of American English, look in a dictionary printed in England and find examples of words or phrases that are unfamiliar. For example, Americans say "elevator," whereas the British say "lift." Write down six words or expressions that are common to your particular dialect of English. (If you are a native speaker of another language, do the same exercise with an appropriate dictionary.)

_____   _____
_____   _____
_____   _____

2. Write a creed for yourself to live by as a citizen of the world.

_____
_____
_____
_____
_____
_____
_____
_____
_____
_____
_____
_____
_____
_____
_____
_____

Group Activities

1. As a group, brainstorm about aspects of your "implicit" culture (those elements taken for granted by individuals). For example, list some fears, values, ideals, or other beliefs common to your culture. If more than one culture is represented in your group, compare and contrast the aspects of implicit culture in each.

Reactions:

_____

_____

_____

_____

_____

_____

_____

_____

2. As a group, brainstorm about aspects of your "explicit" culture (those elements that are visible and can be described verbally.) For example, list some customs, behaviors, and expressions common to your culture. If more than one culture is represented in your group, compare and contrast the aspects of explicit culture in each.

Reactions:

_____

_____

_____

_____

_____

_____

_____

_____

Reaction Paper 2.1

This chapter has suggested that diversity increases the possibilities for progress and for positive change in the world. Explain what that means. Provide a concrete example of progress or change that was made possible by another point of view.

Reaction Paper 2.2

This chapter distinguished between ideal and real culture. Discuss some ideal aspects of your culture and how they contrast with the reality of people's actions.

Notes

Chapter 3

The Rights of People Who are Diverse

Introduction

Although we have seen that exceptionalities fall into many categories, the social climate in a culture tends to affect many of those persons at once. In other words, interest in promoting the rights of all people in general leads to attention to the rights of specific groups. In the United States, the labor movements of the 1930s helped to focus some attention on physical impediments to work and on the needs and rights of children. The 1950s and 60s saw the beginning of the civil rights movement, which focused on the need for social change in regard to African Americans. Gradually, the methods which proved to be effective in raising the consciousness of the American people about the plight of African Americans, such as education and free speech, came to be implemented in the cause of women's rights, gay rights, disability rights, and the rights of all individuals to freedom from discrimination. In all categories of exceptionality, people deserve and demand freedom from personal, social, and economic discrimination.

While we work for fundamental change in individual attitudes which will promote understanding and tolerance of difference, it is important to protect human and civil rights through legislation. Local, state, and federal laws insure opportunities for employment, provide for appropriate education and medical care, and seek to secure access to public buildings and streets for everyone. The struggle for equal opportunity has not been an easy one, nor is it over. However, thanks to the many court decisions which have upheld individual rights, state government and the federal government have gone far to establish a public policy through legislation which recognizes the right to be different.

The following is a brief discussion of some major areas of legislative protection. It is important for every individual in this society to be aware of the laws protecting our rights and the rights of others. Even a cursory study of this list will help you to see some of the difficulties people with exceptionalities may encounter. Such a study should raise your consciousness and increase your awareness of the ways in which individuals are penalized for being different in schools, in the workplace, and in social situations every day.

The Laws of Human Diversity

      The following overview examines the legal aspects of various categories of human diversity. Because state and local laws change frequently, this examination will focus primarily on selected federal legislation that affects all Americans. It is important to recognize that this information is not all-inclusive. Additional reading and study are needed to achieve a complete understanding of laws which impact persons who are diverse.

Age. As longevity increases, our society has the benefit of more and more older citizens who are increasingly physically able to perform in the workplace. These older Americans offer wisdom and experience from which we can all profit. Due to the changing nature of work in the information age, it is even more clear that there is no justification for discrimination on the basis of age.

      The Older Americans Act of 1965 (OAA) is designed to safeguard the rights of senior citizens. The Act focuses on health care, Social Security, and employment. The Administration on Aging (a division of the Office of Human Development Services) is the principal agency designated to carry out the provisions of the OAA. Senior advocacy groups in Washington monitor policy on Social Security, Medicare, and Medicaid.

Disability. The Rehabilitation Act of 1973 provides for a "Barrier-Free Environment" for people with disabilities and defines these individuals as persons who have a physical or mental impairment which substantially limits one or more major activities, have a record of such an impairment, or are regarded as having such an impairment. The Act requires any program or activity receiving federal monies to provide equal access and opportunities for people with disabilities. This includes people with cancer, heart disease, diabetes; cerebral palsy, epilepsy, mental illness, mental retardation; muscular dystrophy, multiple sclerosis; drug addiction and alcoholism; visual, hearing, and communication disorders. This comprehensive Act affects state and local government, education, transportation, housing, and employment.

      The Americans with Disabilities Act (ADA) of 1990 (Public Law 101-336) is considered a "civil rights bill" for individuals with disabilities. The ADA grants civil rights protection to individuals with disabilities in all public services, public accommodations, transportation, and telecommunications. Under ADA, employers with 15 or more employees may not refuse to hire or promote a person with a disability when that person is the most qualified person to perform the job. Additionally, an employer must make reasonable accommodation for a person with a disability if that accommodation will allow the person to perform the essential functions of the job. Public accommodations affected by the ADA include hotels, restaurants, auditoriums, stores, banks, doctors' offices, museums, libraries, parks, zoos, schools, and recreation facilities. According to ADA, it is discriminatory to fail to remove structural, architectural, and communication barriers in facilities where such removal is readily achievable. Telecommunications reform under ADA requires telephone services to provide "Telecommunications Relay Services" for those with hearing or speech impediments.

Education. The Individuals with Disabilities Education Act (IDEA), formerly the Education of All Handicapped Children Act, became law in 1990. Its purpose is to guarantee the availability of special education programs to children and youth with disabilities and to assure that educational decisions relating to such students are fair and appropriate. Additionally, it assists state and local governments in providing special education through the use of federal funds. It requires schools to provide appropriate elementary and secondary education to children and youth ages 3-22. This public law has been amended several times and now includes the provision of services for adolescents who are leaving school programs and beginning adult life, and requires the educational program of a student with a disability to include a plan for transition to post-secondary life. This plan must include appropriate assistive technology which benefits the student, such as microcomputers, alternative speech devices, and keyboards.

Equal Protection. You may have been the well-cared for child of a prosperous parent whose economic and social status offered you many benefits. As a young adult, however, you may be an unemployed student with no health insurance and a social profile which makes you vulnerable to the scrutiny of law-enforcement officers. Later, you may become part of any number of minority groups, either because of your gender, sexual orientation, physical or mental disability, health, or religion. If you live many years, you will certainly be a senior citizen. Even the most fortunate of us will at some time in our lives come to realize the importance of equal protection.

Equal Protection of Laws is your Constitutional right to receive the same protection under state law as any other person. The 14th Amendment to the Constitution says that "No State shall ... deny to any person within its jurisdiction the equal protection of the laws." This clause was meant to prevent state governments from favoring particular groups of people at the expense of other groups. All people are protected, including the poor, children, prisoners, non citizens, and minorities. State constitutions also contain equal protection clauses.

Families. The public policy decisions which have the greatest impact on children and families are made at the state and local levels. Child advocacy organizations speak out for improvement in the condition of the children in their community and state through legislative, executive, and judicial decisions on programs to meet children's needs. They focus on basic income and family support, child welfare, juvenile justice, nutrition, education, and child care programs. The term "family" does not have a precise legal meaning, so most laws include a definition of the term when they use it. In some legislation, the term means only people who are related by blood or marriage and live together. In other laws, family includes relatives who may or may not live in the same household. In still other laws it can mean two people or a group of people who stay committed to one another in a domestic setting for an unlimited period of time, sharing a home and responsibility for financial support and household duties. No specific number of persons is necessary to make up a legal family (Leonard, 1990).

Gender. Ironically, such leaders as English Prime Minister Margaret Thatcher, Indian Prime Minister Indira Gandhi, and Pakistani Prime Minister Benazir Bhutto are often seen as anomalies rather than cited as models for gender equality. Though women have served as senior officers on space shuttles, supreme court justices, chief executive officers of major corporations, and at the highest ranks in the military services, their ability to lead is still seen as a subject of debate. Based upon their exemplary performance in traditional male roles, from combat commander to truck driver, it must be concluded that the debate stems from gender discrimination alone.

Though women are guaranteed equality, many women in the United States are still fighting to claim their full equal rights under the law. Women's advocates seek the passage of an Equal Rights Amendment and constantly monitor legislation affecting women both in the workplace and at home. Title VII of the 1964 Civil Rights Act prohibits sexual discrimination in employment. The Equal Pay Act of 1963 prohibits discrimination in the form of different compensation for jobs with equal skill and responsibility. The Pregnancy Discrimination Act of 1978 prohibits discrimination against employees on the basis of pregnancy and childbirth with respect to employment and benefits.

Race. In one generation we have seen extraordinary progress toward full integration and equality for all races and nationalities. For example, Charlayne Hunter (Gault) became familiar to television viewers across America when, as a child, she had to be protected by the National Guard from protesters as she integrated a southern school. Today, Ms. Gault is widely known as a national television news anchor.

People of all different ethnic, racial, and national origins now have legal protection from discrimination (Coughlin, 1993). The 14th Amendment to the Constitution states that it is illegal to classify a citizen by his or her national origin, since a foreigner is entitled to equal protection under the law once that individual has been naturalized as a citizen. Brown v. Board of Education (1954) established as a matter of law that racially segregated education was unequal. Additionally, Title VII of the 1964 Civil Rights Act prohibits discrimination based upon an employee's race, color, or national origin.

Religion. The U.S. Constitution guarantees that all Americans are free to follow the religion of their choice or none at all. Article I of the Bill of Rights states that "Congress shall make no law respecting an establishment of religion, or prohibiting the free exercise thereof." The government can neither establish a state religion nor force anyone to attend or support any religious institution. Individuals have the right to worship as they please. Title VII of the 1964 Civil Rights Act prohibits discrimination on the basis of an employee's religion.

Although the letter of the law may be followed, as individuals we need to be aware of the spirit of the law. Looking at the wars and dissension around the world in such places as the Middle East, Northern Ireland, and the states of the former Soviet Union, we may congratulate ourselves on our rights to religious freedom. However, though protected by laws, many of us continue to suffer from a subtle bias against certain religions. It is important to be sensitive to the fact that children, for instance, may feel this discrimination when certain holidays are celebrated in school. For example, many public schools in the United States celebrate Christmas in some way, if only by taking a school vacation, while Jewish, Moslem, Buddhist, Hindu, and other minority religions may be hardly acknowledged, if at all. Such oversight has a significant effect on the way our children perceive the importance of these religions.

Sexual Orientation. As of the publication of this textbook, no well-defined body of law guarantees the rights of people who are homosexual. No federal law protects gay men and lesbians from discrimination in employment or housing. Advocacy groups continually focus on combating state-by-state anti-gay ballot initiatives, challenging the military ban, and establishing legal precedents to secure constitutional protections for lesbians and gay men.

As attorney and civil rights expert Donald Cohen explains, most anti-homosexual laws treat gay men and lesbians as a class of criminals who are not entitled to assert their civil rights. In many states, private consensual sexual acts between same sex adults remain criminal, and individuals have been imprisoned simply for expressing their sexuality. Such anti-homosexual laws mistakenly equate being gay, or living an alternative lifestyle, with the criminal act of sodomy. As long as being gay is considered criminal, Cohen suggests, there can be no secure and lasting legal rights for all people (Cohen, 1994).

Cohen considers criminal laws which proscribe consensual sexual activity to be the central obstacle to homosexual rights. In Bowers v. Hardwick (1986), the United States Supreme Court held that states may criminalize sexual activity between consenting adults. "The right to privacy, therefore, did not protect people from being arrested for private sexual conduct even in their own homes," Cohen explains. Yet the battle for homosexual rights on state constitutional grounds continues to be an evolving process, he says, and the tide is turning. For example, in Texas v. Morales (1992), an appellate court held that the Texas State Constitution protected the right to choose one's sexual orientation. And in Kentucky v. Wasson (1992), the Kentucky Supreme Court decided that the Kentucky Constitution protects the freedom to choose one's own sexual partner and struck down the state's anti-sodomy law (Cohen, 1994).

Because our laws still don't protect equal rights on the basis of sexual orientation, people who are gay, lesbian, or bisexual continue to face discriminatory practices. It should also be recognized that people who are heterosexual also have no legal protection on the basis of their sexual orientation.

Size. As of the publication of this textbook, no well-defined body of law guarantees the rights of people who are overweight or excessively tall or short. Advocacy groups seek to fight discrimination against people on the basis of weight or stature. They work to educate lawmakers and serve as national legal clearinghouses for attorneys challenging size discrimination. Our media culture clearly promotes certain physical attributes such as tallness and thinness. Perhaps because height is perceived as a positive attribute, there seems to be little awareness of the challenges of those who are exceptionally tall. The inaccessibility of public facilities is also problematic for those who may not find ample legroom, headroom, or seating space in public transportation, theatres, schools, and other such places.

Socioeconomic Levels. Socioeconomic disadvantage is a complex, multi-faceted problem for many Americans of both genders and all races and national origins. The Equal Protection Clause of the 14th Amendment guarantees equal protection under the law for people living in poverty. Federal Social Security programs provide aid to families with needy dependent children, supplemental security income to persons with disabilities, and Medicaid to ensure health care for low-income families. The Commodities Distribution Act distributes surplus staple foods to needy families, and the Food Stamp Act of 1904 distributes coupons that may be exchanged for food. Advocacy groups monitor state and local legislation, focusing on welfare reform, job creation, public housing, and job training.

The Job Training and Partnership Act (JTPA) of 1982 (Public Law 97-300) authorizes federal funds administered by the Department of Labor to support local and regional employment assistance efforts. The JTPA offers an opportunity to address such diverse elements as basic literacy, skills development, and education in life skills such as job interviewing, budgeting, and parenting skills help. For example, it offers low-income or unemployed single parents the chance they may need to find financial aid, child care assistance, and parenting and legal advice so that theycan address their education needs and learn a skill or trade.

Legal Issues Diverse People May Face

- Dealing with the police
- Knowing when one needs a lawyer
- Finding the right lawyer
- How to conduct oneself during an arrest
- Avoiding legal problems
- Knowing one's legal rights
- Understanding the language of the law
- Understanding how the law works
- How to report a violation of one's rights
- Knowing what constitutes a crime
- Legal expenses
- Becoming the victim of a crime
- Knowing the rights of the accused
- Witnessing a crime
- Going to court
- Courtroom protocol
- Trial procedures
- Serving on a jury
- Being a trial witness

Summary

As we have become educated as a culture about the causes and effects of exceptionalities, we have made some significant, though still inadequate, progress in the development of legal protection of human rights, and through that legislation have begun to undergo real social change. Countless individuals have sacrificed time, money, energy, and sometimes their lives to bring about these changes. For example, civil rights leaders Martin Luther King, Jr. and Madger Evers gave their lives for their causes. Rosa Parks risked her life for integration of public transportation. Col. Margarethe Cammermeyer revealed her sexual orientation at the risk of her military career. Vietnam war veteran Ron Kovic dedicated his life to securing the rights of veterans with disabilities. Madeline Murray O'Hair, an atheist, fought for her freedom *not* to worship. Many challenges remain in the attempt to secure full participation in society for each and every person regardless of race, gender, religion, sexual orientation, ethnicity, age, or handicapping condition. It will take the continued efforts of dedicated individuals to bring about more change.

As time passes, new issues arise which demand attention and resolution. In the 1980's and 90's, a major new source of concern was the question of how to meet the needs of people with AIDS and other contagious diseases while protecting their privacy and insuring their rights. Other on-going issues center around the problem of drug abuse as it has an impact on the society at large. New technology brings new possibilities for treatment of personal and social ills, but the paramount issue is still the preservation of human rights.

References

Cohen, D. G. (1994). The rights of gay men and lesbians. *Legal Interest,* 5-10.

Coughlin, G. G. (1993). *Your handbook of everyday law.* New York: Harper Perennial.

Leonard, R. (1990). *Family law dictionary.* Berkeley, CA: Nolo Press.

Suggested Readings

Curry, H. (1994). *A legal guide for lesbian and gay couples.* Berkeley, CA: Nolo Press.
This is a self-help guide for gay couples which covers various legal statutes affecting homosexuals.

Gifis, S. H. (1991). *Law dictionary.* New York: Barrons.
This is an indispensable handbook covering United States law and defining many important legal terms.

Leonard, R. (1990). *Family law dictionary.* Berkeley, CA: Nolo Press.
Provided in this book are some easy to understand definitions of legal terms and legislation important to families in the United States.

U.S. Deptartment of Justice. (1990). *The Americans with disabilities act.* Washington DC: U.S. Department of Justice.
This pamphlet presents a brief overview of the Americans with Disabilities Act.

Exploration

Individual Activities

1. Do you think that most citizens know about the laws concerning human diversity and their implications? Conduct an informal survey of your friends and family.

Observations:

_____

_____

_____

_____

_____

_____

_____

_____

2. As you go through your daily activities, you often notice the accommodations made for people with disabilities–ramps, lower water fountains, Braille on elevator buttons, etc. Imagine that you are a politician who would like to design a bill to help members of another category of diversity. Describe legislation that you would sponsor to better the quality of exceptional people's lives.

_____

_____

_____

_____

_____

_____

_____

_____

Group Activities

1. Under Equal Protection of Laws, all people are protected, including prisoners and non citizens. Discuss in your group whether or not you believe that prisoners and non citizens are entitled to equal protection.

Reactions:

_____
_____
_____
_____
_____
_____
_____
_____

2. A bill is being debated concerning the rights of excessively tall individuals. This bill, if passed, will grant tall people free college education and low cost housing. Your class is the deciding body for this law. Choose six members of the class to make the final decision based upon the arguments presented by the rest of the class. Arrange to have half the class argue the pros of this bill and the other half the cons.

Reactions:

_____
_____
_____
_____
_____
_____
_____

Reaction Paper 3.1

The Americans with Disabilities Act is legislation that is a civil rights bill for people with disabilities. It states that the workplace must be made to accommodate people with disabilities. Assume that you are an employee in a company where people with disabilities are not being fairly accommodated. What would you do to improve the situation?

Reaction Paper 3.2

Some people believe that laws and legislation are needed to improve the quality of life for low-income families. Others would argue that it shouldn't require laws and legislation to aid the poor, but that members of society should naturally help those in need. What is your position? Why?

Notes

Chapter 4

Racial and Ethnic Diversity

Introduction

More than any other category of human diversity, the concept of "race" is controversial and explosive. Among both politicians and humanitarians there is a growing perception that it is desirable to minimize racial differences and to emphasize human similarities. Some anthropologists have even gone so far as to state that there is no such thing as race at all, maintaining that the study of human differences merely serves to perpetuate prejudice (May, 1971). Yet interracial tensions and hostilities persist, and many people feel that minimizing differences is done at the risk of sacrificing important racial and ethnic distinctions enjoyed by various groups. It seems pointless to deny the existence of different types of people, especially since unity and harmony among peoples do not require that everyone be identical. In fact, the definition of harmony is many *different* voices in accord. The purpose of this chapter, then, is to define the concepts of race and ethnicity in the hope that an understanding of them will encourage a genuine brotherhood and sisterhood among humans.

The Culture of Race and Ethnicity

It is not possible to make any definitive statements about the culture of race beyond the fact that culture and race are generally considered to be separate issues. Much of what we associate as racial culture is actually geographic and social in nature. A person's country of origin and his or her race are distinct. People of African origin, for example, may be of any race. Likewise, how we define "African culture" depends upon where in the world we look. The people of the Congo share much cultural heritage with the French, the people of Somalia are culturally defined by their Muslim heritage, and the African American population has created its own unique culture influenced by America's diverse immigrant population. With exponentially increased immigration and travel worldwide, distinctions of race and culture are blurring.

Ethnicity, on the other hand, can definitely be linked to culture. In fact, ethnicity arises from the cultural commodities that are shared by a number of individuals (Auerbach, 1994). Such commodities are magnets that draw individuals together, providing them with a group identity and consciousness. A shared nationality, language, religion, or history may be the focal point of an ethnic group. Like races, ethnicities often overlap. A person with parents of Cuban and German backgrounds could choose to be called either Cuban American, German American, or simply American, and could celebrate any one cultural heritage or all three.

Terminology

Before we delve into the topic of racial and ethnic diversity, an understanding of the following terms is crucial.

Race. This is an anthropological concept used to divide humankind into categories based on physical characteristics of size and shape of the head, eyes, ears, lips, and nose, and the color of skin and eyes (Bennett, 1993). Race has never scientifically been equated with any mental characteristics such as intelligence, personality, or character.

Racism. This is the belief that one's own race is superior to another. This belief is based on the erroneous assumption that physical attributes of a racial group determine their social behavior as well as their psychological and intellectual characteristics (Bennett, 1986).

Ethnicity. This refers to how members of a group perceive themselves and how they are in turn perceived by others. *Ethnic* describes a group of people within a larger society that is socially distinguished or set apart by others and/or by itself, primarily on the basis of racial and/or cultural characteristics. Such characteristics may include religion, language, and tradition. The beliefs of individuals about their own ethnic group tend to be similar to, and more positive than, the beliefs of those outside the group.

Nationality. One's nationality is not necessarily tied to one's culture, ethnicity, or race. Nationality simply refers to the country where a person was born.

Minority. Although this term should simply be used to describe a subset within a population, it often connotes inferior or lesser status in comparison to the majority. Often the minority is a sociological term referring to a social group that occupies a subordinate position in a society.

Americanization. This term refers to a practice of acculturation that seeks to merge small ethnic and linguistically diverse communities into a single dominant national culture (Garcia, 1994). Americanization is a synonym for the "melting pot" phenomenon.

Prejudice. This is a set of rigid and unfavorable attitudes toward a particular group which is formed in disregard of facts. Prejudice is usually an unsupported judgment accompanied by disapproval. This is a learned concept, not innate. Individuals generally do not realize how prejudiced they actually are.

Bias. This is a personal preference that prevents one from making a fair judgment.

Discrimination. This is differential treatment based on unfair categorization. It is denial of justice prompted by prejudice. When we act on our prejudices, we engage in discrimination. Discrimination often involves keeping people out of activities or places because of the group to which they belong.

Scapegoating. This refers to the deliberate policy of blaming an individual or group when the fault actually lies elsewhere. It means blaming another group or individual for things they did not really do. Those that we scapegoat become objects of our aggression in work and deed. Prejudicial attitudes and discriminatory acts often lead to scapegoating. Members of disliked groups are denied employment, housing, political rights, or social privileges. Scapegoating can lead to verbal and physical violence, including death.

Stereotyping. This is a preconceived or oversimplified generalization involving beliefs about a particular group. Negative stereotypes are frequently the foundation of prejudice. The danger of stereotyping is that it ignores people as individuals and instead categorizes them as members of a group who all think and behave the same way. We may pick up these stereotypes from what we hear other people say, what we read, and what people around us believe. As a group becomes more distinctive in character, a consensus develops regarding stereotypes associated with that group.

Are You a Racist?

Answer yes or no to the following questions (adapted from Patterson & Kim, 1991):

1. Do you believe that your country would have fewer racial problems if different people would keep to their own kind?
2. Would it bother you to learn after an accident that you received a blood transfusion from someone of a different race?
3. Have you ever invited a person of another race into your home for a social occasion?
4. Would your friends be understanding if you married a person of another race?
5. Do you believe that some races are naturally superior to others?
6. Would you be reluctant to adopt a child of a different race?
7. Do you think that people of some races are more intelligent than others?
8. Do you think people of some races are more hard-working than others?
9. Do you think legal immigrants are stealing American jobs?
10. Would you send your child to a private school that did not accept racially diverse students?
11. Do you feel uncomfortable around people of different races?
12. Does it make you uneasy to see a man holding hands with a woman of a different race?
13. Do you have any racially diverse friends?
14. Do you believe that so-called minorities are poor because they fail to take advantage of the opportunities open to them?

Give yourself one point if you answered "yes" to questions 1, 2, 5, 6, 7, 8, 9, 10, 11, 12, 14. Give yourself one point if you answered "no" to questions 3, 4, 13.

How did you score?

9 - 14	= stubborn racist	(you categorize and judge people based solely upon race)
7 - 8	= bigoted	(you are generally intolerant of any race that is not your own)
5 - 6	= prejudiced	(you have preconceived ideas about people based upon race)
3 - 4	= biased	(your personal preferences color some of your judgments)
2	= tolerant	(you grant others their rights but still see differences based upon race)
0 - 1	= color-blind	(you do not categorize or judge people based upon race)

Racial Diversity

Racial differentiation is a product of evolution, natural selection, and genetic mixing, and human races vary greatly across the globe. As Edward Babun pointed out in *The Varieties of Man,* people of genetically diverse populations look different in superficial ways, such as skin color, facial features, body build and size, and hair type. They also differ in less apparent ways, such as resistance to various diseases, tolerance for extreme temperatures, frequencies of blood type, and other aspects of biochemistry and physiology. For all the external and internal differences, however, human races ultimately make up one species, *Homo sapiens* (Babun, 1969).

In the gene pool of any given race is an astronomical number of possible chromosome combinations. Differences among races account for a mere six percent of human genetic variation. Differences among tribes or nations within a race account for only eight percent of variation. Individual variation within local groups, on the other hand, accounts for eighty-five percent of genetic difference (Myers, 1995). Therefore, the average genetic difference between two Siberians or two Cubans is much greater than the difference between the two groups. Not all Japanese people are short with black hair. Not all Norwegians are tall with blond hair. In every race, the range of difference is vast.

The Problem with Racial Classification

The actual number of races has not been clearly defined. Some scientists classify humankind into five major stocks or subspecies (May, 1971):

- **Mongoloid:** yellow, tan and copper-colored Asian people with narrow or almond-shaped eyes, straight black hair, and wide cheekbones.

- **Negroid:** tan, black and brown-colored African people with tightly curled brown or black hair, high foreheads, and large lips and noses.

- **Capoid:** yellow-tan colored South African people with narrow eyes.

- **Caucasoid:** pinkish-white and olive-colored European people with blond to brunette and wavy to straight hair, blue or green eyes, and straight or pug noses.

- **Australoid:** dark brown to black-colored Australian, Indian, and Southeast Asian people with curly or wavy hair and heavy browbridges.

Other scientists consider the traditional five groups to be outdated and have pinpointed as many as two thousand racial populations. The reason for such disagreement is that human races are constantly evolving and changing. Some of today's living races did not exist five hundred years ago, and others are older than written history (Babun, 1969). There hasn't been a pure race for more than 100,000 years (Duvall, 1994), and not all racial populations are completely distinct.

It is common today to find people who have backgrounds in two or more races, making it even more difficult to classify them. In fact, the very concept of race, according to the Census Bureau, now reflects self-identification and does not denote any clear-cut scientific definition of biological stock. How a person defines his or her race ultimately depends upon which race he or she most closely identifies with (Famighetti, 1993).

The problem with racial classification goes deeper than merely what categories or how many categories we choose to use. Geneticists have had trouble even identifying the gene or sets of genes responsible for race, and many now claim that race does not exist.

The idea of race is actually relatively new in human history. The term was coined by the French naturalist George Louis Leclerc Buffon in 1749. Perhaps the concept could disappear just as quickly as it was invented. "If members of society refused to believe that skin color and certain other physical traits were important, the concept of race would not exist" (Auerbach, 1994, p. 1377).

The Uses of Racial Classification

In spite of the fact that racial classification is virtually meaningless, our society categorizes people by race all the time. We use racial labels on birth certificates, marriage licenses, college applications, and other official forms. Race is used to determine eligibility for education

Spotlight on Diversity

My son is adopted. We brought him to the United States from Korea in 1980. When he was old enough, we talked to him about the fact that he was born in another country but that now he was American.

Shortly after he started kindergarten, he began to resist going to school. When we questioned him, he said that the children called him names because he is Chinese.

"But that's silly," we told him. "You're not Chinese, you're Korean." What he said made me realize that I had no way to help him understand racism, because I couldn't understand it myself. "But Mom," he said, "they don't know any names for Koreans, so that's why they call me a Chink." He had already accepted the idea that racism was a given, and he was only 5 years old.

—Dinah L., San Diego, CA

scholarships and grants. Race is also a factor in what majors and courses a school offers, such as programs in Afro-American, Native American, Latin American, and Asian studies. The Census Bureau asks people to assign themselves to a particular racial category. The government uses these census figures to determine voting districts and allot funding for social programs including low-income housing, medical clinics, literacy education, and minority benefits.

A Changing Definition of "Minority"

Just as our conception of what "race" means is changing, our definition of "minority" must change as well. That's because the demographics in the United States are shifting rapidly. In 1995, nearly one out of every four Americans was a member of a so-called minority racial or ethnic group. Estimates of future population predict that by the year 2000 one out of every three Americans will be a minority. By 2050, the percentage of the population that is White (not Hispanic) will decrease from 75.7 percent (in 1990) to 52.7 percent (Landes, 1994). With each passing day, the word "minority" loses both its original meaning (a smaller part) and its connotation (something lesser than the majority).

Stereotypes of People from other Countries

The following stereotypes of racially diverse people are *not* true:

- They are in the United States illegally
- They spend all their money in their home country
- They do not understand English
- They have a large family
- They have a lot of money or come from a wealthy family
- They are stealing American jobs
- They are either work-a-holics or lazy

Issues Racially Diverse People may Face

- Prejudice and bigotry
- Being labeled as a foreigner
- Being treated differently
- Homesickness, separation from family
- Ignorance about country of origin or heritage

- Being perceived as an illegal immigrant
- Being perceived as "Un-American"
- Cultural differences
- Overcoming stereotypes
- Interracial relationships/dating
- Finding peer support
- Socioeconomic issues or assumptions
- Hate crimes

Support Services

Ethnic and racial populations have support groups, churches, and social organizations where people can interact and share their common heritage. Members meet and communicate through newsletters and social opportunities. Affirmative Action policies, which are often the target of debate, assist people who are discriminated against because of their race to obtain equal treatment in housing, employment, and banking.

Interactions

Take a stand against racist behavior. Don't be a guilty by-stander. Remaining silent only makes prejudiced people think you agree with them.

Remove "race" from your vocabulary. There is no scientific definition for race. It is a vague, imprecise category. The concept of race only serves to promote divisiveness.

Practice looking at people and not at labels. It often takes a conscious effort to unlearn prejudices and biases we have grown up with. Since members of any given group are just as diverse as members of any two groups, *everybody* is an "other."

Treat everyone you meet as an equal. Superficial differences have nothing to do with intelligence or ability. Beneath every skin tone and hair color is a human being just like you, experiencing many of the same joys, worries, doubts, and challenges inherent in being alive.

Celebrate a particular ethnic culture. Remember that ethnic groups are made up of people who *choose* to associate with each other. Your ethnicity is whatever you make it, and the celebration of your ethnic group tends to have a positive impact on everyone's lives.

Accept, respect, and celebrate diversity. Different individuals possess unique talents and personalities, and those should be respected, celebrated, and indeed sought after because they enrich all our lives.

Summary

As members of the genetically diverse human race, we need to appreciate our similarities as well as our differences. Skin color is the most common factor people use to separate themselves into smaller groups and "races." However, skin color is the perfect example of how race is relative. Depending upon what society or circumstance you are in, the shade of your skin may be variously interpreted. For example, the Creoles of Louisiana, a French-speaking people of mixed racial heritage, are variously seen as black, white, or Creole, depending upon the context (Auerbach, 1994). Perhaps we cannot ignore our superficial, genetic differences, but we should strive to take such differences at face value, so to speak. Ultimately, we are all members of the *human* race.

References

Auerbach, S. (Ed.). (1994). *The Encyclopedia of Multiculturalism.* (Vol. 5). New York: Marshall Cavendish.

Babun, Edward. (1969). *The varieties of man: An introduction to human races.* London: Collier-Macmillan.

Bennett, C. E. (1993). The black population in the United States. *Current Population Reports*, 20-471.

Bennett, C. I. (1986). *Comprehensive multicultural education: Theory and practice.* Boston: Allyn and Bacon.

Duvall, Lynn. (1994). *Respecting our differences: A guide to getting along in a changing world.* Minneapolis: Free Spirit.

Famighetti, R. (Ed.). (1993). *The world almanac and book of facts 1994.* Mahwah, NJ: Funk and Wagnalls.

Garcia, E. (1994). *Understanding and meeting the challenge of student cultural diversity.* Boston: Houghton Mifflin.

Landes, A. (Ed.). (1994). *Minorities: A changing role in America.* Wylie, TX: Information Plus.

May, J. (1971). *Why people are different colors.* New York: Holiday House.

Myers, D. G. (1995). *Psychology.* New York: Hope.

Patterson, J. & Kim, P. (1991). *The day America told the truth.* New York: Plume.

Suggested Readings

Baker, J. R. (1974). *Race.* New York: Oxford University Press.
This book defines the concepts of race and ethnicity and reviews evidence of the intelligence of four different human races.

Landes, A. (Ed.). (1994). *Minorities: A changing role in America.* Wylie, TX: Information Plus.
With up-to-date charts and diagrams, this book covers population trends that will force us to redefine what we mean by "minorities."

Thernstrom, Stephan. (Ed.). (1980). *Harvard Encyclopedia of American Ethnic Groups.* Cambridge: Harvard University Press.
This comprehensive book examines hundreds of categories of ethnic diversity, providing an informative, easy-to-read essay on each.

Exploration

Individual Activities

1. Thoroughly read today's newspaper. Then answer the following questions (adapted from Duvall, 1994):

a. How many stories involve racism or racial issues?

b. How many members of "minority" groups are mentioned?

c. How many stories are about members of the "majority"? (How can you tell?)

d. In what context are minorities mentioned? (Criminals? Victims? Experts? Prominent members of society?)

e. How often do members of minority groups appear in negative stories as opposed to positive ones?

Reactions:

_____

_____

_____

_____

2. How many stereotypes about your own race can you think of? Are any of them valid?

Reactions:

_____

_____

_____

_____

_____

_____

_____

_____

Group Activities

1. As a group, discuss what constitutes an "Average American." Where did your mental images of the Average American come from?

Reactions:

_____

_____

_____

_____

_____

_____

_____

_____

2. As a group, discuss how life will be different for white Americans when they are no longer the majority. How will life be different in the home, at school, at work, and in the community?

Reactions:

_____

_____

_____

_____

_____

_____

_____

_____

Notes

Reaction Paper 4.1

Today, over half a million immigrants per year are allowed to legally enter the United States. Do you think this country already has enough "foreigners," or should we open more doors to immigrants?

Reaction Paper 4.2

If you had no legal document that stated your race or ethnicity, how would you categorize yourself?

Notes

Chapter 5

Gender and Sexual Orientation

Introduction

Since the moment you were born and the doctor said, "It's a boy" or "It's a girl," your parents, peers, and society have helped to shape your sexual identity. Every human being, whether male of female, has gender and sexual orientation. While members of minority groups often have characteristics which make them apparently different from the majority, such as skin color, language, age, or size, our sexual orientation is invisible unless we choose to reveal it.

Our sexuality is so fundamental a part of who we are that it is a most difficult subject to discuss objectively. There are differing scientific views about gender differences and about the definition and roots of sexual orientation. However, everyone agrees on one point: the issues are complex and few people can address them without emotion. That is probably because we are all sexual beings. The purpose of this chapter is to examine the diversity of human sexuality and to suggest ways we can combat discrimination.

The Culture of Sexuality

The sexual impulse is a powerful driving force of culture. It colors and enriches our lives. The idealization of male and female beauty has given us famous works of art, most notably the ancient Greek Venus de Milo statue and Michaelangelo's sculpture of David. The longing for human connection, both spiritual, emotional, and sexual, is the subject of countless love stories, plays, ballets, and operas. When we think of sexuality, it is important not to confuse it with pornography and perversion. Too often people think of all sexuality as something bad or dirty. To do that is to think of ourselves as unnatural and to ignore an integral part of our being.

The Gender Gap

The gender gap refers to inequality between the sexes. For example, the life expectancy for American men is approximately eight years shorter than that for women. This life span disparity is in part due to the fact that men suffer from a variety of stress-related diseases which are connected to sexism. That is, men try to live up to societal expectations and ruin their health in the process (Hanmer, 1990). Another example of the gender gap is the fact that women in America earn about 70 cents for every dollar men are paid for similar full time employment. This wage disparity exists even though most women are self-supporting heads of households or necessary contributors to a family income. The gender gap arises out of a fundamental belief that men and women are not equal. The gender gap fuels sex discrimination.

Discrimination in Action

Prejudice and discrimination against people because of their gender or their sexual orientation is sometimes an even greater problem than that against other minorities because it potentially involves half the population of the earth. When we have discrimination against either men or women built into our laws and our system of education, for example, we may not even think of ourselves as being biased against one gender or the other. It is merely our way of life. While not everyone is a member of any other minority group, everyone has a particular gender and sexual orientation.

Whether knowingly or unknowingly, individuals and cultures practice sexual discrimination all the time. Masculine and feminine stereotypes define standards of beauty

Spotlight on Diversity

In 1989, when I was 45 years old, my husband retired and for the first time in my life, I entered the work force. I had been a housewife and mother and decided to use my experience and become a cook. I went to a local community college and got a certificate qualifying me as an apprentice chef.

I had a difficult time with my first job at a large hospital kitchen. I was a female in a male profession, which surprised me. I had thought that cooking was women's work. It was even harder for me because of my age and lack of experience. My supervisor came right out and told me I'd never go any higher in my profession because I was already too old and a female.

As it turned out, I left after a few months and took a lower-paying job in a nursing home. I had more responsibility there, since most chefs didn't want to work there. It felt like running away to me, but I just didn't want to work in a hostile environment.

—Sarah K., Denver, CO

which dictate how men and women decorate themselves. Gender role stereotypes have led us to distinguish between "men's" jobs and "women's" jobs and have shaped our legislation for child custody. Jokes, slams, slurs, graffiti, and whistling reveal our biased attitudes about gender and sexual orientation. Rapes and assaults carry sexist attitudes to a violent extreme. Whatever our sexual orientation, and whichever our gender, all of us suffer in some way every day because of our own lack of information and understanding about human sexuality. Fortunately, ignorance is a curable disease.

Stereotypes of Issues Regarding Gender Relations

Below is a list of common stereotypes about women and men. It is *not* true that:

- Men are all sexists
- Men are emotionally strong
- Men never listen
- Men are not affectionate
- All men are homophobic
- Men are over-aggressive sexually
- Men are weak if they have feminine qualities
- Men and women are opposites

- Women cannot be sexist
- Women are emotionally weak
- Women always want to talk
- Women are all affectionate
- Women are not homophobic
- Women do not think about sex
- Women are strong if they have masculine qualities
- Women and men are not different

Common stereotypical language, such as the terms listed below, tend to demean people. Though not all of these terms are demeaning in all contexts, they encourage divisiveness and generalizations.

Terms that belittle, demean, or stereotype men:

- hunk
- jock
- bastard
- effeminate
- fag
- fruit
- queen
- wimp
- dork
- prick
- pig
- mama's boy
- queer
- fairy
- pansy
- sissy

Terms that belittle, demean, or stereotype women:

- broad
- bimbo
- cow
- butch
- amazon
- lesbo
- the wife
- the little woman
- chick
- babe
- bitch
- dyke
- honey
- tomboy
- my old lady
- the ball and chain

Issues People May Face Related to Gender

- Lack of awareness of the other gender
- Sexual assault
- Stereotyped behaviors for men and women
- Stereotyped roles for men and women
- Developing relationships
- Puberty
- Cultural differences in defining masculinity and femininity
- Sexual harassment
- H.I.V. and A.I.D.S.
- Equal opportunity
- Cultural pressures to have a family
- Cultural pressures to get married
- Cultural pressures to have children
- Stereotyped careers for men and women
- Defining masculinity and femininity
- Body image
- Sexism in general
- Sexual behavior
- Finding role models
- Gender equity

The Gender Movements

Whether you are male or female, the way your gender is perceived and treated in the world is no doubt of great importance to you. Though men and women in the United States enjoy more freedom than in much of the world, the struggle for gender equity is ongoing. Sexual harassment, sexist institutions, and domestic violence continue to thwart our fight for rights. The women's and men's movements seek to empower individuals by addressing such issues as:

Power in Society. Women are barely tokens in the decision-making bodies of our nation. In Congress, women make up about 5% of the lawmakers. In state legislatures, the number is less than 20%. In order to achieve equal power in society, the gender movements seek to put more women into policy-making positions in government, business, education, religion, and all the other powerful institutions of society. Many men as well as women support feminist goals and encourage women to be politically active, to run for office from any political party, and to participate in the decision-making processes of the nation.

Traditional Roles. Often even feminists overlook the issue of homemaker's rights. There has historically been little recognition for the economic value of the vital services homemakers, whether male or female, perform for family and society. The gender movements believe that legislation reflecting the reality of marriage as an equal economic partnership would go far to end discrimination against this group.

Because we all have heard and accepted that we live in a male-dominated society, it is easy to overlook some important and disturbing facts about what it could be like to be a modern male. While a small minority of men may indeed hold most of the power in our world, the majority of males are suffering from the deterioration of their traditional roles. The oppression of men can clearly be seen in alarming statistics on male addiction, suicide, and depression. Male teenagers are five times more likely to take their own lives than females. Overall, men commit suicide at four times the rate of women. Men between the ages of 18 and 29 suffer alcohol dependency at three times the rate of women of the same age group. More than two-thirds of all alcoholics are men. Men account for more than 90 percent of arrests for alcohol and drug abuse violations. Sixty percent of all high school dropouts are males. Men's life expectancy is 10 percent shorter than women's (derived from Myers, 1995).

Both gender movements seek to broaden the definition of what it is to be male and female in our society. At the same time, there is clearly a need to consider the positive qualities of traditional roles and to explore emerging roles as well.

Economic Rights. Gender equity requires full economic equality between men and women. Eighty percent of America's homeless are men. At the same time, female-headed families in the U.S. are four times as likely to be poor as male-headed or couple-headed families. The fight to end poverty focuses on equality in jobs, pay, credit, insurance, pensions, fringe benefits, and Social Security, through legislation, negotiation, labor organizing, education, and litigation.

Equal Rights Amendment. Though twice proposed in the U.S. Congress since 1923, the Equal Rights Amendment has yet to be ratified. Women are still not in the fundamental law of the land. Leaders of the gender movements believe that the ERA is essential to establish equality under the law for women, and the gender movements are committed to its passage as a priority. One right the ERA would guarantee is for women to serve in combat in the military and to perform traditional male tasks such as combat piloting. We have been seeing, however, that many of the outcomes sought under the ERA are slowly being adopted without the passing of the amendment.

Reproductive Rights. The question of reproductive rights for women continues to fuel a controversy which deeply divides Americans of both genders. The so-called Pro-Choice advocates support access to safe and legal abortion and to effective birth control. They oppose attempts to restrict these rights through legislation, regulation, or Constitutional amendment. The so-called Pro-Life advocates oppose abortion on moral, ethical, and civil-rights grounds. They support alternatives such as adoption, abstinence, and pregnancy prevention. Beliefs about reproductive rights are frequently fraught with emotion and continue to result in violent confrontation. This is an issue that profoundly needs mutual understanding and one that transcends gender differences, encompassing personal philsophy and religion.

Custody and Child Support: Because our society has redefined gender roles and the meaning of "family," many people in the gender movements feel that laws concerning custody and child support need to be redefined accordingly. The gender movements seek public support for the vital role of fathers, stepfathers, foster fathers, uncles, brothers, and mentors in the growth and development of children while continuing support for the vital role of mothers and other female family members. The movements advocate joint custody for mothers and fathers, equality in child custody litigation, enforcement of children's rights of access to both parents, and equitable financial child support guidelines, orders, and enforcement.

Parental Leave Legislation. The so-called "Lost Father" syndrome refers to the fact that men too often do not take an active role in child rearing. To help remedy this situation, the gender movements support parental leave legislation, which gives working parents the right to take time from work to care for children. The movements also encourage fathers to push for changes in the workplace, including more flexible hours, part-time work, job sharing, and home-based employment so they can play more of a role in child care.

Harassment and Assault. More and more often, formerly feminist issues such as sexual harassment and gender discrimination in the workplace have become men's issues as well as women's. As our societal consciousness is raised, our justice system is recognizing that women aren't the only victims of sexual and physical abuse, including rape. Both women and men are frequently victims of sexual assault and spousal abuse. Rape and spousal assault legislation and support programs for battered women and men address the problem, but in spite of widespread attention and tremendous effort, the problem for both sexes continues to grow.

Education. In many communities–especially inner cities–men are often absent from the homes as well as from the schools. The gender movements have as a primary goal the re-establishment of a male voice in education. They seek to provide men with greater opportunities to be teachers and role models in early-grade classes. Such a male presence can help fatherless male children develop self-esteem.

Community Involvement. The gender movements seek to revive men's and women's concern for their community by encouraging the participation of men and women in community-based boys' and girls' clubs, scout troops, sports leagues, religious organizations, and big brother and sister programs.

Sexual Orientation

We all necessarily use labels to describe actions and attributes. However, it is problematic even for doctors and mental health professionals to find appropriate and accurate labels for sexual orientation. The subject is too complex, and human feelings, thoughts, and actions are seldom easy to objectify. We use the terms *gay* (men), *lesbian* (women), or *homosexual* to describe people who are attracted to persons of their same sex. We use *heterosexual* to describe those attracted to the opposite sex. *Bisexual* refers to men and women who may be attracted to both genders. *Straight* refers to men and women who are exclusively heterosexual. However, virtually all experts on human psychology agree that within everyone there exist both feminine and masculine traits. There is no "normal" or "abnormal" orientation, and homosexuality is not a disease (Reiss, 1980). Both aggression and sensitivity can be found in every emotionally healthy person, regardless of gender.

Our sexuality is an invisible quality. Scientists disagree about whether we choose our orientation, are led to it by our environment and social interactions, or are born with it. Many experts now believe it is a combination of factors. We cannot use the term *sexual orientation* to divide people into two groups, heterosexual and homosexual. Sexuality is not black or white. Rather, many people fall into some category between the two extremes. It is important to note that sexual behavior and sexual orientation are not the same. Some people engage in sexual activity with same sex partners who do not consider themselves gay or lesbian.

Incidence of Homosexuality

Suppose there are twenty people in your class, some male and some female. It's likely that two or more of your classmates are not heterosexual. Estimates of the incidence of homosexuality vary depending upon how strictly homosexuality is defined and the methodology of the study. The Kinsey Report of 1948 estimated that ten percent of the adult population was homosexual, and most current estimates tend to lean toward the ten-percent level. However, a University of Chicago survey in 1994, where researchers who were strangers to the respondents asked questions regarding sexual orientation, put the number at about three percent (Gallagher, 1994). Such low figures need to be considered carefully due to the methods utilized in the study. Due to

---

Spotlight on Diversity

When I was 14, I realized that I was gay. It was not an easy thing to face because I grew up hearing nothing but negative comments and jokes about homosexuality from everyone around me. I was very afraid that people would change their impressions of me if they ever discovered my sexual orientation. I even developed several health problems as a result of the turmoil that I felt.

One night I vented my frustrations in a letter to my parents. I never intended them to read it, at least not consciously. My mother found the note the next day while I was away at school, and she left another note for me in its place. She was deeply saddened by the entire situation: my sexuality in general, the stress I had forced upon me, and my fear of discussing it with anyone. My parents then began to send me to a therapist to discuss my emotions and to attempt to "repair the problem."

After quite a bit of therapy, I ended up feeling even better about my sexual orientation than before. Family counseling later encouraged my parents to accept and love me regardless of the way I was. I then had the self-esteem to come out to my friends and other relatives and have since felt very positive about my life and my relationship with my parents.

—*Jeffery B., Richmond, VA*

social stigmas and people's reluctance to confide private information to a relative stranger, any statistic on sexuality must be taken with a grain of salt.

Your best friend may be gay or lesbian and you may not even know it. In maturity, people sometimes realize that they have a different sexual orientation than they believed themselves to have had in youth. As sexuality expert Margaret Hyde noted, many gays never admit their feelings to any of their friends. One cannot necessarily identify homosexual people by the way they talk, dress, or act (Hyde & Forsyth, 1994). Just as heterosexuals fall into many different types, so do homosexuals.

Labeling

Labeling not only promotes prejudice, but it is pointless when it refers to sexual orientation. It is impossible to know what someone feels or what his or her point of view is unless you are told by that person. We can observe behavior, but even behavior can be misleading. Many gay men and women are married to opposite sex partners, are parents, and in every way fit stereotypes for heterosexuals. Conversely, many heterosexual people fit stereotypes we may have for homosexuals. Women may dress in a masculine way, have short haircuts or deep voices, for example. Men may dress in flamboyant clothing, have long hair, or wear a lot of jewelry. We accept these variances from the traditional in many contexts every day. For instance, we don't label entertainers or people from different cultures as readily as we do those in our own social circles. If we look closely at our reactions and examine our labels, we will see how useless and sometimes silly they actually are.

Stereotyping

There are many different manifestations of sexual prejudice. *Chauvinism* is a belief that one gender is superior to the other. *Sexism* is discrimination against a particular gender. *Homophobia* is dislike or distrust stemming from feelings about a person's sexual orientation or lifestyle.

Biases and discrimination arise from and feed misinformation and fear. Some biases grow out of myths about sexual orientation. For instance, many people believe that men who feel a compulsion to wear women's clothes are homosexual. In fact, these men, called *transvestites,* are predominately heterosexual. *Pedophiles,* adult men or women who seek sexual satisfaction from children, fall into neither heterosexual or homosexual categories. Though pedophiles are often erroneously thought to be homosexual, it is not the gender of the child they are attracted to but rather the child's prepubescence. *Transsexuals* are individuals who have undergone or are in the process of undergoing a sex change operation because they do not like the gender they were born with. Transsexualism is not related to sexual orientation, but rather has to do with physiology. A person who is *asexual* has no sexual feelings for either men or women.

There are many myths about homosexuals. The following popular stereotypes (adapted from Papish, 1995) are likely to sound very familiar to you, even though they are recognized as being myths:

Stereotypes of gay men:

- high voice
- gourmet cook
- fashion oriented
- one night stands
- not attractive to women
- have A.I.D.S./H.I.V.
- limp wrists
- sissies
- small, slight build
- not interested in sports
- want to be women
- body builder
- physical weakness
- lisp
- recruit new gays
- effeminate
- molest children
- promiscuous
- had distant fathers
- good dancers
- had overbearing mothers
- female impersonators
- artistic

Stereotypes of lesbian women:

- masculine
- aggressive
- fat/husky
- athletic
- strong
- ugly
- short hair
- tough
- short
- hiking boots
- hairy legs
- not attractive
- wear men's clothes
- non-sexual
- want to be men
- wear flannel shirts
- have tatoos

Occupations believed (most often incorrectly) to be "typical" for gay men:

- hairdresser
- art gallery owner
- interior decorator
- ballet dancer
- actors/theatre
- airline flight attendant
- musician
- antique dealer
- gourmet chef
- artist
- fashion designer
- male model

Occupations believed (most often incorrectly) to be "typical" for lesbian women:

- construction worker
- military
- camp counselor
- truck driver
- fire fighter
- professional athlete

- mechanic
- gym teacher
- law enforcement
- bartender
- old-maid teacher
- folk singer

Issues People May Face Regarding Sexual Orientation

- Harassment
- Alienation
- Inability to share about their lives
- Inability to share relationships
- Sexually transmitted diseases
- Self-awareness and self-esteem
- Disclosure or coming out
- Religious issues
- Finding a peer group
- Finding support
- Fair and equal treatment
- Confidentiality
- Lack of legal support
- Finding mentors or positive role models
- Fitting some stereotypes
- Rejection from close friends
- Rejection or alienation from family
- Rejection from society or the community
- Gay bashing and threats
- Fear of being alone
- Rejection from careers
- Sexism and heterosexism
- Acceptance and/or respect
- Understanding
- Living arrangements
- Pressures to be heterosexual or get married
- Oppressive laws in their states

Support Services

The National Organizations of Men and Women sponsor local support organizations for abused spouses, including shelters and counseling for abused spouses, gender support groups, and social groups. Gay-Lesbian-Bisexual owned and operated hotels, restaurants, bookstores, and travel agencies cater to the interests of their clients. Many churches welcome people of different sexual orientations and sponsor support groups. Telephone hotlines operate 24-hours a day in most cities, providing general counseling and crisis intervention for men and women of all orientations.

Interactions

Don't assume that anyone or everyone is heterosexual. Assume that you do not know anyone's sexual orientation for certain. Accordingly, do not use language that may be offensive.

Help to stop sexist behavior. Notice and ask people not to tell sexist jokes or use sexist language. At the same time, try to acknowledge when someone takes even small steps in the direction of tolerance and sensitivity.

Avoid discussing others' behavior. Refer only to your own behavior.

Work to safeguard the basic rights of all people. Some people may be uncomfortable with their own sexuality and may need friendly support.

Be sensitive to labels. Call people what they prefer to be called, and make an effort to determine what is appropriate in a given situation. If you are unsure what designations to use, ask. But avoid labeling people whenever possible. Differences should be mentioned only when relevant.

Avoid biased speech and writing. We can help to remove bias in our speech and in writing by using terms such as "same-gender," "male-male," "female-female," and "male-female" sexual behavior when referring to sexual pairings.

Avoid patronizing. Sometimes when we try to stretch beyond our prejudices, we make patronizing statements unintentionally, such as "You don't *seem* gay."

Treat others as you would like to be treated. Sexual orientation has nothing to do with ordinary daily living. Treating others as you would like to be treated yourself is just a simple matter of respect for human diversity.

Demonstrate change. If people are responding negatively to you, instead of sticking on that point, show them something positive they can respond to. Draw upon their optimism rather than their fears. Find a common point (for example, you both cheer for the same team) so that it gives the person something different to focus upon. We can break down prejudices one person at a time. Provide a model through your own behavior. You will experience change in yourself as you change other people (Kaye, 1994).

Summary

The varieties of human sexuality defy easy categorization, even though labels are pervasive in our society. Though a minority of people are strictly heterosexual and strictly homosexual, most others fall somewhere in the middle. Biases about gender, sexual orientation, and men's and women's "natural roles" have led to sexual discrimination. Until we remove sexism from our institutions and sexist attitudes from ourselves, human beings will continue to be limited (Hanmer, 1990).

References

Gallagher, J. (1994). 10%: reality or myth? The Advocate 15 Nov., 23.

Hanmer, T. J. (1990). *Taking a stand against sexism and sex discrimination.* New York: Franklin Watts.

Hyde, M. O. & Forsyth, E. H. (1994). *Know about gays and lesbians.* Brookfield, CT: Millbrook Press.

Kaye, K. (1994). *Workplace wars and how to end them.* New York: American Management Association.

Myers, D. G. (1995). *Psychology.* New York: Hope.

Papish, R. (1995). Diverse works. Gainesville, FL: University of Florida.

Reiss, B. F. (1980). Psychological tests in homosexuality. In J. Marmor, (Ed.), *Homosexual behavior* (pp. 296-311). New York: Basic Books.

Suggested Readings

Berbards, N. (1989). *Male/female roles: Opposing viewpoints.* San Diego: Greenhaven Press.
In this book, various authors debate how sex roles were established and how men and women respond to changes in sex roles.

Deegan, M. J. & Brooks, N. A. (1985). *Women and disability: A double handicap.* New York: Transaction Books.
This book discusses the way disability magnifies the effects of sexism on women and the way that disability changes relations of disabled women with men and with other women.

McCauslin, M. (1992). *The facts about lesbian and gay rights.* New York: Crestwood House.
This book examines various myths, fears, and misconceptions about homosexuality and current attempts to gain fair treatment of homosexuals in the areas of housing, the media, the church, and the military.

Persing, B. S. (1983). *The nonsexist communicator: Solving the problems of gender and awkwardness in modern English.* Englewood Cliffs, NJ: Prentice-Hall.
This book proposes ways to avoid using sexist language and suggests non-gender-specific alternatives.

Exploration

Individual Activities:

1. As you get dressed in the morning, observe what articles of clothing you put on. What elements of your wardrobe or personal grooming adhere to a gender stereotype? Write your thoughts below:

_____

_____

_____

_____

_____

_____

_____

2. Think back on your own childhood and on children whom you know today. In our culture, how are children led to stereotypical interests through toys, books, games, etc.? Write your observations below:

_____

_____

_____

_____

_____

_____

_____

Group Activities:

1. As a group, think of role models who transcend stereotypes. Write the names of the role models below and explain why you chose them:

_____

_____

_____

_____

_____

_____

_____

_____

_____

2. Imagine that you are presented with the business cards below. What is your immediate assumption about their owners' gender and/or sexual orientation?

Dr. N. R. Jones	**Pat Smith**	**Chris Brown**	**Capt. Terry L. Black**
Dept. of Women's Studies	*Smith's Gym*	*Massage Therapy*	*U.S. Air Force*

Discuss with your group why you made certain initial assumptions about these people. Write your reactions below:

_____

_____

_____

_____

_____

_____

_____

_____

Reaction Paper 5.1

Have you ever seen a person on the street and thought he or she was gay or lesbian? Describe what dress, features, or behavior made you think so. What other factors besides sexual orientation may have explained what you saw? How valuable was your labeling?

Reaction Paper 5.2

Are there some types of work which you consider inappropriate for females or for males? Explain why.

Notes

Chapter 6

Religious Diversity

Introduction

Religion involves powerfully-charged feelings, passionate dedications, and deep loyalties. Religion is as old as humankind. In a very real sense, the history of humankind has been driven by religion. In the name of religion, wars have been fought, new territories have been discovered, and conflicts have been resolved. Though there are myriad expressions of spirituality across the globe, the underlying religious impulse is shared by all faiths. The purpose of this chapter is to define what religion means, present an overview of the major and minor belief systems of the world, and examine steps you can take to understand people who follow faiths different from your own. The ultimate aim of this chapter is for you to view your own religion in a universal context.

The Culture of Religion

Our culture is enriched by religious traditions. The passing of our years is marked by festivals, rituals, and holidays which honor figures and events from many faiths. Such celebrations typically involve special costumes, foods, dances, and songs. The constant repetition of religious stories has kept alive some of the world's finest literature through the ages. Much of the most beautiful architecture and art in the world, from the pyramids in Egypt to the Sistine Chapel in Rome, have come from our attempt to express religious feelings.

Not all religions survive. The gods of Ancient Greece, for instance, are no longer worshipped. It takes people to keep a religion alive, and people incorporate religion into their daily lives in such profound ways that we are often unaware of them. People of many faiths welcome the coming of spring with a religious-based holiday, the harvest with a thanksgiving feast, and the new year with a celebration often related to religious beliefs. Even those who profess no faith usually participate in rituals such as weddings, funerals, and baby-showers, all of which have their roots in religious rituals.

What is Religion?

Religion has been defined as the attitude of individuals in a community toward the powers which they conceive as having ultimate control over their destinies and interests (Lewis, 1968). But don't let that definition confuse you. Religion is simply the part of culture associated with people's deepest convictions. Through religion we seek to explain awe-inspiring, mysterious concepts: What is God? Why does evil exist? Is there a soul? What happens when we die? How did humanity begin and when, if ever, will it end? People need general ideas that give meaning to their lives by explaining their place in the universe. Different religions attempt to give different answers to these human questions.

There is talk today that the world is becoming one and that people are uniting under a "New World Order." Innovations in technology are certainly tying people together. Over the worldwide computer Internet, for example, a Baptist student in Kansas can bump into a Buddhist student in Japan and strike up a conversation. Although we live in a "global village," not everyone agrees about how to live, how to govern, or how to worship. Yet if we intend to live together, we must understand each other's deepest convictions. The majority of the world's population adheres to one of four religious categories: Hinduism, Buddhism, Christianity, or Islam. In order to appreciate and understand another belief system, we do not necessarily need to agree with it. Rather, we need only seek to understand and respect the differing viewpoint and the person who holds it.

The Major Religions of the World

It is impossible in this context to fully discuss every religion practiced in the world, much less the particular denominations and offshoots within each religion. However, a brief overview of the world's major belief systems is practical and useful. The following summaries, therefore, are intended to introduce some key concepts at the foundation of each religion.

Animism/Shamanism

Animism and Shamanism are religious systems typically found in the tribal societies of Africa, Australia, and North and South America. Animism is a belief that God is present everywhere, in a multiplicity of expressions that inhabit natural objects such as rocks and trees and rivers. All beings and things were created by God and can be used for either good or bad purposes. Gifted people called Shamen (priests, prophets, medicine men) believe they can go into a visionary state and communicate with the great power of the universe. Such a communion helps to sustain nature and the relationship between human beings and the universe.

Buddhism

Buddhists are found in the greatest numbers in eastern Asia. Buddhism is a religion founded by Buddha, a prince who lived in India several hundred years before Jesus. This prince renounced his wealth and status and began teaching a philosophy of physical discipline, moderation, silent contemplation (meditation), and universal brotherhood as a means of liberation from the physical world. Buddhists believe that our desires trap us in the "Wheel of Life," a cycle of rebirths. The goal of the Buddhist is to attain Nirvana, a state of complete peace and bliss in which one is free from the inability to fulfill desire.

Christianity

Christianity has its roots in Judaism. Christianity is a religion of love, compassion, and fellowship, based on the life and teachings of Jesus Christ. Christianity sees God as a trinity—the mystery of three in one. Christians believe that Jesus is the Messiah (or savior) sent by God. They believe that Jesus, by dying and being resurrected, made up for the sin of Adam and thus redeemed the world, allowing all who believe in Him to enter Heaven. Christians rely on the *Bible* as the inspired word of God.

Confucianism

Confucianism is a system of ethics based upon the teachings of Confucius. This system has dominated Chinese culture for 2,000 years. Confucius emphasized moral perfection for the individual and social order for society. He believed world harmony could be attained if people possessed such virtues as loyalty, respect, integrity, piety, righteousness, wisdom, benevolence, and courage. While Confucianism is not strictly a religion, its followers are certainly religious. Confucianism has no priesthood, churches, or system of gods, but Confucius himself is revered and worshipped as the ideal man, and Confucians believe that the goodness in human nature comes from Heaven.

Hinduism

Hinduism, a religion of India, is one of the world's oldest living religions. Its holy scriptures, the *Rig-Veda*, date all the way back to 4000 B.C. and make reference to the genesis of the universe. Hindus believe in a personal creator God who sustains the universe. They follow the principle of Karma, a law of cause and effect in which every action one does, whether good or bad, eventually comes back to him or her. Hindus also believe in reincarnation, a cycle of never-ending births and deaths in which ignorant people are reborn according to the deeds (or Karma) of their past lives. Enlightened people are not reborn. Hindus see the material world as being an illusion which can be changed by one's viewpoint. They also believe that all people are actually facets of Brahman, the eternal web of the universe.

Islam

Islam is the dominant faith in the Arab nations and is growing in other parts of the world. Like Christianity, Islam has its roots in Judaism and worships the same indivisible God (called Allah in Arabic). Islam was founded by Mohammed, a prophet (messenger) of God who dictated the *Koran.* The fundamental belief of Islam is that "There is only one God, and Mohammed is his prophet." The word *Islam* means "submission to the will of God." Followers of Mohammed, called Moslems, are obliged to pray five times a day, to avoid pork and alcohol, to give to the poor, and to make a pilgrimage to Mecca (Mohammed's birthplace) at least once in their lives.

Jainism

Jainism is a native religion of India, founded by a man named Mahavira. This religion grew out of Hinduism and teaches a doctrine of non-injury, or *ahimsa.* Jains believe in the law of Karma (cause and effect) and reincarnation. Jains do not eat meat, and they seek to avoid harming anything believed to have a soul. Jains attempt to achieve *moksha,* or salvation, though self-discipline, knowledge, faith, and right conduct.

Judaism

Judaism, the religion of the Hebrews, centers around a personal God, Yahweh. A succession of great prophets (spiritual messengers), such as Abraham, Moses, Elijah, and Isaiah, spoke in God's name and taught Jews how to know and serve Yahweh. In Judaism, a permanent covenant with God and his chosen people allows heaven to come to earth. Jewish law, legend, and history is embodied in the *Talmud* and the *Torah.* Jewish worship takes place in a synagogue and is led by a rabbi (a scholar of Jewish thought).

Shinto

Shinto is the national religion of Japan. The word *Shinto* means "The Way of the Gods." Many Gods are honored, representing natural forces, ancestors, former emperors, and national heroes. Over 100,000 shrines have been built to the Gods. However, these shrines are not meant for the assembling of worshippers but rather as dwellings for the Gods. Many of the shrines are very small and are focal points for festivals and patriotic holidays. Shinto promotes national loyalty.

Sikhism

Sikhism is a faith that arose in India as a result of the coming of Islam. It features elements of Islam and Hinduism, but maintains a separate identity. The founder of the movement was named Nanak. He taught that the way of salvation was through *bhakti* (devotion). Sikhs worship Hari, the one God. Sikhs believe in reincarnation and hope to break out of an endless cycle of rebirths to merge with the soul of God. The sacred book of the Sikhs, the *Granth,* contains Nanak's poems and songs of devotion.

Taoism and Chinese Folk Religion

Taoism is a philosophical religion native to China. It was founded by a great philosopher named Lao Tse. Taoists attempt to live according to the Tao (pronounced *DOW*) , or "Way," which they believe governs the universe. Lao Tse called for people to be peaceful, inactive, and quiet. He believed that bringing these qualities into daily life would put one effortlessly in touch with the universe. The *Tao Te Ching,* or Book of the Way, spells out the doctrine of Lao Tse. Chinese folk religions combine Taoism, Buddhism, Confucianism, ancestor worship, and local deities.

New Religions

New Religions have grown up in Asia, mostly since 1945. Some of these popular new beliefs were inspired by Buddhism and Shintoism. They were founded by visionaries who preached a fresh new social ethic. Most stress gratitude for God's creation, social rather than individual good, and hard manual labor. The Nichiren Shosu religion, founded in Japan earlier this century, has spread to other countries in both the East and the West.

World Membership of Major Religions

Christians	1,833,022,000
Moslems	971,328,000
Nonreligious	876,232,000
Hindus	732,812,000
Buddhists	314,939,000
Atheists	240,310,000
Taoists & Chinese folk religionists	187,107,000
New Religionists	143,415,000
Tribal/Shamanists	96,581,000
Sikhs	18,800,500
Jews	17,822,000
Confucians	6,028,000
Baha'is	5,517,000
Jains	3,794,000
Shintoists	3,222,800
Other religionists	18,586,000

Caution: these numbers may be misleading. Definitions of membership vary greatly from one religious body to another. For example, some count children who have been received into the faith, and others count only adults (Famighetti, 1993).

Denominations and Minor Religions

Within the major religious systems are numerous denominations, all with their own special beliefs and practices. For example, Christianity is divided into four main denominations: Catholic, Protestant, Orthodox, and Anglican. Each of those is divided into smaller affiliations—Methodist, Baptist, Lutheran, Mormon, Pentecostal, Presbyterian, Seventh-Day Adventist, Jehovah's Witness, Greek Orthodox, Shaker, and so on.

In addition to the major religions, there are dozens of minor religions, branches, and offshoots, including:

Celtic religions. These include the ancient nature cults of Great Britain, such as Druidism.

Caribbean religions. These religions of the Caribbean islands include Voodoo and Santeria. Though frequently misunderstood and stereotyped, Caribbean religions have a unique and rich cultural heritage.

Eckanar. Eckanar focuses on the personal experience of the sound and light of God.

Esoteric Brotherhoods. These exclusive, philosophical societies include the Rosicrucians and the Freemasons. They have a long history, dating back to ancient times.

Krishna Consciousness. Originating in India, this movement was made popular in the West during the 1960s by A. C. Bhaktivedanta Swami Prabhupada. It focuses on love, service, and devotion to Krishna, the personal aspect of God. Followers of Krishna avoid eating meat, engaging in illicit sex, the use of intoxicants, and gambling. They frequently chant the name of God (Prabhupada, 1969).

Magick systems. The ancient practice of Witchcraft is a magick system. Though often confused with Satanism, many magick systems practice "white magic" and stress personal empowerment through the energy of nature.

Natural Law systems. These are not religions in terms of doctrines or dogmas. Practitioners of these systems view individual life from a universal perspective. Based upon modern and ancient science and reports of higher states of consciousness, they recognize the intelligence and creativity underlying the order in the universe. Such a recognition offers one the choice regarding a personal relationship with the divine. Practitioners observe the natural rhythms and cycles of the universe, including the cycle of creation-maintenance-evolution-dissolution. The Transcendental Meditation movement, developed by Maharishi Mahesh Yogi, is a natural law system which can be followed from within any religious tradition (Yogi, 1972).

North, Central, and South American Indigenous Religions. These are ancient regional belief systems, many of which are tribal in origin. Followers of these religions are usually descended from a particular area's native population.

Satanism. Satanism is the worship of the Devil.

Scientology. This movement, founded by L. Ron Hubbard, teaches a modern science of mental health and social betterment.

Spiritualist systems. These systems include New Age beliefs (such as channeling).

Sufism. This is a system of Islamic mysticism which teaches that repentance, abstinence, poverty, patience, and trust lead to union with God. Love is the key to Sufi ethics. Some Sufis, called dervishes, engage in a devotional exercise which involves a whirling dance.

Unification Church. The Unification Church was established in Korea by the Rev. Sun Myung Moon in 1954 to bring about spiritual and social reform.

Zoroastrianism. This is a religion founded in Iran, based upon the philosophy of a man named Zoroaster. Zoroastrians worship the god Ahura Mazda, creator of goodness and light, and view life as a constant battle between good and evil. Good thoughts and deeds are the keys to salvation.

Other Categories of Belief

There are, of course, people who do not adhere to any faith at all. Some people call themselves skeptics or Agnostics. Agnosticism is a denial of knowledge about whether or not there is a God. People who are agnostic are open to the possibility that God exists but believe that there can be no proof either way.

Spotlight on Diversity

I always thought talk about religious persecution was just paranoia until last year, when the son of a friend of mine was chased by a gang of his sixth grade classmates and beaten up. The boy is Jewish and some boys in his class started playing a game called "Nazis." They had all been friends before, but now they targeted him to harass for fun.

The teacher sat them all down and told them about what Nazism is about and explained what Judaism is. They discussed the importance of religious freedom and so on, and the games stopped, at least at school.

I know that my little friend will never take his safety for granted again, though, and neither will I. There is so much fear of anything different from the majority, and it is so near the surface. The scariest thing is that wherever you go in the world, somebody is different.

—Anna M., Trenton, NJ

Other people, called Atheists, go so far as to reject all religions outright. Atheism is the denial that there is any God, no matter how God is defined.

On the opposite end of the spectrum, there are people who follow the wisdom of more than one faith. The Unitarian and Universalist movements, for example, tolerate various religious beliefs and study both Eastern and Western spiritual writings in a quest for universal brotherhood. Similarly, the Baha'i faith (which originated in Iran) emphasizes the spiritual unity of all humankind. A movement called Ecumenism promotes worldwide unity among churches and religions through greater cooperation and improved understanding. Another specialized church is the Metropolitan Community Church, which is an international Christian-based church for persons who are lesbian, gay, or bisexual, and their friends and family.

Religious Prejudice

Unlike racial prejudice, religious prejudice is directed against groups that people *choose* to join as a matter of faith (Kronenwetter, 1993). Religious prejudice stems from the belief that one's particular faith is favored by God. Ironically, virtually all of the world's religions teach against prejudice in favor of tolerance, unity, and love.

Perhaps people will never agree about the fine points of religious doctrine, but such agreement is not necessary. One does not have to convert to another religion in order to honor the piety of its followers. The challenge is to practice what you preach. Do you believe that your actions will one day be judged by God, or that your deeds in this life will come back to you the next time around, or that you are answerable only to yourself? No matter how we express it, virtually everyone agrees that people are all accountable for their actions. Whether all humankind are facets of God, or part of the web of the universe, or descendants of Adam, everyone is entitled to respect. Regardless of our religion or lack thereof, we are all travelers on the journey of life. If you are convinced that yours is the best path, be a respectable representative and give others the opportunity to be drawn to your example.

Stereotypes of Persons of Different Faiths

The following stereotypes regarding people of different faiths are *not* true:

- They are ignorant or unenlightened
- They are misguided
- They are sinful, "ungodly," or devil-worshippers

- They are strange
- They are fanatics
- They want to convert you to their religion
- Their religious heritage is primitive
- All are religious
- All are experts on their religion
- All observe holidays or religious practices
- All hate people who don't adhere to their faith

Issues Persons of Different Faiths May Face

- Understanding the cultural issues of their religion
- Dating and marriage within or outside the faith
- Religious persecution
- Stereotypes about people of their religion
- Other people being ignorant about their religious culture
- Group identification
- Understanding the importance or lack of importance of certain holidays
- Finding peer support
- Not knowing a lot about their culture themselves
- Understanding religious practices
- Finding mentors or role models
- Maintaining a cultural identity
- Careers that allow for cultural observance and participation
- Maintaining self-esteem and pride
- Comfort wearing special clothing or other symbols of religious pride and observance
- Stigma of being identified as a minority

Support Services

Most religions have formal places of worship where members of the particular faith can gather together. Such places of worship are listed in the Yellow Pages. Some smaller congregations may meet in houses, in rooms rented by other churches, or even outdoors. Wherever they meet, members of a particular faith form social networks to support one another in times of crisis or need and to sponsor activities for singles, children, adolescents, families, and senior citizens. Many churches offer evening classes which provide additional instruction on their particular belief system or on other faiths practiced around the world.

Interactions

Resist trying to force others with another faith into the categories of your own belief system. Take them on their own terms, giving their experiences and beliefs respect.

If another religion seems foreign or confusing, remember that it is simply another human attempt to make sense of life's mysteries. Keep in mind that *your* belief system may seem just as foreign to someone who doesn't follow it.

Before you form an opinion about a believer of another faith, remember the key quality you have in common. Both of you carry on the tradition of a long line of believers stretching back through time.

Do not be embarrassed by your ignorance of a person's faith and customs. Ask questions in an open, friendly, interested manner and you are likely to find that the person will be eager to discuss and share his or her religious culture.

Approach another religion in the light of what it contributes to the life of its followers. Ask followers of this religion how their faith has changed their lives, or empowered them, or comforted them. Ask how religious holidays involve the participation of their families.

Summary

Religion is a universal experience of awe and wonder in the presence of the mysterious. In different lands and different times, throughout human history, religion has helped people to understand their lives in a larger, cosmic context. Religion concerns the deepest and most sensitive area of a person's experience. The only way to be sympathetic and objective toward others of another faith is to be knowledgeable about their belief system.

References

Famighetti, R. (1993). *The world almanac and book of facts 1994.* Mahway, NJ: Funk & Wagnalls.

Kronenwetter, M. (1993). *Prejudice in america: Causes and cures.* New York: Franklin Watts.

Lewis, J. (1968). *Religions of the world made simple.* Garden City, NY: Doubleday.

Prabhupada, A. C. B. S. ((1969). *Sri Isopanisad.* Los Angeles: Bhaktivendanta Book Trust.

Yogi, M. M. (1972). *The science of creative intelligence: Teacher training course.* Fairfield, IA: Maharishi International University.

Suggested Readings

Carmody, D. & Carmody, J. (1983). *Eastern ways to the center.* Belmont, CA: Wadsworth Publishing Co.
This is a readable introduction to the belief systems of Asia.

Eliade, M. (1987). *The encyclopedia of religion.* New York: Macmillan.
This encyclopedia breaks down world religions into geographical categories and features informative, comprehensive discussions of each faith and its offshoots.

Ferm, V. (1945). *Encyclopedia of religion.* New York: Philosophical Library.
This encyclopedia offers essay-length discussions of world religions and important figures.

Notes

Exploration

Individual Activities

1. Compare the wisdom of another scripture (such as the *Koran, Rig-Veda,* or *Talmud)* to the wisdom of your own scriptures.

What similarities do you notice?

_____

_____

_____

_____

What differences do you notice?

_____

_____

_____

_____

2. Visit the church of another faith. You will notice that every religion has a system of rituals or ceremonies, no matter how elaborate or simple. Even a bowed head, folded hands, and the repetition of sacred words are ceremonial. Describe a ceremony you witness. How is it similar to or different from a ceremony you are more familiar with?

_____

_____

_____

_____

_____

_____

_____

Group Activities

1. Have each person in your group represent a different faith. Defend your assigned faith against charges that it is "strange," "illogical," "ungodly," etc.

Reactions:

_____
_____
_____
_____
_____
_____
_____
_____

2. Have each person in your group explain his or her particular belief system. Why do you believe what you do? What does your belief system teach about human diversity?

Reactions:

_____
_____
_____
_____
_____
_____
_____
_____

Reaction Paper 6.1

Imagine that you belong to a particular religious minority. What day-to-day experiences or encounters might be striking reminders that the people around you don't share your faith?

Reaction Paper 6.2

Ancestor worship is a component of many Eastern religions. Altars are set up in a family house in reverence of deceased family members. Here, on the birthdays of the deceased, candles are lit, prayers are said, and food is offered. At the grave site, monuments and arches are erected. In what similar ways does your own culture and religion honor its dead?

Notes

Chapter 7

Socioeconomic Perspectives

Introduction

The realities of family diversity and the challenges of global transformation have recently evoked a social reaction. In a brief flurry of media coverage during the 1992 Los Angeles riots, many Americans saw for the first time how our inner cities actually function.

Poverty, crime, drug use, and unemployment plague America and developed countries across the world. We send hundreds of millions of dollars abroad each year to assist third world countries, yet our own children comprise the majority of America's poor. Unfortunately, ingrained prejudice and voluntary ignorance exist throughout America.

The United States Bureau of the Census measures people's economic condition with a criterion called socioeconomic status (SES). Socioeconomic status includes income, level of education, and the social status implied by the occupations of its wage earners. This chapter will highlight various statistics related to children, adults, and persons who are elderly. We will discuss poverty, wealth, and related SES societal issues.

Children

The United States ranks second in the world in per capita gross national product. However, we do not rank as well in measurements related to the health and well-being of children (Children's Defense Fund, 1990). Children today make up only 26 percent of the population and yet are the poorest of any age group in the nation. More than 22 percent of American children live in poverty, an increase of more than one-third since 1970. The United States has a lower poverty level than Switzerland, Sweden, Norway, West Germany, Canada, the United Kingdom, or Australia (Children's Defense Fund, 1990).

Our schools are having difficulty preparing children for the twenty-first century. Approximately 500,000 children in the United States drop out of school each year (Children's Defense Fund, 1990). Among 18 selected nations, the United States ranked 12th on eighth-grade mathematical achievement tests. Students of the United States scored lower than students in Japan, Hungary, the United Kingdom, and eight other countries. Many researchers have suggested a relationship between poor school achievement and lower socioeconomic status. Numerous federal programs have been initiated to provide children from poor families with food, clothing, and other services so that they have better opportunities to learn.

The fastest growing segment of the homeless population in the United States is families with children. One-half of preschool children in 1995 had mothers employed outside the home. This figure will rise to nearly seven in 10 in the near future. Children are spending more time alone, in day care, and with siblings. Less time is spent with parents. Part of this change in childrearing is due to transitions in the American economy and both parents requiring outside employment to support a perceived lifestyle.

Adults

Since 1980, young workers' earnings have declined while more single-parent families developed. Compared to 1980 statistics, median incomes for young families with children dropped by 24 percent, even with massive numbers of women entering the work force. Low income housing assistance has been reduced by 76 percent (adjusted for inflation since 1980).

Not all of the facts are negative, however. In 1993, Congressional leaders took several important steps to assist families in meeting basic needs. Expansion of the Federal Earned Income Credit and improvements in the Food Stamp program were the most significant changes, incorporated in the Budget Reconciliation Act of August, 1993. This Act represents the single largest measure designed to give income support to poor families and children in more than two decades.

Persons who are Elderly

As the average life span of Americans increase, funding is required for medical service and health care needs. Elderly persons draw upon savings or borrow funds to support healthcare and medical needs. Out of necessity, many extended families are living together in one household.

The multigenerational family can provide many benefits. Multiple incomes pay the rent or mortgage, children can care for elderly relatives, and childcare services can be shared. Some elderly Americans who wish to participate in the labor force are more likely to be unemployed. Poverty levels are high among the elderly.

Poverty

Bell (1994) used Orshanksy's 1965 definition to define poverty as "three times the dollar amount needed to buy a nutritious but low-cost diet." Bell reported that another significant method for identifying poverty incomes is to survey consumers for an opinion. Ask people for the month sum income to be used as a poverty line comparison.

The United States Census Bureau has used a mechanical formula to figure poverty levels since 1965. According to this formula, in 1994 the poverty threshold for a family of four was $13,749. The racial and gender gap in poverty rates has persisted over the past 30 years, despite changes in legislation providing for equal opportunity, family structures, attitudes about two-income families, and government housing opportunities. African Americans, Native Americans, and Hispanic Americans are burdened by the most severe economic deprivation of all ethnic groups in this country (Gollnick & Chinn, 1994).

Women, as a group, earn less and are more likely to be plagued by poverty than any other group. Women of color feel the greatest oppression of poverty. Perhaps this is due to the rigid gender and racial divisions of labor historically seen in this country. Both ends of the lifespan (female children and elderly adults) show high incidences of poverty.

Although poverty makes life inordinately difficult, it alone does not explain human difficulties. Some people are apathetic, some are militant, some are ill, and some are mature enough to manage despite overwhelming odds (National Institute of Child Health and Human Development, 1994). Some welfare programs help underprivileged persons learn job skills and go to school.

Housing

The growth of the American economy between World War II and 1973 allowed incomes at all levels to increase at a faster rate than expenditures (Gollnick & Chinn, 1994). These increases allowed families in lower income brackets to purchase homes, and luxuries for the home. The annual median income of persons above age 13 nearly tripled between 1947 and 1973, from $1,787 to $5,004 (Gollnick & Chinn, 1994).

Spotlight on Diversity

I lost my job six months ago. My kids do not have any shoes, and I cannot afford to feed them every day. They don't complain, though. They're tough.

We live in an abandoned building. I found all of our furniture on the streets. We have a table, a chair, a sofa, and a bed.

I look for aluminum cans to sell for money. I worry about my kids when I am gone all day. I feel very sad all the time. I don't know where we will be to-morrow.

—*Beth H., Dallas, TX*

However, in 1973, the cost of living began to increase faster than income. In constant dollars, the median income in 1986 was less than that in 1973 (Bureau of the Census, 1992).

While the government subsidized suburban housing and middle-class social mobility in the 1950's and 1960's, government policies promoted a rigid private enterprise system for the inner cities, for the poor in general, and for African Americans in particular. In the 1990's, African American families were three times more likely to be poor as compared with Caucasian families. Southern, non-metropolitan African American families, especially female householder families, continue to have a high incidence of poverty (Ghelfi, 1990).

The government spends four times as much on housing subsidies for middle-income Americans as it does for low-income ones. In 1991, households with adjusted gross incomes of more than $100,000 a year received $11.2 billion dollars in government housing subsidies (Salmon, 1992). In 1994, taxpayers spent $25 billion for food stamps, compared to $29.2 billion on subsidies to agribusiness. The difference between welfare for the poor and welfare for the rest is that the handouts to the middle class and to the rich are not stigmatized.

The Children's Defense Fund estimates the number of homeless individuals varies from 228,000 to 600,000 per evening and from 1.7 million to 3 million per year, depending on the definition of homelessness and the method of counting (1990). While homelessness is a viable manifestation of the nation's housing crisis, millions of other American families live in unstable, substandard, or overcrowded housing.

Housing has become incredibly expensive. In 1991, some 2.7 million renter families were forced to spend at least half of their income on housing. Some people eligible for Federal housing assistance are not aware they are eligible, and therefore do not apply to receive it.

Unemployment Rate

The unemployment rate for persons who are foreign born was 7.8 percent in 1990, compared with 6.2 percent for the native born citizens. Persons who were foreign born had a higher per capita income than the native born ($15,033 vs. $14,367) in 1989, but their median family income was almost $4000 less than that of persons who are native born ($31,785 vs. $35,508). By March of 1993, the Department of Labor reported unemployment rates for workers without a high school diploma were 75 percent higher than individuals with a high school diploma and 250 percent higher than individuals with a college degree. Unemployment rates are highest for persons with disabilities and the elderly.

Communities

Where we live is a reflection of our wealth. A postal worker once confided, "Tell me the zip code and I will tell you what type of a community it is." Most working class Americans live in suburban subdivisions and commute to work. They usually socialize on some basis other than geographic proximity. Many Americans do not even know their geographic neighbors. However, a common denominator among the neighbors is a similar income. Their educational backgrounds are likely to be similar, the taxes they pay are roughly the same, and they indulge in similar consumer impulses.

Students at a wealthy suburban high school may enjoy a campus with a closed-circuit television network to all classrooms, an Olympic-size swimming pool, a state-of-the-art science laboratory/planetarium, a state-of-the-art computer lab connected to other schools and businesses, and paid classroom assistants in every classroom. Such a school district would pay approximately $7,500 a year to educate each student, almost twice that spent per student in an inner city school in the same area.

Wealth

In America, one of our greatest failures remains the inability to effectively deal with poverty. We cannot live peaceably when the gap between affluence and poverty is as wide as ours has become (Lavelle, 1995). In 1994, the top one-fifth of working Americans earned more than the other four-fifths of Americans combined. This is the highest ratio in postwar history. These high earners inhabit a different economy from other Americans (Lavelle, 1995). However, this

> ### *Spotlight on Diversity*
>
> *I don't really know what it would be like to have to consider money when making decisions. I never wanted for anything in my life. My father supported everyone in my family. Even my married sisters kept their credit cards, which were paid for by Dad. We attended the best private schools, traveled, and lived in a large house with all the luxuries we could want.*
>
> *I married a wealthy man, too, and continued a lifestyle which allowed me to indulge all my desires. We have a plane, three homes, and a large yacht. We travel frequently—sometimes as often as once a month. Essentially, my life is one of leisure.*
>
> *I do some charity work, and we contribute generously to several causes. I don't feel guilty about my good fortune, but I do try to be a responsible citizen and help the poor where I can. I think people who have to struggle to support themselves must live in an entirely different world.*
>
> *—Tamara K., Portland, OR*

lifestyle is not particularly typical of the rest of the nation.

The top percentage of the income earners have discovered ways to match individual self-interest with self good. The challenge is to match the affluent individual self interest with collective good. For example, the high earners in our society take pride in their many charitable acts. However, a close examination of the receiving charities reveals that most of the contributions go to places that entertain and educate wealthy Americans (such as elite universities, private hospitals and schools). During 1994-95, American households with incomes of less than $10,000 gave an average of 5.5 percent of their earnings to charity or to a religious organization (Schorr, 1995). If even one quarter of those contribution dollars flowed to social services for the poor, our nation would be a better place to live. Typically, wealthy people know about poverty only what they perceive from the facts, figures, and sensational stories on the evening news.

Persons who are considered wealthy often attend the best schools, have the finest medical care, and, due to status and connections, usually achieve professionally at the highest level. However, children and adults who are from the most wealthy group of citizens—just as those who are poor—are often mistrusted by the vast middle class of Americans and excluded from daily activities. Although wealth may seem to be a wonderful lifestyle, as it is often depicted on such television shows as *Lifestyles of the Rich and Famous,* there are problems, stereotypes, and stigmas that persons who are wealthy face. It must be recognized that whether wealthy or poor, most individuals still are similar physically, intellectually, and emotionally.

Support Services

Occasionally, members of families lack the skills needed to balance a check book, find proper housing, or seek a job. There are numerous family service associations in the United States. These associations provide special services for domestic violence, divorce, substance abuse and delinquency prevention.

In addition to job referral services, most communities have a labor service agency that assists with job placement and referral to retraining programs. These agencies assist persons to identify rehabilitation programs in their community, provide emergency assistance and case management for the homeless. These services can be found in the Yellow Pages of the local community.

Poverty and low income are often related to a limited education. Local YMCAs/ YWCAs, Jewish community centers, adult alternative education centers, church organizations, and community clubs offer education-based classes for little or no fee. Additionally, most states have a community college system which includes a low-fee set of education and literacy courses.

Stereotypes of People Living at Poverty Level

It is *not* true that people living at poverty level:

- Are all homeless
- Are prone to substance abuse
- Are unemployed
- Are all lazy
- Are uneducated
- Choose to live in poverty
- Cannot hope to escape poverty
- Are born into poverty
- Have the same opportunities as everyone else

Stereotypes of Wealthy People

It is *not* true that wealthy people:

- Are all hard workers
- Are all employed
- Are all greedy
- Are not generous
- Are neither perpetrators nor victms of crime
- Have greater or less social consciousness than other people
- Make better parents
- Cannot lose their wealth quickly
- Are born into wealth
- Are highly educated

Economic Issues Individuals May Face

- Whether or not to relocate in order to find work
- Paying taxes
- Whether to send a child to private or public school
- Whether or not to live in the suburbs or inner city
- How much to give to charity
- Which charities to support

- How to spend discretionary income
- Investment opportunites
- Planning for retirement
- Finding health care

Interactions

When you are interacting with people who have less than you, do not give them only what they might need. Give disadvantaged people dignity and respect by taking them seriously, conversing with them, and establishing a human connection.

Carefully consider assisting a charity. Strongly consider donating to organizations that will truly enhance the way of life for persons who live in poverty.

Find out about the per student spending at your local school and compare it to other areas in the state. Talk to the local school board and show the numbers to them. Recommend ways to improve per student spending.

Be an appropriate role model for children. Patterns of lower achievement and underparticipation begin early in the educational process. Encourage children to attend school, to read, and to participate in extra-curricular activities.

Encourage members of your family to talk about inequities based on income and wealth. Discuss ways to provide equality within the family structure.

Stay informed. Read the newspaper, watch the news, and review editorials. As we become informed, we learn ways to assist with various projects.

Summary

*Unfortunately, many Americans live on the outskirts of hope—
some because of their poverty, some because of their color, and
all too many because of both. Our task is to help replace their
despair with opportunity.*
–President Lyndon B. Johnson's inaugural address, Jan. 8, 1964.

President Johnson declared a war on poverty in March, 1964. Since then, statistics show communities are poorer and the gap between the wealthy and other Americans has widened. Opportunities for education, nutrition, and job-training are still absent in many areas of society. It's time to stop declaring a war and to start fighting it.

References

Bell, C. S. (1994, July 14). What is poverty? *The Boston Globe,* p. A5.

Bureau of the Census. (1992). *Statistical Abstract of the United States*, 1992 (108th ed.). Washington, DC: Government Printing Office.

Children's Defense Fund. (1990). *Children of 1990: A report card, briefing book, and action primer.* Washington DC.

Ghelfi, L. M. (1990). Poverty among black families in the nonmetro south, *Rural Development Research Report, 52.* Washington, DC: Department of Agriculture.

Gollnick, D. M. & Chinn, P. C. (1994). *Multicultural education in a pluralistic society, (4th ed).* New York: Merrill.

Lavelle, R. (1995). *America's new war on poverty.* San Francisco: KQED books.

National Institute of Child Health and Human Development. (1994). *Perspectives on human deprivation: Biological psychological and sociological.* Washington, DC: U.S. Department of Health, Education & Welfare.

Salmon, J. (1992). Reaching new deductions about mortgage tax breaks. *Washington Post National Weekly Edition, 25*(31), 21.

Schorr, D. (1995). In Lavelle, R. *America's new war on poverty.* (p. xvi-xxiv). San Francisco: KQED Books.

Suggested Readings

Butler, R. N. & Lewis, M. I. (1991). *Aging and mental health: Positive psychosocial and biomedical approaches* (4th ed.). New York: Macmillan.
This book contains xcellent information for persons interested in the elderly population.

Glazer, N. (1988). *The limits of social welfare policy.* Cambridge: Harvard University Press.
This book explains how the civic values presumably held by Americans temper and limit the kinds of political strategies adopted for reducing poverty.

Gollnick, D. M. & Chinn, P. C. (1994). *Multicultural education in a pluralistic society,* (4th ed.). New York: Merrill.
This text contains an excellent chapter on class and status.

Hodgson, B. F. (1911). *The secret garden.* New York: Harper Collins.
This book explains how friendship and love can bring happiness into the lives of people who have nothing.

Kozol, J. (1991). *Savage inequalities: Children in America's schools.* New York: Crown.
This book presents descriptions of poor and rich schools interwoven with stories of persons living in each area.

Kozol, J. (1988). *Rachel and her children: Homeless families in America.* New York: Crown.
This is a chronicle of the lives of homeless families including a description of how services are received and of the humiliation felt by women and children receiving the services.

Rose, S. J. (1992). *Social stratification in the United States.* New York: New Press.
This report analyzes data on wealth, race, martial and occupation, and income. It provides a vivid description of the U.S. social structure.

UNICEF. (1995). *The state of the world's children.* New York: Oxford University Press.

This report discusses the progress made since the 1990 World Summit for Children, providing ideas for where the world needs to be in order to fight the war on poverty.

U.S. Bureau of the Census. (August, 1991). *Poverty in the United States: 1990.* Washington DC: U.S. Bureau of the Census.

This report provides a comprehensive overview of poverty and some of the latest official indicators and characteristics about poverty.

Wilson, W. J. (1987). *The truly disadvantaged: The inner city, poverty, and public policy.* Chicago: The University of Chicago Press.

This book examines how broad social and economic transformation has impacted negatively on poor and working-class communities in urban America.

Notes

Exploration

Individual Activities

1. How would you categorize your economic status? Upon what criteria did you base your answer?

_____

_____

_____

_____

2. *Forbes* magazine publishes an annual list of the top 500 wealthiest people in the world. Who were the top three wealthiest people last year? How did they become wealthy? What do they do with their money?

_____

_____

_____

_____

_____

_____

_____

_____

Group Activities

1. As a group, list five characteristics of wealthy people and five characteristics of poor people. Discuss why you thought of these common stereotypes.

_____
_____
_____
_____
_____

_____
_____
_____
_____

2. As a group, come up with ten things that money can't buy.

_____
_____
_____
_____
_____
_____
_____
_____
_____

3. As a group, come up with five disadvantages to being wealthy.

_____
_____
_____
_____
_____

Reaction Paper 7.1

Suppose that someone dared you to wear a button stating your annual salary, and you had to wear this button everywhere you went. Would you do it? Why or why not?

Reaction Paper 7.2

The United States Census Bureau has set the poverty threshold to a single dollar amount for all Americans. Discuss ways in which such a specific figure could be misleading. For example, how could the same income level be comfortable for one family and grossly inadequate for another?

Notes

Chapter 8

Physical Differences

Introduction

People come in every size and shape. Have you ever thought what it might be like to be the smallest person in your class or the largest person in your workplace? Someone reading this may fall into one of these categories. When you were a child, your parents may have told you, "Regardless of what we look like on the outside, it is what is inside that counts." That advice could be difficult to accept if you are a 5 foot, 1 inch male, a 6 foot, 3 inch female, or if you weigh 350 pounds. The same frustrations and difficulties experienced by someone who may look different from the norm are often experienced by persons with physical disabilities.

Persons with physical differences are people just like you. They share some of the same likes and dislikes. They may strive for individuality or conformity, just like the rest of us. However, society poses a challenge for people with physical differences because it sees the difference first and the person second. Many people refrain from greeting persons with physical differences because they see the physical abnormalities and assume the person might not be able to communicate, to socialize, or to think. However, many highly successful individuals have had physical differences, including Alexander Pope, Franklin Roosevelt, and Mohammed. Their physical difference did not hinder them from achieving their goals in life. This chapter will help define various physical differences and provide information on interaction with a person with a physical disability.

Types of Physiognomy

The practice of reading a person's character from his or her facial and bodily form dates back to the ancient Greeks and is still found in some parts of the world. We often judge a person's character by facial qualities: "He has an open face," "She gave a frank look," "He had a sinister appearance," "She gave a furtive glance." The age-old art of interpreting physiognomy took all sorts of physical characteristics into account: one's stature, build, posture, forehead, nose, ears, chin, eyebrows, eyes, cheeks, mouth, and hair. Bumps on the head were also interpreted (in a pseudo-science called "Phrenology,") as were lines on the palm of the hand ("Palmistry"). Today, we never make judgments on such superficial bases. Or would we?

People do sometimes fall into general "body types," and certain characteristics *are* associated with physical features. The study of this phenomenon is called morphology. For thousands of years and up to the present day, the traditional medical practitioners of China and India have relied upon morphology to classify and treat their patients. Do you fall into one of these three morphological categories?

Type 1	Type 2	Type 3
Moderate frame	Thin frame	Thick frame
Tend to be skinny	Moderate weight	Tend to be overweight
Dry hair	Soft, oily hair	Thick, wavy hair
Small eyes	Penetrating eyes	Big, attractive eyes
Very active	Moderately active	Lethargic
Irregular sleep	Little but sound sleep	Heavy sleep
Variable appetite	Good appetite	Slow but steady appetite
Restless mind	Sharp intellect	Calm, slow mental activity

Some people very clearly fall into one of these categories. Many other people exhibit combinations of these traits. Looking at these charts, we can see that we cannot always take a person at "face value," nor should we be quick to judge others according to physical attributes. Surface differences don't necessarily reveal the important qualities of the person inside.

Size and Stature

Body size is a variable of the human condition. However, people whose size varies from the average often find themselves physically and emotionally isolated. It is inappropriate to publicly despise and harass persons who are obese, excessively thin, smaller, or taller than average.

Weight. An estimated 38 million Americans are significantly heavier than average and face societal and institutional bias because of their size (National Association to Advance Fat Acceptance, 1995). People who are obese are discriminated against in employment, education, access to public accommodations, and access to adequate medical care. In addition, people who are obese are stigmatized and are the victims of tasteless jokes and assaults on their dignity. Despite evidence that 95-98% of diets fail over three years, our thin-obsessed society continues to believe that people who are overweight are at fault for their size. In fact, most weight problems may be hereditary. Scientists have recently isolated a "fat gene" which could genetically predispose a person to be overweight. More and more doctors are now suggesting that remaining at a stable weight, making sensible food choices, and concentrating on personal fitness rather than thinness may be the healthiest way to deal with one's propensity to be overweight.

Just as with people who are obese, not all people who are excessively thin have eating disorders. Thinness is often associated with a person's metabolism, and someone may be genetically predisposed to thinness. Anorexia, a lack of appetite and/or inability to eat, is a specific disease. One should never use labels such as "anorexia" to describe a person's weight unless one is a trained diagnostician.

Spotlight on Diversity

Imagine wearing a sign on your forehead that reads, "I was an abused child," or "I have problems with my boyfriend," or even "I am afraid of the dark." People would stare at you and make snide remarks. They might laugh as you walk by. The luxury of those problems is that they can be hidden in you mind, and the note on your forehead doesn't really exist.

People who are overweight wear their problem on the outside, for all the world to see. Fat. It's a three letter word that I am pretty familiar with. I am not looking for sympathy, but if losing weight were easy I would have done it by now.

I was put on my first diet in second grade. Now I am happy with who I am. I have self-esteem and friends. However, I know that I would be happier thin. I know that because I was there once, too. When I was 14, I spent two summers at a weight loss camp, and I was doing great. Then I blinked, and the weight was back on. It is a part of me.

There are some good things about being overweight. You make real friends because people who are superficial tend to steer as far away as possible. Also, my parents and I always have something to talk about. We discuss what diet I should go on next, or whether I have been exercising.

I want the world to realize that I know I am overweight. Don't censor conversation in the room when I walk in. Don't avoid serving me french fries! Let me make my own choices, and when I am ready, if I am ready, then I will take on the task of losing weight.

—Tracy A., North Miami Beach, FL

Height. The pituitary gland, located at the base of the brain, releases growth hormones which stimulate cell reproduction. Growth hormones, then, help to increase body growth. Deficiencies or excesses of growth hormone in early life typically cause extreme variations in a person's height.

An excess of growth hormone in an adult results in a characteristic overgrowth—in thickness, not length—of facial bones and bones of the hands and feet. These are the features of a disorder called *acromegaly.* Oversecretion of growth hormone in early life, usually caused by a pituitary tumor, results in gigantism. An individual with *gigantism* may reach a height of seven to eight feet. Sometimes surgery is successful in halting abnormal growth.

Dwarfism. Height below the fifth percentile plotted on an incremental growth chart often results in a formal diagnosis of *dwarfism.* Delayed growth and short stature are symptoms of this condition. Causes of dwarfism can be environmental or genetic. Delayed growth may be due to a growth hormone imbalance, an initial manifestation of malnutrition, or deficiencies in iron, zinc, or vitamins. Chronic uncontrolled diabetes, cardiopulmonary, hematologic, or autoimmune disorders can all be associated with delayed growth. Today, genetically engineered growth hormones can be periodically injected in children to spur their growth.

Defining Physical Disabilities

Physical disabilities are problems that result from injuries or conditions affecting the central nervous system, difficulty of movement, and/or a lack of function of some part of the body and related functions. These problems interfere with an individual's mobility, coordination, communication, behavior, learning, intellectual ability, or personal adjustment. The number of persons with physical disabilities is increasing as modern medical treatment keeps more individuals alive. With children, physical disabilities are usually diagnosed by physicians early in life. It is critical that communication be maintained among physicians, families, and educators.

Federal guidelines place students with physical disabilities under the categories of orthopedic impairments, and traumatic brain injury. These two categories will be discussed in the following sections.

Orthopedic Impairment

Orthopedic impairments are typically caused by:

- A congenital anomaly such as clubfoot or absence of a limb
- Impairments caused by disease, such as poliomyelitis or tuberculosis
- Impairments from other causes, such as cerebral palsy, amputations, and fractures or burns that cause contractures

Spinal cord injuries, cerebral palsy, multiple sclerosis, muscular dystrophy, limb deficiencies, and other physically limiting disabilities all can be categorized as orthopedic impairments.

Spinal cord injury. Spinal cord injury is used to describe permanent injury to the spinal cord. The injury usually causes paralysis in specific areas of the body. The extent of the paralysis is often specifically related to the location of the injury. Causes frequently cited for spinal cord injury include diving, automobile accidents, and other forms of trauma.

Spina bifida. Spina bifida is a congenital disorder caused by a failure of the spinal cord to develop properly in the womb. "Bifid" means short, thus a "short spine." Spina bifida is the most common birth defect in North America. There are two major types. *Spina bifida occulta* occurs when a defect of the vertebral arch causes failure of posterior fusion of the vertebrae. *Spina bifida cystica* is the most severe form of spina bifida. In this defect, some as yet unidentified initial assault causes abnormal development of the spinal cord and the overlying bone and skin. The spinal cord is left open and exposed to the amniotic fluid. Characteristics include unilateral foot deformity, weakness of foot muscles, urinary infections and bladder disturbances. Hydrocephalus, a condition in which the spinal cord and brain become abnormally bathed in spinal fluid, occurs in a large percentage of these children, perhaps as much as 70 to 90 percent (NICHCY, 1993).

Spina bifida is the major cause of paraplegia in young children. In addition to paralysis and deformities of the lower body, those affected may also develop hydrocephalus, incontinence, and sometimes mental retardation. These children have weak muscles and poorly developed legs. Physical therapy can delay atrophy of healthy muscles, and antibiotics control secondary illness, but neither treatment helps the dystrophy process. The cause of spina bifida is not known, although many factors are suspected (Batshaw & Perret, 1986).

Cerebral Palsy. Cerebral Palsy (CP) is a disorder of posture (ability to remain still) and movement (ability to move) caused by damage to the brain. Most children who have CP acquired it either prenatally or perinatally. An estimated 3,000 children are born with CP each year in the United States. Another 100 or so preschool children acquire CP annually as a result of head injuries or illness such as meningitis. Several of the more common prenatal causes of cerebral palsy are heredity, maternal infection (i.e. Rubella), fetal anoxia (lack of oxygen), RH incompatibility, and overexposure to X rays (Cartwright, Cartwright, & Ward, 1995). Perinatal causes may include lack of oxygen and birth injury.

Anything that results in oxygen deprivation, poisoning, cerebral bleeding, or direct trauma to the brain can be a possible cause of cerebral palsy. Contrary to popular belief, CP is not a disease and it is not life-threatening. Instead, CP is a group of conditions caused by damage to the brain that is nonprogressive.

People with cerebral palsy are not paralyzed. The brain is unable to send correct movement messages to muscles. People with CP exhibit differing degrees and combinations of motor, speech, vision, hearing, and learning disabilities. Although CP cannot be cured, the associated conditions can be managed (and frequently improved) by early diagnosis and therapeutic intervention. There are several types of cerebral palsy. The following definitions have been adapted from Lessen (1991) and Cartwright, Cartwright, & Ward (1995).

- **Spasticity** is characterized by involuntary contractions of the muscles when suddenly stretched, sometimes inaccurate and difficult voluntary motion, and flexing of the arms and fingers.

- **Athetosis** is characterized by involuntary, purposeless movement of the limbs with explosive and jerky uncontrolled movements. Additionally, involuntary motions are more pronounced under stress or emotional tensions.

- **Ataxia** is characterized by impaired balance and equilibrium with dysrhythmic and flailing movements, plus a weaving and stumbling gait.

- **Tremor** is characterized by a variation in constancy and pattern of movement and shakiness of an involved limb.

- **Rigidity** is a severe form of spasticity due to high levels of muscle tone and lack of voluntary motion.

- **Atonia** is characterized by no muscle tone.

- **Mixed Cerebral Palsy** is characterized by a combination of spasticity and athetosis.

According to the United Cerebral Palsy Association, the odds of having a child with CP are approximately 1 in 1,000 births. Classification according to the extremities involved applies not only to CP, but also to all types of motor disability or paralysis. The most common classifications are as follows:

- **Hemiplegia** is characterized by an involvement of one-half of the body (one-side).

- **Diplegia** is characterized by the involvement of the legs to a greater extent than arms.

- **Quadriplegia** refers to entire body involvement, both arm and leg paralysis. All limbs are involved.

- **Paraplegia** refers to involvement of the legs or lower half of the body.

- **Monoplegia** is characterized by involvement of only one extremity.

- **Triplegia** refers to a situation where three limbs are involved.

Cerebral palsy can be a multi-handicapping condition. Several secondary or associated disabilities are commonly associated with cerebral palsy. These can include speech and language disorders, mental retardation, vision and hearing impairments, perceptual and visual-motor disorders, sensory deficits, convulsive disorders, and social emotional difficulties (Cartwright, Cartwright & Ward, 1995). The intelligence levels of persons with cerebral palsy range from severely retarded to extremely gifted. There is no direct relationship between intelligence and severity of physical disability.

Multiple sclerosis. Multiple sclerosis is a degenerative, progressive disease of the central nervous system with hardening, or sclerosis, of the tissue throughout the brain. The symptoms include muscle weakness, spasticity, balance difficulties, recurring and progressively severe episodes of numbness in the appendages, blurring or loss of eyesight, and paraplegia. Persons with multiple sclerosis can experience times of incapacity and times of remission. When symptoms are relieved, they can lead active lives. Although there is much disparity among experts in the field, most doctors concede the disease is caused by either slow-moving and long-lasting viruses and/or environmental factors. Most frequently, multiple sclerosis is not diagnosed until adulthood. On average, a person can live an additional 20-35 years after diagnosis.

Muscular Dystrophy. Muscular Dystrophy is a common name for a group of inherited conditions resulting in progressive weakening and deteriorating of muscular tissue. The several types of muscular dystrophy are classified according to age of onset, distribution of muscular involvement, mode of inheritance, and rate of progression of weakness (Cartwright, Cartwright, & Ward, 1995). Duchenne is the most common and most severe type of muscular dystrophy. Although the outward physical appearance is one of health, the muscles are being replaced by fatty tissue. Muscular dystrophy occurs primarily in males because 90% of cases are due to a sex-linked disorder. The disease often is not diagnosed until a child is three years old. As this is a progressive disorder, the person becomes more and more disabled over time. The exact biological mechanisms responsible for muscular dystrophy are not known, and currently there is no cure. Various additional forms of muscle weakness include the following:

- **Atrophy** is a degeneration of tissue, such as muscles or nerves.

- **Dystrophy** is hereditary, progressive weakening and deterioration of muscle tissue in which there is no evidence of neurological disease.

- **Myotonic dystrophy** is a characterized by weakness of fingers, hands, forearms, feet, and lower limbs. This dystrophy usually appears in early adulthood. Occasionally, myotonic dystrophy is also known as Steinut's disease.

Limb deficiencies. Limb deficiencies refer to the loss of one or more limbs. Limb deficiencies can be congenital (present at birth) or acquired (occurring later in life). Occasionally, the cause is genetic; other causes include viruses, chemicals and radiation. If the condition interferes significantly with performance in school or at the job, the person can receive special education services.

Traumatic Brain Injury

Traumatic Brain Injury (TBI) means an acquired injury to the brain caused by an external physical force, resulting in total or partial functional disability and/or psychosocial impairment. TBI adversely affects a child's educational performance. The term applies to open or closed head injuries resulting in impairment in one or more areas. The areas include cognition, language, memory, attention, reasoning, abstract thinking, judgment, problem-solving, sensory, perceptual and motor abilities, psychosocial behavior, physical functions, information processing, and speech. The term does not apply to brain injuries that are congenital or degenerative, or brain injuries induced by birth trauma. Partial functional disability or psychosocial maladjustment could be the result of the injury. When the injury occurs by traumatic causes, one or all parts of the brain could be affected. The result may range from mild to profound and be temporary or permanent. As the brain rebounds within the skull during the injury, neurons stretch and tear. The consequential swelling and bleeding could cause further damage. Problems can be of varying duration and severity. The person with the brain injury may also experience transient states of fatigue, irritability, inattentiveness, and mental confusion.

Support Services

Many persons with limitation (permanent or temporary) in locomotion or motor functions require supportive services. Individuals with mobility disabilities use braces, canes, and wheelchairs for mobility assistance. Environmental adaptations, such as elevators, ramps and lifts, specially-designed buses, and special cafeteria trays and utensils have assisted with the opportunities for independence for a person with a disability. A significant impact on the number and quality of mobility opportunities available to persons with disabilities has been expanded because of technology.

Examples of assistive technology include beeper baseballs, motorized wheelchairs, adapted skis, bathing and grooming devices, electronic communication devices, specialized hand tools, computer workstations, memory aids, spelling aids and educational software.

A physical therapist should be consulted regarding the therapeutic positioning of persons with physical disabilities. The therapist can identify positions that maximize participation and independence. Cartwright, Cartwright & Ward (1995) provide several noteworthy examples. The therapist could recommend a prone position that involves use of a wedge, to encourage spontaneous head lifting and development of strength in the shoulders. The therapist could also recommend side-lying, which allows eye-hand activities and proper spine alignment.

It is very common to meet a person with a physical disability and/or health problem who uses a dog as a companion. A canine companion enhances the life of a person with a disability by helping him or her overcome physical barriers and by being a loyal friend. A dog provides constant companionship, love, and assistance. Whether pulling a wheelchair or alerting a person of an object in the path, a canine companion helps make independent living a reality for a person with a disability.

One agency that trains dogs for working with persons with disabilities is Canine Companions for Independence (CCI). The canine companion begins specialized training in a volunteer's home. The "puppy raiser" is responsible for socialization and the teaching of basic commands. At approximately one-and-a-half years of age, the puppy is returned to a CCI regional training center for eight months of advanced training by a professional CCI instructor. The dog then attends "boot camp," an intensive two to three week training course where recipients learn to work with a canine companion.

Treat the person like everybody else. Do not make a big deal over someone's size or stature. Do not use "cute" little names like "chubby" or tap the person with dwarfism on the head. Do not perpetuate the harassment that many persons of different stature live with today. Accept them for who they are.

Never lean against or hang on someone who uses a chair or cart . A person with a disability views the equipment as an extension of his or her body. Wheelchairs assist the person in moving around, taking the place of legs. If you lean on chair, as if it were a post, the person may be uncomfortably jolted. The jolt is equivalent to someone walking by and bumping you.

Ask the wheelchair user if he or she would like assistance *before* you help. A wheelchair provides mobility for the person using it. Don't assume the person wants to be helped; he or she will usually ask for assistance if needed.

Listen attentively when talking to people who have difficulty speaking. Wait for a response. Be patient when talking to a person with a physical disability. Listen carefully and never pretend to understand. It is acceptable to ask the person to repeat a statement.

Place yourself at eye level when speaking to someone in a wheelchair or who is significantly shorter than you. If a conversation lasts longer than a few minutes, sit or kneel to place yourself at the same level as the person. Consider the strain on your neck and back when you are seated and speak to someone standing over a given period of time. Correspondingly, do not talk to someone when you are out of the line of sight.

Always offer to shake hands when introduced. Shaking hands is an important part of greeting someone in western culture. People with disabilities are often excluded during social interactions. A limited use of hands does not mean a person is unable to shake hands. Persons with disabilities are people too and everyone wants to relate on a personal level. Place your hand in front of the person in greeting as you greet others, and the person with the disability will do the rest.

Avoid portraying successful people with physical disabilities as remarkable, superhuman, or inspirational. This implies that it is unusual for people with disabilities to have talents or skills.

Do not use the disability to describe the person. Labels set people apart. Labels tend to emphasize differences, and they do not provide any real information about the affected person. When you talk about a person, use the name first and mention the disability only if that information is relevant.

Avoid giving the impression that a disease is present when talking about a disability. A physical disability may result from a disease, such as polio, but is itself not a disease. Neither is the person with the disability unhealthy or contagious. People with disabilities should not be referred to as "patients" or "clients" unless under medical or counseling care.

Summary

Always remember that a physical difference is a condition that may interfere with a person's ability to be successful. People with physical disabilities and differences have capacities, gifts, and contributions to make. Their differences only need give them opportunities to contribute as individuals. The words we use must convey this message.

References

Batshaw, M. L. & Perret, Y. M. (1986). *Children with handicaps: A medical primer.* Baltimore: Paul H. Brookes.

Cartwright, G. P., Cartwright, C. A., & Ward, M. E. (1995). *Educating special learners.* Cincinnati, OH: Wadsworth.

Lessen, E. (1991). *Exceptional persons in society.* Needham, MA: Simon and Schuster.

National Association to Advance Fat Acceptance. (1995). *Fighting Size Discrimination and Prejudice.* Sacramento, CA: Author.

National Information Center for Children and Youth with Disabilities. (1993). *Fact Sheet Number 12: Spina Bifida.* Washington, DC: Author.

Suggested Readings

Beisser, A. (1989). *Flying without wings.* New York: Doubleday.
This is a first hand account of living with a physical disability.

Bergman, T. (1989). *On our own terms: Children living with physical disabilities.* Milwaukee: Gareth Stevens.
This is an excellent children's book presenting pictures of children with various disabilities in everyday situations.

Brimer, R. (1990). *Students with severe disabilities: Current perspectives and practices.* Mountain View, CA: Mayfield Publishing Company.
This book provides excellent global introductions to many severe physical disabilities. A historical perspective and theories related to causes and cures are included.

Brown, T. & Ortiz, F. (1982). *Someone special just like you.* New York: Henry Holt.
This book was written to give children and adults a better understanding of disabilities.

Savage, R.C. & Wolcott, G. F. (1988). *An educator's manual: What educators need to know about students with traumatic brain injury* (2nd ed.). Southborough, MA: NHIF.
This is an essential guide for dealing with students with traumatic brain injuries.

Exploration

Individual Exercises

1. There are many people who have difficulty performing tasks that are usually taken for granted. This activity will give you a perspective on how these people feel about and deal with these tasks. Hold one arm behind your back and try to do the following activities: tie your shoes, open a can or a bottle, get dressed, eat something, and play a sport that normally requires two hands. Now, remember, only one hand and no cheating.

Describe how well you did. Also describe the difficulties you encountered.

_____

_____

_____

_____

2. Assume that you are confined to a wheelchair and are about to start your first day in college. But wait. Your college campus is not set up for wheelchairs. How do you feel?

_____

_____

_____

_____

List some things that may be obstacles to you.

_____

_____

_____

_____

_____

_____

_____

148
Group Activities

1. As a class, take a trip to the local mall or to your college's student union. Today, you will have a physical handicap. You are to interlock your fingers from both hands and place them on top of your head. If you feel silly, remember that everyone else is doing it also! The task assigned to you is to pair off in groups of two with only one person at a time acting as the person with the disability. While disabled, have your partner feed you and wash your face. Also, play a video game, bowl, or play some other type of game. As you walk around the mall or union, open doors for yourself and be as independent as possible.

Reactions:

_____

_____

_____

_____

2. A town meeting is being called to order and your class is the community. Five people need to be appointed to the town council to weigh the information presented to them by the community—namely, the rest of the class. The issue of concern in your town is a petition being circulated to keep overweight students out of the local public schools. Divide the class into sides: one to argue for these students to be given the right to attend the school, and the other side to argue against the action. The town council will be the decision-making body. Before the meeting begins, take 5 to 10 minutes and brainstorm ideas supporting your side of the issue. Allow time for opening comments, the actual arguments, rebuttals, and closing comments. After the town council members have made a decision on how they will vote, ask for their reasons.

Reactions:

_____

_____

_____

_____

Reaction Paper 8.1

You are a world-famous inventor and one day you see a little child in a wheelchair. This sight affects you deeply and at this moment you decide to dedicate your life to inventing items that will be of use to people of all ages who are physically disabled. Identify two or three inventions you will create and how they will help people who are physically disabled.

Reaction Paper 8.2

Have you ever felt left out? When you were younger, possibly even now, were you ever the last one picked to play a sport? Did people ever laugh at your abilities while you tried to do something such as dancing, reading, drawing, or music? Using your own experiences, discuss how a person with physical differences might feel when unable to do a specific task well or when alienated from the group.

Notes

Chapter 9

Learning Differences

Introduction

When you learn a new game, what do you do first–read all the rules, watch others play, or just start playing and learn as you go? When you are introduced to new information, do you remember it better if you see it on paper, hear it, write it, or say it aloud? No two people learn in exactly the same way. People with learning differences may be good at processing information in one way but not in another.

We frequently rely upon technological aids to make learning easier–calculators for difficult math calculations, word processors to check our grammar and spelling, and tape recorders to record or play back information. Books on tape often sell as well as their printed counterparts. Computer programs help us to master foreign languages, learn to draw, and balance our checkbooks. Clearly, many of us take advantage of ways to augment our learning. And many of us are underachievers, whether academically or professionally. People with learning disabilities, though, may not have poor achievement as they have learned good coping strategies. Learning disabilities can be related to disorders of thinking, learning, and sometimes of communication. They are called by different names, and there are many types, but we will use the general term *learning disability* to describe the exceptionality in general, and briefly discuss a few of the specific types in more detail.

A learning disability is an invisible disability. Because individuals with learning disabilities are in the normal range of intelligence and may function perfectly well in certain contexts, it is sometimes difficult to assess their problem. Individuals with learning disabilities look and act like everyone else for the most part. Until they are asked to read, write, solve mathematical problems or do some other academic skill, or until they exhibit the inability to organize their learning tasks, it may not be apparent that they have any problem at all. Someone with a learning difference may be able to recite sports statistics, remember song lyrics, or show artistic talent, for example, but in some particular areas be unable to perform adequately.

It may be frustrating for both the person with a learning disability and for that person's family, friends, and teachers to understand what is happening and to cope with the problem, especially until such time as the difficulty is properly diagnosed. The reason for the frustration is that frequently the student with a learning disability has average to high intelligence and cognitive ability. This chapter seeks to introduce the many facets of learning disabilities so that you will be better equipped to understand friends and family members who learn differently.

The Culture of Learning

People with learning differences are frequently successful because they have developed techniques for camouflaging their differences and getting by in the world. For example, a business executive who has trouble reading or writing might dictate letters and have a secretary type them. In this case, the potential disability is circumvented. Another person might rely upon digital watches to tell the time, or calculators to solve math problems. Such a person can accurately tell time and solve math problems by using assistive technology. A traveler lost on the road might ask for directions rather than consult a map, again taking advantage of other sources of information. Someone may even pretend to read a book or newspaper while sitting on the city bus in an effort to fit in with the crowd. Indeed, an entire culture of learning has arisen to aid people with learning differences in succeeding in life and going unnoticed.

Identifying the Problem

Learning disabilities are the newest categories of exceptionality, having been identified only since the 1960's by educators and parent groups. According to the National Association of State Directors of Special Education (1991), forty-nine percent of children between the ages of six and twenty-one during the 1988-89 school year were identified as having learning disabilities. However, others have suggested figures at ten percent. Many people are not diagnosed with learning disabilities until college level. Three to five percent of college students are diagnosed with learning diabilities, even though they experienced no difficulties in their earlier school experiences. It has been estimated that over one million children will have received stimulant medication in the 1990's in attempts to treat learning disorders (Associated Press News Service, 1989). Of all categories of exceptionality, learning disability (LD) affects the greatest number of individuals and requires the greatest number of instructional personnel. It also is the subject of the most disagreement about definition and diagnosis, as well as treatment methods and educational services.

Some exceptionalities, such as race, gender, physical disability, size, or age, for example, are obvious because of their characteristic features or behaviors. Learning disabilities, however, are very difficult to identify because individuals with LD are more like those without it than not. There is an extremely broad range of problems associated with learning disability, and its effect varies in degree from very mild to severe. The primary way that the exceptionality of LD is identified is by comparing a person to other people in his or her age bracket to determine if there is a discrepancy between expected achievement and actual performance. This discrepancy model is the basic method for identifying an individual with a learning disability. For example, if an eight-year-old girl is not performing at the average or expected level for her age, I.Q., educational opportunity, and ability, her poor performance is most likely due to some sort of learning disability. The girl is also likely to be exhibiting some social or behavioral problems as a result of the way the LD affects her feelings and/or the responses of the people around her.

Categories of Learning Disability

First, let us examine some generalities about learning disorders and disabilities. Traditionally, perception, memory, and attention have been areas of concern, and educators, doctors, and psychologists have all had their different ways of assessing and addressing the problems. For example, educators may use such terms as *specific learning disabilities*. Psychologists may talk about *perceptual disorders* and *hyperkinetic behavior*. Speech and language specialists use such terms as *aphasia* and *dyslexia*. Doctors may use such labels as *dysfunction*, *impairment*, or *brain injury*.

We can say as lay persons that individuals with LD have, at some point in their lives, all experienced poor achievement in some context, and that that poor achievement was associated with learning needs. Since performance and achievement affect self-concept, and learning disabilities may inhibit

Spotlight on Diversity

When I was sixty-seven years old, I had to learn to read. My husband had a heart attack and all of a sudden I was faced with bills from doctors and letters from family which I couldn't read, let alone answer. I was brought up in south Louisiana and my family spoke Cajun French. I never learned to read at all, but it didn't matter because my husband took care of all that. When he got sick it was terrible, though. I couldn't drive, and even after I took a cab to the hospital, I had trouble finding my way around. I couldn't read the signs, and at night there was almost no one to ask for directions.

I finally went to an adult education center where they assigned me a reading tutor. We studied one-on-one, and by the end of the first book I could read most traffic signs and could write my name and numbers so I could write checks. Now, after two years, I can read pretty much everything.

I like the feeling of being independent. I can find new recipes, read labels on cans, and look for sales at the store. Best of all, I don't have to hide anymore. I always pretended or avoided people in the past. Now I'm just like everybody else. It feels good.

Marian J., —Port Allen, LA

the development of social and interpersonal skills as well, often individuals with LD may suffer emotionally and socially, though this is not always the case.

Following are some broad, thumbnail definitions of a few categories of the exceptionality called learning disability. It is a good rule to be cautious about using these terms without the guidance of a professional. This list is offered solely for the purpose of introducing you to a few of the most commonly used terms.

Specific learning disability: A legal definition which has been incorporated into federal law is that specific learning disability is a "disorder in one or more of the basic psychological processes involved in understanding or in using language, spoken or written, which may manifest itself in an imperfect ability to listen, think, speak, read, write, spell, or to do mathematical calculations" (Individuals with Disabilities Education Act, 1990).

Brain injury: An individual with brain injury is described as having an organic impairment which results in perceptual problems, thinking disorders, and emotional instability (Hardman, Drew, Egan & Wolf, 1993).

Minimal brain dysfunction: A person who shows behavioral but not neurological signs of brain damage is sometimes diagnosed with "minimal brain dysfunction" or "minimal brain injury." People with minimal brain dysfunction are often average or above average in intelligence.

Hyperactivity: This is a behavioral characteristic which is also often termed *hyperkinetic*. Hyperactivity is typically a general excess of activity. Individuals may be described as fidgety, nervous, or distractible.

Perception disorders: Perception problems for individuals with LD may include a wide range of difficulties, including visual, auditory, and haptic (touch, body movement) sensory systems. Visual and auditory difficulties in LD should not be confused with the characteristics associated with hearing and vision exceptionalities. These perceptual problems are entirely different. They have to do with perception, rather than with hearing and vision, per se. An example would be clearly seeing a word on paper yet reversing the order of letters.

Dyslexia: Impairment in the ability to read is called dyslexia. People with dyslexia may have trouble spelling certain words and may invert letters of the alphabet. They may also have difficulty with comprehension as a side-effect of the dyslexia.

Dysgraphia: Impairment in the ability to write is called dysgraphia. People with dysgraphia may know how to spell a word but be unable to write it on paper. They may also have difficulty with handwriting, word spacing, or letter formation, or they may write very slowly.

Dyscalculia: Impairment in arithmetic or computation skills is called dyscalculia. People with dyscalculia may have trouble counting, writing numbers, or solving even simple addition or subtraction problems because they are unable to relate to the numerical figures.

Aphasia: Aphasia is the loss or impairment of the ability to use spoken or written language. A person experiencing aphasia may not be able to recall the name of a familiar person or object.

Causes of Learning Disability

Learning disabilities have different causes, and any one disability may have many causes. Some types of LD are caused by neurological damage (typically acquired at birth, either due to lack of oxygen or during delivery), genetic abnormality (passed on from parent to child), or environmental factors (including lack of reinforcement for learning by parents and, according to some experts, radiation stress, flourescent lighting, and unshielded television tubes). Factors such as poor nutrition, food additives, drug or alcohol consumption, and smoking are also thought to play a role in the development of a person with LD. Research into the causes of this complex exceptionality is on-going, though no one factor has been proven conclusively.

Stereotypes of Persons with Learning Differences

The following stereotypes about people with learning differences are *not* true:

- They can't understand
- They represent a small minority
- They are not trying hard enough
- They all have brain damage
- They are "slow"
- They always have trouble academically
- They cannot read or write
- Their social and emotional well-being is not affected
- They usually outgrow their learning disabilities
- They are stupid
- They need special classes
- Teachers can always identify children with learning disabilities

Issues Persons with Learning Differences May Face

- Receiving appropriate service
- Ridicule from others
- Identifying the learning difference
- Classroom problems
- Mainstreaming v. non-mainstreaming
- Finding support or acceptance
- Finding role models and mentors
- Relationships
- Labeling
- Finding the best treatment
- Instructor's perceptions
- Adaptable or appropriate equipment
- Acknowledgment of difference
- Adaptation of classroom teaching strategies to adjust for learning differences
- Getting a job where the boss accepts or is willing to recognize issues related to learning challenges
- Others considering them slow or stupid
- Feelings regarding their need for assistance or different educational strategies

Support Systems

Adult education is provided by local schools and community colleges to teach basic skills, General Equivalenvy Diploma (GED) preparation, and vocational education. Volunteer tutors participate in adult literacy programs in which individuals with low reading and writing skills are placed with tutors for one-to-one private instruction. Churches and synagogues frequently provide tutorial services, and colleges and universities offer community education classes.

In elementary and secondary schools, students with LD are often included in special education programs. In addition to studying their subject matter in these programs, they are often taught how to learn using widely accepted "learning strategies" developed at the University of Kansas.

Interactions

Following are some suggestions for interaction with a person who has a learning disability (LD).

Learn about advocacy groups which provide information and act to secure treatment and protective legislation for those with LD. Offer your help and support.

Volunteer as a tutor for children or adults with learning disabilities. Many organizations provide training for volunteers at no cost.

Promote the development of functional academic programs for LD students in your local schools. Talk to school personnel to determine what programs are currently being offered for LD students, and suggest the development of a program if necessary.

When you experience a problem, or see a problem that a person with LD is having, focus on the environment rather than on the learner. For instance, try to express directions more clearly, or in another way, or try demonstrating instead of telling the instructions.

Model the behavior you desire or are trying to teach. Modeling is much more effective than telling, either in speech or in writing.

Do not give individuals with LD too much information at one time. Present instructions or information in small increments, so that the person is not overwhelmed.

Write down information when possible. Check to be sure the person understands the instructions.

Establish eye contact before giving or repeating instructions. Establishing eye contact helps to make a stronger connection between you and the person with whom you are communicating.

Review information. It is helpful to repeat frequently, so that learning is reinforced.

Ignore inappropriate behavior whenever possible, and reward and reinforce positive or appropriate behavior. Whatever you put your attention on will increase and grow, so why not put your attention on positive behavior?

It is important to be patient and to remember that the difficulties of individuals with LD do not come from lack of motivation or intelligence. Think of the problem as a challenge to you to communicate more clearly.

Encourage persons with LD to seek assistance from agencies which offer special help. Newspapers, talking books, and many other services are available in most communities.

Encourage a positive attitude toward the exceptionality of LD among your friends, family, and neighbors, because they, like you, will certainly encounter and interact with many people in their lives who have learning disabilities. The information you share may help them to identify their own LD in some cases, as well.

Summary

This chapter has introduced an exceptionality which is complex and comprehensive, and so offers you special challenges. You have seen that the term *learning disabilities* is broad and generic and that it involves different specific problems. The study of this exceptionality is relatively new, and though a variety of disciplines such as medicine, education, and psychology have undertaken it, even the conceptual development and terminology related to LD are still in the formative stages. The field is growing at a rapid pace, and our understanding is increasing. At the present time we can only say that those individuals exhibiting the characteristics of learning disabilities are so varied that we cannot describe them with any one concept or term.

References

Associated Press News Service. (1989, June 3). 750,000 children take stimulants researchers say.

Hardman, M., Drew, C., Egan, M., & Wolf, B. (1993). *Human Exceptionality: Society, School, and Family* (4th ed.). Boston: Allyn and Bacon.

National Association of State Directors of Special Education. (1991). *Reference notes for speechmaking or for understanding the forces at work which are driving social policy.* Washington, DC: author.

Individuals with Disabilities Education Act. (1990). Washington, DC: U.S. Government Printing Office.

Suggested Readings

Ellis, E. S., Deshler, D. D., Lenz, B. K., Shumaker, J. B., & Clark, F. L. (1991). An instructional model for teaching learning strategies. *Focus on Exceptional Children, 23*(6), 1-24.

> *The strategies instructional approach developed at the University of Kansas Institute for Research in Learning Disabilities is described in this paper. An eight-stage model fo promoting learning by students with learning disabilities is described.*

Hall, D. E. (1993). *Living with learning disabilities: A guide for students.* Minneapolis: Lerner Publications.

> *This guide describes various LDs such as attention deficit disorder, fine motor problems, and difficulties with visual information, and offers positive advice on how to cope.*

Hampshire, S. (1982). *Susan's story: An autobiographical account of my struggle with dyslexia.* New York: St. Martin's Press.

> *This book presents one woman's first-hand experiences with dyslexia.*

Ingersoll, B. D. (1993). *Attention deficit disorder and learning disabilities: Realities, myths, and controversial treatments.* New York: Doubleday.

> *This book examines the symptoms, development, prognosis, causes, diagnosis, and treatment of learning disabilities and ADD.*

Notes

Exploration

Individual Activities

1. Read the following paragraph quickly:

> Down syndrome si a disaes dezirertcarahc by wol I.W., shrot
> and broad hands, and woleb average thgieh. Ti is more birth
> DNA there is no crue.

This is how an individual with a severe learning disability may see words. Did it take you longer than usual to read and understand it?

_____

_____

Imagine having to deal with all reading materials in this fashion.

Now quickly write your name and address, but write all of the words backwards. Do you think people with learning disabilities feel the way you do now when faced with a difficult task?

_____

_____

_____

Reactions:

_____

_____

_____

_____

_____

_____

_____

_____

166

2. Imagine that you have a learning disability. Write a letter to a newspaper advice column about your problem. Then write a response to your letter that offers helpful advice.

Letter:

_____
_____
_____
_____
_____
_____
_____
_____
_____
_____
_____

Response:

_____
_____
_____
_____
_____
_____
_____
_____
_____
_____
_____

Group Activity

A learning disability may not just be trouble recognizing words or memory. It may affect one's ability to take notes. Have one member of your group read aloud a short paragraph from your textbook as quickly as a teacher would speak during a lecture. Take notes on this information in the space below. However, don't write with your preferred hand. Use the other! How well did you do compared to the other members of your group? Are you LD?

Reactions:

_____

_____

_____

_____

_____

_____

_____

Notes

Reaction Paper 9.1

One major problem with people who live with learning disabilities is not their skills but their self-concept. It is difficult to advance when you are constantly thinking that you are not as good as everyone else. If you had a child with learning disabilities, what would you say or do to get the lower expectation out of your child's mind?

Reaction Paper 9.2

We all take advantage of learning aids to make the job of processing information easier. What are some learning aids that you frequently use, and why?

Notes

Chapter 10

Intellectual Differences

Introduction

Intellectual diversity surrounds us. Intellectual abilities cross over every race, ethnicity, gender, family, or socioeconomic status. Intelligence is vitally important to our world. The debate over whether intelligence is measurable or is inherited will not be solved here. Rather, we use the term intelligence to refer to a person's cognitive powers and intellectual abilities. Everyone requires stimulation to nurture those powers and abilities. This chapter will focus on two categories of exceptionalities commonly connected with intelligence: giftedness and mental retardation.

Giftedness is a condition of significantly advanced abilities above the normal population in such areas as intelligence, leadership, psychomotor, academics, and the creative and performing arts. Mental retardation is a condition of globally-limited intellect existing concurrently with a lower level of adaptive behavior and identified before the age of 22. This chapter provides an historical background to the field of intelligence, examines definitional issues of gifted and mental retardation, and proposes ways to successfully assist people to use their cognitive abilities.

What is Intelligence?

Individual characteristics are recognized by our society. However, norms have been determined for human development and intelligence. These norms are the standards against which persons are evaluated. Present-day norms are constructed when researchers select a large sample of individuals representing different elements of the population (age, culture, etc.) and study the characteristics assessed for a person. The scores then emerge as standards.

Scores that a person receives on an assessment can be compared to those of others in the norming group. Society can then determine how average individuals function and differentiate people who do not function easily in that range. The deviation ranges from gifted (for surpassing the established range) to disabled (for an inability to meet it). A look at a short history of defining intellectual levels can establish a progression to the acceptable definitions of today.

Historical Perspectives

Historical events have contributed to the evolution of our ideas about the nature of intelligence. Charles Darwin (1859) asserted that some individuals were the "fittest" of each species. In the late nineteenth century, Darwin's cousin, Sir Francis Galton, conducted a study of intelligence, concluding that intelligence is wholly determined by heredity. Galton described intelligence as a function of sensory acuity, believing that "the only information that reaches us concerning outward events appears to pass through the avenue of our senses; and the more perceptible our senses are of difference, the larger the field upon which our judgment and intellect can act" (1907, p.19). Galton's work was unchallenged for many years and led to an established belief that an individual's intelligence was genetically determined at birth.

Alfred Binet, a French psychologist, offered the first significant counterclaim to this view. In 1869, he reported that intelligence was "educable." His most significant contribution was to develop a scale to distinguish between normal and "dull" students in Parisian schools. Binet inductively created a series of 30 practical tasks (i.e. tying shoestrings, recalling digits and sentences) and ranked them in order of increasing difficulty. Using his own children and their friends as a norming sample, Binet determined the "mental age" at which most people could accomplish each task. He then made comparisons of the responses of unknown test subjects with his scale and determined whether the subject was in the normal or dull range of human intelligence. His scale became the most widely accepted theory of heredity and intelligence in the twentieth century. Binet believed that with appropriate education and training, an individual could learn to accomplish the tasks and thus raise the "mental age" score.

Intelligence Testing

Louis Terman, an American teacher and principal, was interested in studying the differences between bright and dull children. After graduating from Clark University in 1905, he went to work at Stanford University where, in 1910, he acquired English translations of Binet's scales for research purposes. He adapted and altered the tasks to fit American subjects and named the new scale the Stanford Revision of the Binet Scale, which became known as the Stanford-Binet Intelligence Test. Terman incorporated a new method of calculating the score on the test. He calculated the ratio between the chronological age and the mental age, multiplying the result by 100 to eliminate decimals. The resulting "Intelligence Quotient" or IQ is represented by the following formula:

$$IQ = \frac{\text{Mental age} \quad x \quad 100}{\text{Chronological age}}$$

Terman's intelligence test and scoring method was immediately accepted as the best measure of intelligence available in the United States. It was so well respected that as other instruments were developed to measure intelligence, the new instruments would be validated by correlating them with the Stanford-Binet. Terman believed that the Stanford-Binet test measured innate, unchanging ability or aptitude, and persons who scored well on the test would become the future leaders of our society. Based on his research, he concluded that a score of 130 and above is a mark of "giftedness," while an IQ of 150 and above signifies "genius" (Feldman, 1979).

In 1930, a University of Chicago psychologist, L.L. Thurstone, challenged the single-score concept of intelligence. In his view, IQ scores only predicted verbal academic achievement and not other endeavors. He advocated for intelligence testing consisting of seven distinct, primary mental abilities using verbal comprehension, word fluency, number facility, spatial visualization, associative memory, perceptual speed, and reasoning. He believed each of the factors represented an independent aspect of intelligence. California psychologist J. P. Guilford expanded upon the Thurstone view and described a three-dimensional "Structure of the Intellect" model of intelligence, consisting of 120 separate elements or basic factors of intelligence.

Guilford critiqued Terman's work, claiming it was simply a practical adaptation of Binet's model and was not guided by scientific research. Paradoxically, while Guilford criticized Terman's concept of intelligence for being too general, others criticized Guilford's model for being too specific. In practice, the Structure of Intellect Test is very difficult and time consuming to administer, score, and interpret.

In 1939, David Wechsler presented the education world with the Wechsler-Bellvue scale for adults. This intelligence scale incorporated the notion of a general intelligence consisting of specific intellectual abilities. He incorporated this philosophy into the development of a series of scales, including the Wechsler Intelligence Scale for Children (WISC) ages 6 though 16, which he revised to its present form in 1974 (WISC-R). These tests provided a welcome alternative to the Binet or Guilford models.

There are several differences in the Stanford-Binet IQ and the WISC-R. The WISC consisted of 10 subtests, independently scoring intelligence performance and verbal abilities, each measuring a different ability. Combined they assess global intellectual capacity. The verbal score on the WISC-R correlates highly with the Stanford-Binet IQ, and the performance score is designed to measure a different, less verbal set of abilities (Wechsler, 1974). Furthermore, the WISC-R replaced the IQ ratio with a deviation IQ score. Instead of applying a derived mental age to a ratio formula, Wechsler converts the raw scores on each subtest to standard scores, normalized for the examinee's age group, and adds them for a total standard score, called the deviation IQ (Patton, Beirne-Smith & Payne, 1990).

Specialized training is required for administration of all intelligence tests. Usually, psychologists and/or other professionals who are certified or licensed administer the test. Intelligence tests have often been criticized due to cultural bias and actual predictability issues. They are designed to provide global estimates of a person's intellectual ability and by doing so, may predict that student's potential to profit from instruction in a specific area. The Stanford Binet Intelligence Scale and the Weschler Intelligence Scale for Children-Revised (Weschler Scales are also available for preschool children and for adults) remain the two most commonly used intelligence tests.

Exceptional Intellects

Each culture defines giftedness within its own image, values, and lifestyles. Outstanding individuals are unusual by definition and therefore fall into a category of exceptionality. Furthermore, exceptional persons tend to be under constant public scrutiny and subjected to all sorts of pressures and temptations. For example, pop stars are typically young people with one particular talent. This talent assists in bringing these people into a world where fame and money remove all the rules of their usually very average childhood. Even the most remarkable prodigies, such as Mozart, did not produce work of lasting merit until their teen or adult years.

Intellectual ability is often compared to success. Several studies have examined the attributes of successful people. These studies have concluded that basic characteristics are common to each of the individuals studied. These basic characteristics include commitment to a task, flexibility, courageousness, decisiveness, risk-taking, high energy, enthusiasm, alertness, and self-confidence.

Many people can be exceptional in more than one way. Some prominent examples of gifted and talented people with disabilities include humanitarian Helen Keller (blind, deaf, and mute), Leonardo da Vinci (learning disabled), Franklin D. Roosevelt (orthopedically disabled), and musician Stevie Wonder (blind).

Eugenics

The science of producing the finest offspring, especially human, is called *eugenics*. Selective breeding was a prominent idea during the early 1900's, derived partly from centuries-old experience of breeding livestock and partly from Darwinian evolutionary theory.

Nearly 60 members of the Bach family appear in at least one musical reference work, suggesting that musical talent may run in the family. It was examples like this that led Sir Francis Galton to produce *Hereditary Genius* (1969). He collected large amounts of biographical data on nearly 300 eminent families. Galton's work drew the conclusion that the more closely related an individual was to a genius, the more likely that individual would also be eminent. His work has been attacked, citing the basis that he confused inheritance of ability with social opportunity. Thus, it can be said that music was the Bach family occupation into which new members could enter with good prospects.

Directly altering genetic material is another form of eugenics. Geneticists are on the threshold of making this practical. Researchers are working on producing a complete analysis of the human genetic make-up. Once this is accomplished, it will certainly lead to control over many inherited illness such as hemophilia, muscular dystrophy, and sickle-cell anemia. It is sure to be quite controversial, however, when geneticists begin altering such basic skills as intelligence.

Gifted

Many heterogeneous and societal stereotypes come to mind when discussing persons who are gifted. Being gifted goes far beyond the traditional stereotype of the highly intellectual being. The term gifted means people who show evidence of high performance capability in areas such as general intellectual ability, specific academic aptitude, creative or productive thinking, leadership capacity, or visual or performing

Spotlight on Diversity

At age twenty-five, I don't feel terribly different from the way I felt when I was in college, and fourteen. I still like to chat with professors, travel around the country in vans (or Greyhound buses), write for publications, and I've even ended up on a university campus again, finishing up coursework for a Ph.D. The lesson I draw from my experiences is that those who wish to understand the lives of gifted children or teenagers might well consider how they would respond if they found themselves in similar situations as adults.

People ask if I didn't feel out of place as a fourteen-year college student, and if that might not have had all sorts of awful effects on my social life. At age 16, I got a brief look at what might have been. Through a stroke of luck, I won a contest which provided me with a chance to go, free of charge, to a summer tennis camp. The fresh-faced campers taunted me mercilessly for my lack of tennis skills, and their disgust increased tenfold when they found out that my blue jeans came from K-Mart. At night, the tennis camp boys stayed up after hours, trying snuff, risking a punishment measured in pushups.

Most of these boys were as old as me, or older. When I returned to college in the fall, I felt more than ever that by ducking out of high school, by doing what mattered to me, I was doing the right thing.

—*Thomas K., Farmington, ME*

arts who require services or activities not ordinarily provided by the school or jobsite in order to fully develop such capabilities and talents. Many children are talented in one area and ordinary in others.

Distinguishing potentially gifted people from the rest of the population causes conflicts because not everyone agrees on a global definition of gifted education. School district personnel, and the communities they serve, usually identify gifted persons yet have widely disparate values and attitudes about who is gifted. The prevalence of giftedness is a function of the definition chosen. The federal figure most quoted for giftedness ranges from 3 to 5 percent of the population.

In 1972, a federal task force was formed to study gifted children. Sydney Marland, the U. S. Commissioner of Education, directed the task force in response to a congressional mandate that gifted children should benefit from federal funding. The document produced by this committee became known as the Marland Report. The report defined contemporary gifted education.

The very definition of giftedness suggested diversity. The report noted six diverse areas and stated children capable of high performance include those with demonstrated achievement and/or potential ability in any of the key areas of giftedness, either singly or in combination. The U.S. Congress altered the definition several times in subsequent laws. The most current definition of the six areas are listed below. Examples are provided as necessary.

General intellectual ability. A gifted intellect is a reported intelligence quotient above 130 on a normal curve.

Specific academic aptitude. For example, Adragon Eastwood DeMello achieved specific academic achievement in his selected field. DeMello was 11 when he graduated with a degree in mathematics from the University of California in 1987. Historically, Karl Friedrich Gauss (1777-1855) is considered by many to be one of the three greatest mathematicians that ever lived, next to Archimedes and Newton. It is reported that Karl noticed and corrected a mistake in his father's weekly payroll at the age of 3!

Creative or productive thinking. History is full of illustrations of highly creative, gifted people. Many of them were not recognized for their creative gifts until they were older. For example, a newspaper editor fired Walt Disney because he had "no good ideas," and Winston Churchill failed the sixth grade!

Leadership ability. Jessie Jackson, George Bush, Bill Clinton, and other political leaders are said to have exceptional leadership ability. Heads of major corporations, such as IBM, AT&T, Chrysler, and Macintosh, would likewise fit in this category.

Visual and performing arts capability. Without doubt, Mozart (1756-1791) is one of the most famous musical prodigies. He played the harpsichord at age 3 and accomplished his first public performance at age 5. Pablo Picasso (1881-1973) was said to be a prodigy in the arts world. He entered the Barcelona Academy of Fine Arts at age 14.

Psychomotor ability. In the 1948 Decathlon, Bob Mathias was, at age 17, the youngest Olympic athletic gold medallist. Sonja Henie was Norwegian figure skating champion at age 11 and Olympic gold medallist in 1928, just four years later. In 1983, Samantha Bruce became the youngest girl (age 12) to swim the English Channel. Certainly oustanding record-setting athletes fit into this category of giftedness no matter when they began to excel in their sport.

Characteristics of Gifted and Talented People

A few of the more prominent characteristics of gifted people include:

- Unusual ability to lead others
- Extraordinary talents
- Unusual empathy and concern for people
- Excellent verbal skills
- Ability to grasp ideas well beyond chronological age
- Genuine interest in learning
- Originality of thought
- An interest in designing, developing, and creating
- Curiosity
- Flexibility
- Ability to appreciate beauty
- Unusually large vocabulary
- Persistence
- Ability to concentrate for long periods of time
- Reads often
- Has a good memory
- Shows good judgement and logic

Stereotypes of Gifted People

It is *not* true that gifted people:

- Are physically weak
- Are socially inept
- Have narrow interests
- Are emotionally unstable
- Are "superhuman"
- Are usually bored in school
- Do everything well
- Always make high scores on tests
- Are always successful

Gifted Underachievers

Four major characteristics that separate underachievers from achievers are feelings of inferiority, less perseverance, less self-confidence, and no life goals. As an example, suppose a child who is academically inclined in general education, is a leader, and has artistic abilities transfers to a class full of gifted children. In the new class, he or she is the bottom achiever, competing with many children who are leaders and have artistic abilities (Karge, 1988). This setting would foster one or more of the four characteristics.

The term gifted underachiever is an ambiguous one. People have many reasons for underachievement. Perhaps they have no particular interest in achieving good grades, in conforming to school rules, or in academics in general. Anyone can be an achiever, when motivated in the proper way.

Mental Retardation

Life for a person with mental retardation, often referred to as a person with a mental handicap, is not the stereotype one might expect. Persons with mental retardation are no longer institutionalized but are integrated into families, taught in special classes, or mainstreamed into general education classes at public schools. Many graduate from high school and progress to minimum-wage or better jobs. Many adults remain at home, but others live independently in group homes assisted by private or public organizations. Many marry and have children of their own.

Historic conceptualizations of persons with mental retardation have included subhuman organisms, objects of pity, holy innocents, eternal children, objects of ridicule, diseased organisms, and menaces to society (Wolfensberger, 1972). Until the 1970's, persons with mental retardation were generally excluded from and ignored by society. We concealed them from our communities, schools, private enterprises, and public facilities. This situation changed dramatically, and the story of that change is an important part of our recent history.

"Normalization" was a major concept in the 1970's, as was "deinstitutionalization." These two concepts promoted the integration of persons with disabilities into the mainstream of life to as great a degree as was appropriate. The decade of the 1970's marked the end to institutionalization of those who were mentally retarded, mentally ill, and who had multiple handicaps. The period also marked the beginning of the shift of public resources into local communities with significant attempts at creating better societal understanding and receptivity toward persons with disabilities.

Today, we recognize that people with intellectual differences need the chance to develop to the best of their abilities, just like everyone else. Respect for what people can do has taken the place of pity for what they cannot do.

The definitions of mental retardation have evolved from the 19th century categorizations of idiots, feebleminded, and imbeciles (terms which are inappropriate today), to distinct definitions based on IQ, to the present abandonment of IQ levels. From 1959 to 1983, many revisions to the definition of mental retardation were integrated. In 1973, mental retardation was categorized using the following IQ levels:

IQ = 50-70	mild retardation
IQ = 36-49	moderate retardation
IQ = 20-35	severe retardation
IQ = <20	profound retardation

Today, traditional levels of IQ have been abandoned

Spotlight on Diversity

I remember one day in school. It was a long time ago but I remember. Someone painted the words "Wip Room" on the door to the class. Our teacher was real mad. Some of the girls was crying. That's because the other kids always teased us cause we was retarded. I used to be late lots so the other kids wouldn't see me going in there. But I learned a lot. And now I got a good job. I work on the 30th floor. I wrap up packages. And I deliver them all around the city. I use the subway to deliver the packages. Sometimes I have to get them there real fast.

I like my job and where I live. I like my friends at the group home. And I like spending the money I make at my job. And I like to go to movies.

—Russell W., New York City

by some and are used less by others. System advocates now use intensity of support services required and subclassify the need (not the person) into four levels (Beirne-Smith, Patton, & Ittenbach, 1994, p. 71):

- Intermittent
- Limited
- Extensive
- Pervasive

These same levels are applied to the adaptive skill areas. The new definitions reflect the changing values in America. We no longer place importance on intelligence levels; rather we need to nurture and support people as they grow.

According to the American Association on Mental Retardation (AAMR) "Mental retardation refers to substantial limitations in present functioning. It is characterized by significantly subaverage intellectual functioning, existing concurrently with related limitations in two or more of the following applicable adaptive skill areas: communication, self-care, home living, social skills, community use, self-direction, health and safety, functional academics, leisure and work. Mental retardation manifests before age 22" (AAMR, 1992, p.5).

The AAMR also reports that four additional assumptions are essential to the application of the definition (as stated by Beirne-Smith, Patton, & Ittenbach, 1994, p. 75):

1. Valid assessment considers cultural and linguistic diversity, as well as differences in communication and behavior factors.

2. The existence of limitations in adaptive skills occurs within the context of community environments typical of the individual's age peers and is indexed to the person's individual needs for support.

3. Specific adaptive limitations often coexist with strengths in other adaptive skills or other personal capabilities.

4. With appropriate support over a sustained period, the life functioning of the person with mental retardation will generally improve.

Characteristics Commonly Associated with Mental Retardation

Persons with mental retardation may exhibit one or more of the following characteristics:

- Language ability below their age group
- Play interests that are immature for their age
- Difficulty in generalizing
- Poor attention span
- Poor sensory skills
- Poor motor coordination skills
- Low frustration level
- Poor social skills
- Poor self concepts
- Need to hear things many times to learn them
- Need to repeat activities many times to understand them

Stereotypes of Persons with Mental Retardation

It is *not* true that persons with mental retardation:

- Always look different from nondisabled people
- Tend to be gentle people who make friends easily
- Should not be expected to work in the competitive job market
- Are always identified in infancy
- Are defined solely upon scores on an IQ test

Self-fulfilling Prophecy

Rosenthal and Jacobson (1968) demonstrated that to some extent, children's performance can improve if relatives and friends are led to believe they have superior ability. Labels often become self-fulfilling prophecies. For example, persons labeled as gifted stereotypically perform well on most tasks, and persons who are labeled as mentally retarded stereotypically perform poorly. Stereotypical beliefs affect what people expect and the attitudes projected to the susceptible person (Ysseldyke & Algozzine, 1995). Individuals learn to perform and conform with what is expected of them. When people learn they are expected to perform slowly, their accomplishments could meet the low goals.

This can be positive when the expectations are high, but extremely damaging when expectations are low. Support personnel must look past the cause and help the individual. This is impeded due to the lack of known causes of many forms of mental retardation.

Etiology

Etiology is defined as all the causes of a disease or abnormal condition. In the study of intellectual diversity, only a few causative-correlational factors relate to mental retardation. Eighty percent of the cases of mental retardation have an unknown etiology. We do know that prenatal factors affecting mental retardation occur twice as often as perinatal or postnatal factors. Two popular methods are used for prenatal detection of possible disabilities: amniocentesis and chorionic villi biopsy.

Amniocentesis is the surgical insertion of a hollow needle to draw amniotic fluid and obtain cells generated by the fetus. The cells are analyzed for detection of chromosomal disorders, biochemical disorders, blood abnormalities, sex-linked disorders, and neural tube defects. The amniocentesis procedure is often suggested by medical experts if the expectant mother is over the age of 35. Possible side effects include infection, hemorrhage, fetal damage, and, in some instances, miscarriage.

Chorionic villi biopsy (CVB) is a procedure whereby a sample tissue is taken by a tube passed through the cervix or abdomen from an outer membrane enveloping a fetus early in development. CVB detects the same disorders as amniocentesis.

If an abnormality is detected, the patient and physician can explore all options prior to birth. Sometimes the mother miscarries the fetus. Almost half of all miscarriages are due to chromosomal disorders.

Down syndrome, Phenylketonuria, toxic agents, and infectious diseases are known causes of mental retardation.

Down syndrome. The most common cause of mental retardation, and the most effectively detected by amniocentesis, is Down syndrome. Down syndrome was first discovered by Dr. J. L. H. Down in 1866. The syndrome is a genetically linked disorder caused by a chromosomal abnormality. For some unexplained reason, an accident in cell development results in 47 instead of the usual 46 chromosomes. Down syndrome occurs with the presence of an extra #21 chromosome, resulting in distinctive facial characteristics and body features. In most cases, the diagnosis of Down syndrome is determined according to results from a chromosome test administered shortly after birth.

Approximately 4,000 children are born in the United States each year with Down syndrome, or about 1 per 1,000 births. Although parents of any age can produce a child with Down syndrome, the incidence is higher for women over 35.

Characteristics of Down syndrome include a small head, short stature, almond-shaped eyes with folds of skin at the inner corners, flattened nose, poor teeth, small mouth, short fingers, wide hands and feet, and small ears. Individuals with Down syndrome could also experience congenital heart disease, greater risk of leukemia, hypothyroidism, skeletal and digestive problems, speech difficulties, and loss of hearing and vision. Any level of retardation is possible. Very few people who are diagnosed with Down syndrome exhibit all of these characteristics, and there is a wide range of intellectual ability among individuals.

Phenylketonuria. Phenylketonuria (PKU) is a hereditary condition in which the absence of an enzyme essential to protein ingestion affects the metabolism of the body and results in a gradual buildup of toxic substances in the blood and urine. The person has difficulty breaking down phenylalanine, an amino acid found in protein. Because phenylalanine cannot be metabolized properly, high serum levels could build up in the blood. These levels of phenylalanine are toxic to the brain, causing damage in the same manner as poison. PKU interferes with normal development and results in brain damage if not treated immediately. PKU is possibly the most widely known abnormality of metabolism that causes mental retardation. Common characteristics include low IQ, seizures, behavior difficulties, temper tantrums, and schizophrenic outbursts. Physically, most children with PKU have fair skin, blond hair, and blue eyes. They could experience eczema and underdeveloped tooth enamel. An early and accurate diagnosis usually determines the most efficient dietary treatment program which is often highly effective in reducing retardation and other difficulties.

Toxic Agents & Infectious Diseases. There is research to support toxic agents and infectious diseases as sources of the cause for mental retardation. These may include, but are not limited to:

- Fetal Alcohol Syndrome
- Substance exposure (including drugs and tobacco)
- Lead poisoning
- Viruses (such as Rubella)

Developmental Disability

Developmental disability is a generic term applied to physical or mental disabilities occurring before a person's twenty-second birthday. A developmental disability is not a disease, nor should the disability be confused with mental illness. Persons with developmental disabilities do learn, but often slowly and with difficulty. People with developmental disabilities have the capacity to learn, to develop, and to grow. The great majority of these citizens can become productive and full participants in society. Many persons prefer the term developmental disability rather than mental retardation or mentally handicapped because the label does not convey the same negative connotations.

Support Services

Many levels of services are provided as a part of the educational system. Teachers and administrators must be properly trained to identify and work with persons of all intelligence levels (Lasky, Karge, Mortorff & McCabe, 1995). Initial contacts should be made at the local school district level.

Intellectual levels can be appropriately advanced when all support persons collaborate to work effectively with the person (Karge, McClure, & Patton, 1995). Job support persons, educational professionals, parents, and specialists must plan together to collaborate on services that will enhance the person's intellectual growth.

Interactions

Do not criticize or ridicule. Killer statements are destructive! For example: "For someone who is supposed to be so smart, you sure are dumb!" or "We have gone over this eight times—I can't believe you are so retarded."

Be consistent, fair, and honest in all interactions. Many people complain because others "change the rules" or become manipulative. Do not adapt for the gift or intellectual deficit unless the person makes the request.

Teach values. Tell the person what you value and why. Teach self-discipline, hard work, and patience. Explain and demonstrate how manipulation to gain favor is not valued in most places and could be destructive to a relationship.

Encourage problem solving and creative thinking. Instead of telling the answer, ask a question to further define the problem. Solving a problem with guidance provides ownership to the individual.

Congratulate people on their achievement, then move on. It is wonderful to have someone be interested in your achievement—and frustrating to repeat every step necessary to attain the success. This scenario can be true for all persons, regardless of intelligence.

Provide a safe environment for exploration. Encourage people to explore and find an answer or solution that works. It is easy to tell people how to accomplish a task, harder to accomplish the task for them, and most difficult to lead them through the exploration process.

Summary

How we define intellectual ability, from giftness to mental retardation, has changed dramatically over time. Today we realize that labeling people's intellectual ability merely serves to limit their potential. Even people with Down syndrome or PKU have varying intellectual abilities. Respect for what people *can* accomplish should take the place of pity for what they cannot do.

References

American Association on Mental Retardation. (1992). *Mental retardation: Definition, classification, and systems of supports.* (9th ed.) Washington, DC: AAMR.

Beirne-Smith, M., Patton, J. R., & Ittenbach, R. (1994). *Mental retardation.* (4th ed.) New York: Merrill.

Darwin, C. (1859). *On the origin of species.* London: Murray.

Feldman, D. (1979). Toward a non-elitist conception of giftedness. *Phi Delta Kappan, 60*(3), 660-663.

Galton, F. (1907). *Inquiries into human faculty and its development.* New York: Dutton.

Galton, F. (1969). *Hereditary Genius: An inquiry into its laws and consequences.* London: Macmillan.

Karge, B. D. (1988). *A methodological study of the self-concept of third grade system identified gifted and learning handicapped children.* University Microfilms International (Number 8822051).

Karge, B. D., McClure, M.A., & Patton, P. (1995). Collaborative Resource Programs for Students with Disabilities at the Middle School Level. *Remedial and Special Education, 16*(2), 79-89.

Lasky, B., Karge, B. D., Robb, S. M., & McCabe, M. (1995). How principals can help the beginning special education teacher. *National Association of Secondary School Principals, 79*(568), 1-14.

Patton, J. R., Beirne-Smith, M., & Payne, J. S. (1990). Mental Retardation. Columbus, OH: Merrill.

Rosenthal, R. & Jacobson, L. (1968). *Pygmalion in the Classroom*. New York: Holt, Rinehart & Winston.

Ysseldyke, J. E. & Algozzine, B. (1995). *Special education: A practical approach for teachers*. (3rd ed.) Boston: Houghton Mifflin.

Wechsler, D. (1974). *Wechsler intelligence scale for children-revised*. New York: Psychological Corporation.

Wolfensberger, W. (1972). *Normalization*. Toronto: National Institute on Mental Retardation.

Suggested Readings

Adderholdt-Elliott, M. R. (1987). *Perfectionism: What's bad about being too good*. Minneapolis: Free Spirit.
This is an excellent overview of the genius, the perfectionist, the highly gifted person.

Armstrong, T. (1993). *Seven kinds of smart: Identifying and developing your many intelligences*. New York: Plume Books.
This book takes the reader beyond the norm and discusses how to identify and develop many different types of intelligences.

Beirne-Smith, M., Patton, J. & Ittenback, R. (1994). *Mental Retardation* (4th Ed.) New York: Merrill.
This book is a detailed coverage of all aspects of mental retardation.

Clark, B. (1988). *Growing up gifted: Developing potential of children at home and at school*. (3rd ed.) Columbus: Merrill.
This is an excellent introduction text covering all aspects of giftedness.

Davis, G. (1986). *Creativity is forever*. Dubuque, IA: Kendall-Hunt.
This is a summary of the various types of creativity.

Parker, J. P. (1989). *Instructional strategies for teaching gifted*. Boston: Allyn and Bacon, Inc.
This is an excellent guide for persons working with gifted students. The book outlines cognitive, effective, and creative strategies, and discusses how to use these strategies in the content areas.

Rimm, S. B. (1986). *Underachievement syndrome: causes and cures*. Watertown, WI: Apple.
This is a text written for parents who value achievement in their children and for the teachers who are challenged to motivate all students. The author believes underachievement syndrome is epidemic and discusses how to work with persons who are underachieving.

Scheerenberger, R. C. (1987). *A history of mental retardation*. New York: Brookes Publishing Co.
This is a summary of the history of the national movement on behalf of persons labeled mental retarded.

Smith, J. D. (1985). *Minds made feeble*. Rockville, MD: Aspen Systems Corporation.
This book explores the devastating impact which the Eugenics Movement had upon persons with disabilities.

Tyor, L. & Leland, V. (1985). *Caring for the retarded in America: A history*. Westport, CT: Greenwood Press.
This text looks at the history of caring for persons with retardation.

Notes

Exploration

Individual Activities

1. Have you ever tried to complete a task or participate in an activity and found it beyond your grasp (such as playing a sport you were not familiar with, trying to play a musical instrument, or beginning a class in a hard subject)? This is a very awkward feeling and, unfortunately, how most people with mental retardation feel every day. They have feelings just like you. List 10 feelings that you have felt when placed in uncomfortable situations due to your lack of ability.

_____   _____

_____   _____

_____   _____

_____   _____

_____   _____

Can you now relate to the feelings of a person with mental retardation? Put a check in front of those items which are probably similar for people with mental retardation.

2. When you think of gifted people, what descriptors or labels cross your mind? List the first 10 thoughts that come to mind. Then check the ones which are accurate labels for gifted people.

_____   _____

_____   _____

_____   _____

_____   _____

_____   _____

Group Activities

1. Divide up into groups of five or six students. Your assignment is to brag. Have each person describe his or her special talents. You will probably be surprised to learn how many of your fellow students are gifted in specific areas.

Reactions:

_____

_____

_____

_____

_____

_____

_____

_____

2. It is highly probably that many people in your class know someone or have a family member who is mentally retarded. Ask those classmates to tell everyone about that person's abilities, limitations, and personality.

Reactions:

_____

_____

_____

_____

_____

_____

_____

Reaction Paper 10.1

Your best friend has just called to tell you about the birth of her new baby. You are surprised to learn that the infant is mentally retarded. Write a letter of support to your friend and offer any appropriate suggestions.

Reaction Paper 10.2

Some have said that gifted children who are not identified and who do not receive appropriate school interventions may be our most wasted resource. Do you agree or disagree with this statement? Why?

Notes

Chapter 11

Challenges Related To Health

Introduction

C hallenges related to health include problems of limited strength, vitality, or alertness due to chronic or acute health impairments. Persons with various health difficulties are often recognized because of visible (observable) differences. The symptoms are medically diagnosed and require a medical remedy. Impairments may occur as the result of conditions present at birth or may result from disease. Health impairments are defined as conditions affecting performance that result in "limited strength, vitality, or alertness due to chronic or acute health problems such as heart condition, tuberculosis, rheumatic fever, nephritis, asthma, sickle-cell anemia, hemophilia, epilepsy, lead poisoning, leukemia, or diabetes" (Federal Register, 1977, p. 42478). Acute impairments are time-limited, while chronic disorders are considered to be treatable but not curable. This chapter will examine numerous common health impairments. Special attention is given to AIDS due to its current spread among college-age individuals.

AIDS/HIV

Acquired Immune Deficiency Syndrome (AIDS) is a life-threatening disease that is easily prevented (Colson & Colson, 1993). If you are sexually active (whether heterosexual, homosexual, or bisexual), have shared intravenous needles, have received a blood transfusion prior to 1985, or have been involved in any activities where blood or bodily fluids are transmitted, then you are at risk of becoming infected. If this description fits your sexual partner, then you are also at risk. Human Immunodeficiency Virus (HIV) has been linked to the onset of AIDS. Not everyone infected with the HIV gets AIDS. When you are infected with HIV, your immune system attempts to fight the virus but is unable to destroy it.

AIDS is a serious condition that destroys the body's natural defenses against disease. A physician will diagnose an HIV-positive individual with AIDS if one of the serious opportunistic infections associated with being positive develops. These opportunistic infections cause malignancy, serious weight loss, AIDS-related dementia, or if the T-cell count drops to below 200 (versus a normal count of between 900 and 1500 T-cells).

AIDS can be stopped through awareness, compassion, commitment, and community support for safer sexual activities (AIDS Foundation, 1995). The AIDS Foundation provides information on activities considered *safe* by most medical professionals. These include:

- Abstinence from sexual activities
- Casual contact
- Touching
- Hugging
- Fantasizing
- Masturbating

Professionals further point out that AIDS is not spread through such activities as these:

- Coughing
- Sneezing
- Breathing the same air
- Eating together
- Eating food prepared by an HIV-positive person
- Donating blood
- Working or socializing with someone who is HIV positive

HIV is spread by blood-to-blood contact, sharing body fluids during sexual contact, and breast milk. A pregnant woman may be able to pass HIV to her baby before or during birth. Caution should always be taken. If you have questions, contact your doctor or the AIDS Foundation.

The most common way to pass HIV is through sex. The following activities are presumed *risky*:

- Deep (french) kissing
- Vaginal/anal intercourse
- Fellatio (mouth/penis contact)
- Cunnilingus (mouth/vaginal contact)
- Sharing non-sterile needles for drugs, steroids, tattooing, or body piercing

These activities can be additionally hazardous if performed under the influence of alcohol and/or other substances (AIDS Foundation, 1995).

The only 100% "safe-sex" is abstinence. Protection devices are never guaranteed. Condom usage is strongly recommended by AIDS researchers. When used correctly, condoms collect semen that is discharged before and during ejaculation while acting as a barrier to prevent sperm from entering a partner's body. Latex condoms containing a spermicide to kill sperm and sexually transmitted diseases are recommended.

Symptoms commonly associated with HIV infection are persistent and unexplained swollen lymph glands, weight loss, tiredness, loss of appetite, night sweats, diarrhea, fever, and mental disorders. If these symptoms continue for more than two weeks, a person should see a physician. None of these symptoms individually means a person has AIDS.

It is critical that an HIV antibody test be performed if AIDS is suspected. The test determines the presence of HIV antibodies in the blood. If there are antibodies present, you are infected with HIV. Counseling sessions should be offered both at the time of the test and when the results of the test are known.

If the diagnosis is HIV-positive, early medical help is one way to remain healthy. It is vital for people who are HIV-positive (or at risk for HIV) to strengthen their immune systems. A proper diet, regular exercise, stress-reducing programs (such as meditation or other relaxation techniques), abstinence from drugs and alcohol, regular massage therapy, and loving relationships have all been shown to dramatically boost one's immunity and general well-being. Medical research into treatment and cure of AIDS is ongoing.

Asthma

Asthma is a chronic respiratory condition in which air passages become blocked, resulting in episodes of breathing difficulty, especially exhalation. The symptoms include labored breathing, shortness of breath, coughing, and wheezing. Emotional factors can contribute to asthmatic conditions. The increasing emotion of a situation could create a tightening of the muscles around the bronchial tubes, with increased secretions and swelling of the tissues. Many new drug treatments have been successful in controlling the symptoms of asthma.

Diabetes

Diabetes is a metabolic disorder characterized by the inability to properly utilize carbohydrates in the diet. The pancreas fails to secrete an adequate supply of insulin, or the insulin secretion process functions improperly in the digestive process. The result is an abnormal concentration of sugar in the blood and urine. Symptoms are excessive thirst, frequent urination, weight loss, slow healing of cuts and bruises, pain in joints, and drowsiness. Long-term problems could include blindness, kidney failure, heart attacks, and infection. An onset of gangrene, in the most severe cases, may require amputations of one or both feet.

There are two types of diabetes: insulin-dependent and insulin-independent. Insulin-dependent persons must take daily insulin to continue normal growth and metabolism. If the insulin is neglected, the body cannot properly use and store glucose and instead will use protein and fat as energy sources. If the process continues, the body produces acids called ketones, and an excess of ketone bodies in the blood can lead to a diabetic coma. In extreme cases, it can lead to death (Balik & Haig, 1988). Individuals who are insulin-independent are able to control their diabetes with diet and exercise and do not depend upon supplemental insulin. A person's diet and level of exercise provide a base for the amount of insulin utilized. Changes in either exercise or diet can trigger an insulin imbalance. The imbalance could lead to hypoglycemia (low blood sugar) or hyperglycemia (high blood sugar). Symptoms of the sugar-based imbalances include a rapid heart rate, sweatiness, weakness, drowsiness, confusion, and hunger (Balik & Haig, 1988). Recommendations for treatment must be provided by a physician. However, if these symptoms occur, try to follow these three guidelines:

1. *Be sensitive to the need for blood sugar regulation.* For example, following vigorous physical activities, a person may require fruit juice, dried fruit, or hard candies to regulate blood sugar levels.

2. *Provide a place to rest.* Occasionally, a few minutes of quiet sitting can calm a person and provide an extra energy boost.

3. *Obtain medical assistance.* If symptoms do not change immediately, seek professional assistance.

In some instances, normal levels of glucose are maintained by an insulin infusion pump, which is worn by persons with diabetes and powered by small batteries. The pump operates continuously and delivers the dose of insulin determined by the physician.

Drug and Alcohol Abuse

Nearly 14 million Americans abuse alcohol or illicit drugs to the point of dependence each year. Pregnant mothers who abuse drugs place themselves as well as their babies at risk for a variety of serious and sometimes life-threatening problems. Seizures, shortness of breath, lung damage, nasal membrane burns, respiratory paralysis (by overdose), cardiovascular problems, anorexia, and premature labor are all examples of potential problems (Smith, 1991). Current information regarding the long-term impact of substance abuse, cocaine addiction, and drug use is unclear. Some have argued that the impact is permanent and severe. Others have suggested that the problems can be successfully treated without lasting damage to the affected children (Greer, 1990; Select Committee on Narcotics Abuse and Control, 1988).

Fetal Alcohol Syndrome (FAS) is caused by a mother drinking alcohol while pregnant. There is no safe level of alcohol consumption during pregnancy. FAS can cause physical and mental disabilities or can lead to behavior problems (Kavale & Karge, 1986). Characteristics include low birth weight, an abnormally small head, and facial deformities. Additionally, mental retardation, attention deficits, motor development delays, hyperactivity, and sleep disturbances have been observed in patients with FAS.

Snuff, chewing, or smoking tobacco products are popular sources of the drug nicotine. Although the number of American men who smoke is decreasing steadily, the percentage of female smokers has been rising. As a result, today more women die of lung cancer than breast cancer each year. The use of snuff or chewing tobacco has increased in the U.S., and tobacco smoking in other parts of the world remains prevalent. Recent cancer studies have proven the dangers of second-hand smoke, and most government and public establishments— such as restaurants, schools, hospitals, and airplanes—are now designating themselves "smoke-free zones" to prevent an unhealthy environment. All cancers caused by smoking could be prevented entirely. Nicotine is highly addicting, and people in the process of breaking the habit may exhibit irritability, anxiety, cravings, headaches, and lethargy. Symptoms of withdrawal may continue for 4-8 weeks and cravings may continue indefinitely.

Epilepsy

Epilepsy is a chronic central nervous system condition characterized by periodic seizures, convulsions of the muscles, and (with the more severe attacks) loss of consciousness. Seizures are involuntary muscular contractions resulting from neurological impairments. Seizures fall into three major categories:

- *Petit mal.* Petit mal seizures are slight and last only a few seconds. They are demonstrated by a blank stare with a loss of awareness and/or dizziness. The seizures can vary in frequency from one to 200 times a day, lasting from 5 to 20 seconds each.
- *Grand mal.* A grand mal seizure occurs when the person loses equilibrium and convulses. During an akinetic grand mal seizure, the person experiences a temporary loss of consciousness and falls in a passive manner. A myoclonic grand mal seizure is characterized by jerking of the arms and bending of the trunk of the body, and could result in a fall.
- *Psychomotor.* A psychomotor seizure is evidenced by extreme physical movement. The person may run, jump and/or yell uncontrollably, then afterward be unaware of the behaviors.

A major epileptic seizure is often dramatic and frightening to those who have little knowledge and experience. Typically, a seizure lasts only a few minutes and does not require expert care. The following intervention procedures are provided courtesy of the *Epilepsy Foundation of America* (1987 & 1992):

1. *Remain calm.* You cannot stop a seizure once it has started. Let the seizure run its course. Do not try to revive the person. It isn't generally necessary to call a doctor unless the attack is followed almost immediately by another seizure or the seizure lasts more than ten minutes.

2. *Remember these simple procedures*:

- If the person is upright, ease the individual to the floor and loosen the clothing.
- Do not insert anything between the person's teeth or in the person's mouth.
- Try to prevent the individual from striking his or her head or body against any hard, sharp, or hot objects; but do not otherwise interfere with this movement.
- Turn the person's face to the side so that saliva can flow out of the mouth. Do not be alarmed if the person seems to stop breathing momentarily.
- After the movements stop and the person is relaxed, allow him or her to sleep or rest if required.
- Notify the person's family that a seizure has occurred. Some persons carry a chart with them to record such incidents.
- After a seizure, many people can carry on as before. If, after resting, the person seems groggy, confused, or weak, it may be a good idea to accompany him or her home.

When monitored to achieve optimal effects, epilepsy can be controlled by medication. Unfortunately, ignorance, superstition, and prejudice toward people who have seizures is still prominent in our society.

Heart Condition

Each year, heart disease kills twice as many people as cancer and eight times as many people as car accidents or infections. Heart conditions are characterized by improper circulation of blood by the heart (Ysseldyke & Algozzine, 1995). Congenital heart conditions can be traced to maternal infections, radiation, chromosomal aberrations, and other environmental factors. Acquired heart conditions typically result from infectious diseases such as rheumatic fever or from unhealthy personal habits like smoking. The battle to defeat heart disease is being fought on two fronts: the research lab and our homes. New medicines and therapies are helping to prevent heart attacks, blood clots, high blood pressure, and strokes. Cardiologists are also encouraging their patients to follow proper diet, stress reduction, and exercise programs. Cardiopulmonary resuscitation (CPR) has been shown to keep heart-attack victims alive until emergency medical help is available.

Hemophilia

Hemophilia is usually a hereditary condition characterized by failure of the blood to clot following an injury. Profuse bleeding, internal as well as external, occurs from even minor injuries. Hemophilia is found primarily in males because of hereditary determination factors. Females carry the hemophiliac gene, passing it to their male children (Bigge, 1991).

Leukemia

Leukemia is a cancerous disease of the blood-forming organs. The number of white blood cells increases, resulting in progressive deterioration of the body. Much progress has been made recently in the treatment of leukemia. For example, persons with leukemia who have successful allogeneic bone marrow transplantation (genetically different, though of the same species) appear to be cured.

Nephritis

Nephritis is a noninflammatory disease of the kidneys characterized by blood protein escaping through the urine, which reduces proteins in the body. Fatty substances are then able to increase in the blood. The resulting imbalance in body functions could result in serious illness and, if not treated, severe kidney deterioration will occur.

Spotlight on Diversity

When my mother was diagnosed with leukemia when I was 13 years old, it was as if we were all diagnosed. My brother's, my sister's, and my life were changed forever. We had the disease, too, in a way, because we had to deal with all the symptoms. Mom was hit unusually suddenly, and she went from healthy to unable to walk or feed herself in a matter of weeks. It took everybody pulling together to cope with the added responsibilities and medical expenses. We cried and cursed a lot, but we all pitched in.

We learned a lot from Mom's strength and also learned a lot about our own ability to do what was required. We actually got stronger individually and as a family in spite of all the hurt and worry. People don't appreciate their health until they lose it.

—William R., Springdale, PA

Rheumatic Fever

Rheumatic fever is a disease characterized by acute inflammation of the joints, fever, nervous disorders, skin rash, nosebleeds, and abdominal pains. The disease can be serious because of the potential for heart damage caused by the scarred tissues and valves. Rheumatic heart is a general term referring to heart murmurs or irregular heartbeat as a result of rheumatic fever. Rheumatic fever often appears after a streptococcus infection. Streptococcus infections manifest themselves as pharyngitis (abrupt onset of sore throat, fever, malaise, nausea, and headache) and skin infections.

Sickle-cell Anemia

Sickle-cell anemia is a blood condition in which the red cells assume a sickle shape and impair circulation by not properly carrying oxygen. No cure is available for sickle-cell anemia. Any activity that reduces oxygen in the blood (for example hiking to high altitudes) may precipitate a crisis. The condition is genetic and largely limited to persons of African descent. The symptoms are low vitality, pain, shedding of blood cells, interference with cerebral nutrition, and chronic illness. If severe enough, sickle-cell anemia may cause mental retardation or premature death.

Tuberculosis

Tuberculosis is an infectious, chronic, communicable disease caused by the tubercle bacillus, a bacterium that destroys tissues of body organs and bones. The lungs are most often affected. However, the larynx, bones and joints, skin, gastrointestinal tract, genitourinary tract, or heart may also become infected. Fatigue, weight loss, fever, night sweats, and a cough are common characteristics associated with tuberculosis. A positive tuberculin skin test reaction can diagnosis tuberculosis. Almost all properly treated persons with tuberculosis are cured. Treatment often includes hospitalization and drug therapy.

Support Services

Treatment of a health impairment depends upon the condition and the desires of the individual. Many community-based organizations provide support services to people with various health impairments. In response to rising health care costs, current trends in healing are focusing more and more on prevention and holistic health, which treats the entire person and his or her lifestyle, not merely the disease itself. Today, hospitals and doctors' offices are not the only places one can turn to for help. People with health issues are finding guidance, support, and treatment from dieticians, massage therapists, chiropractors, acupuncturists, herbalists, psychiatrists, physical therapists, exercise and fitness counselors, families, and friends.

Interactions

Cultivate loving relationships. Caring, understanding, attention, and touch are some of nature's most potent medicines. Giving someone your time, support, encouragement, and love will, without question, ease the stresses of being ill. You will receive support and encouragement in return, plus the knowledge that you did something to measurably increase someone's quality of life.

Know the medications a person must take and be able to administer them. Friends and family members should be aware of medications, their uses, and doses. There may be a time you will need to give the medication.

Be inclusive rather than exclusive. Involve the health-challenged person in all activities that you normally would do, given his or her abilities and interests.

Talk about coping with the health challenge. Since many health conditions are controlled rather than cured, it is appropriate to talk about coping with the ongoing symptoms.

Listen to your friend's concerns. Simply listening to someone's feelings can be very helpful to both of you.

Learn about your community's services. There are usually local support groups and information networks for most types of health problems.

Summary

For the most part, people with health impairments do not appear different and can engage in most typical life activities. Health impairments are frequently not noticeable to the general public unless an acute episode occurs. During periods of good health there may be no disease symptoms. Breakthroughs in medical technology extend life but often necessitate lengthy and costly treatments. Advocacy and support groups are available for all categories of health issues. Caregivers and persons with health impairments are encouraged to join a network of people interested in the same issue and learn to cope with the associated challenges. No two health challenges are the same, nor do they affect people in the same way. Each disease has individual causes, symptoms, cures, and interventions. It is critical to support the people around us in a loving manner. Talking and touching are two key ways we can improve the lives of people with health problems.

References

AIDS Foundation. (1995). *Together Project Life Guard: We can stop HIV/AIDS.* San Diego: AIDS Foundation.

Balik, B. & Haig, B. (1988). The student with diabetes. In G. Larson (Ed). *Managing the school age child with a chronic health condition.* Minneapolis, MN: DCI.

Bigge, J. L. (1991). *Teaching individuals with physical and multiple disabilities* (3rd ed.). Columbus, OH: Merrill.

Colson, S. E. & Colson, J. K. (1993). HIV/AIDS education for students with special needs. *Intervention in School and Clinic, 28,* 262-274.
This is an excellent overview of several AIDS training/prevention programs.

Epilepsy Foundation of America. (1987). *Epilepsy school alert.* Washington, DC: Author.

Epilepsy Foundation of America. (1992). *Seizure recognition and observation: A guide for allied health professionals.* Landover, MD: Author.

Federal Register. (1977). *United States Code of Federal Regulations* 34 CFR, Ch. III, Sec. 300.7. p. 42478.

Greer, J. V. (1990). The drug babies. *Exceptional Children, 56,* 382-384.

Kavale, K. A. & Karge, B. D. (1986). Fetal alcohol syndrome: A behavioral teratology. *The Exceptional Child, 33*(1), 4-16.

Select Committee on Narcotics Abuse and Control. (1988). *Cocaine babies.* Washington, DC: U.S. Government Printing Office.

Smith, J. (1991). The dangers of prenatal cocaine use. *American Journal of Maternal Child Nursing, 13*(3), 174-179.

Ysseldyke, J. E. & Algozzine, B. (1995) . *Special education: A practical approach for teachers.* 3rd Ed. Boston: Houghton Mifflin.

Suggested Readings

Althea. (1987). *I Have Epilepsy.* London: Dinosaur Publications.
This is a children's book explaining epilepsy in easy to understand terminology.

Jennings, C. (1993). *Understanding and preventing AIDS: A book for everyone.* Cambridge, MA: Health Alert Press.
This is an essential guide for anyone interested in gaining knowledge about AIDS.

Johnson, A. N. (1993). *The story of Terry Fox.* New York: Value of Communications Inc.
This story is about Terry Fox's battle with cancer of the knee. The content goes beyond a personal story and provides suggestions for persons living and/or working with someone with a health challenge.

Jones, M. L. (1985). *Home care for the chronically ill or disabled child: A manual and source book for parents and professionals.* Washington DC: Association for the Care for Children's Health.
This book is a beautifully written account of parent perspectives on issues concerning family members who care for persons with disabilities.

Positively Aware. (1995). *The Journal of Test Positive Aware Network.* Chicago: Test Positive Aware Network.
This journal is published bimonthly by Test Positive Aware Network, 1258 West Belmont Avenue, Chicago, Illinois 60657-3292. This is a Network for persons interested in AIDS.

Shelton, T. L., Jeppson, E. S., & Johnson, B. H. (1987). *Family-centered care for children with special health care needs.* Washington DC: Association for the Care of Children's Health.
This book provides resources for technical assistance, programs and audiovisuals related to family-centered care.

Notes

Exploration

Individual Activities

1. When you think of diabetes, asthma, epilepsy, and AIDS, there are several personal problems that may go along with these conditions. Describe a few problems associated with each condition. Suggest strategies to overcome these problems.

Diabetes

_____

_____

_____

_____

_____

Asthma

_____

_____

_____

_____

_____

Epilepsy

_____

_____

_____

_____

_____

AIDS

_____

_____

_____

_____

_____

214

2. How would it feel not to eat your favorite foods, play sports, or have to take medication or injections on a daily basis? These are considerations that people with health impairments may face every day. List 10 thoughts that are going through your mind while you think about this.

_____

_____

_____

_____

_____

_____

_____

_____

_____

_____

Group Activities

1. How would you feel if a member of your family had a severe health impairment? With four or five other students, discuss ways you would deal with the situation.

Reactions:

_____

_____

_____

_____

_____

_____

_____

_____

2. Arrange a class visit to a nursing home which specializes in caring for patients with severe health impairments. While there, be sure to notice the level of care that is required for some patients. Try to focus on the attitudes of both staff members and patients.

Reactions:

_____

_____

_____

_____

_____

_____

_____

_____

Notes

Reaction Paper 11.1

Assume that you just read a letter to the editor of your local newspaper which suggested that persons with AIDS should not be allowed to shop in your community's food stores. Write your own letter to the editor in response.

Reaction Paper 11.2

Maintaining a good quality of life is important for persons who have a permanent health disabilities and for members of that individual's family. What do you consider a good quality of life to be? Suggest what can be done toward maintaining a good quality of life.

Notes

Chapter 12

Communication Diversity

Introduction

C ommunication is a relationship–a human connection. The word *communicate* comes from a Latin word which means "to share." Communication is a means of transmitting information, ideas, or feelings from one person to another. The ability to communicate often means survival, as when we need to signal our need for help.

Through communication we share our knowledge, ideas, dreams, and hopes. We communicate in many ways, including speech, gestures, drawings, written language, sign language, and facial expressions. Language is the primary means by which people communicate. Ironically, however, it is also the primary means by which people *fail* to communicate. Anyone who has traveled has no doubt encountered either an unfamiliar dialect or a totally foreign language. In different cultures, people communicate with different gestures as well. The purpose of this chapter is to look at the diverse ways in which people exchange ideas and to examine methods to break down communication barriers.

The Culture of Communication

Our reliance on language is so fundamental that we often take it for granted. It is through language that we organize our social structures and learn how to coexist. The communication of messages plays a vital role in expressing and transmitting our culture. In fact, culture itself has been defined as "any system in which messages cultivate and regulate relationships" (Gerbner, 1990, p. 423). Whenever you speak and write your language, you also speak and write your culture. The cultural assumptions and understandings of many generations are embedded in your words.

A culture's myths, legends, and folk ballads are products of communication. Before our ancient ancestors invented writing, they preserved their history through the "oral tradition." They recited or sang their history over and over again, thereby passing it down to the next generation. Over time, the stories changed and kept only the most important and profound meanings—ideas about the beginnings of life, the nature of humanity, and the mysteries of death. These stories survive today as mythology, folklore, legends, allegories, fables, and parables.

A culture's visual arts are another important product of communication. The earliest records of human communication are the prehistoric drawings on cave walls in France and Spain, depicting human figures and animals. To this day, art continues to serve as an important visual means of sharing information and imagination, whether in the form of a painting in a museum or an illustration in a magazine advertisement. Written language, too, can reach artistic proportions in poetry and literature. Even the alphabet itself can be a means of artful expression, as seen in calligraphic handwriting.

There are yet other facets of cultural communication found in the performing arts. Dance, for example, is a system of body language that expresses meaning through movement, gestures, poses, and pantomime. In many parts of the world, such as India, Japan, and Thailand, complex systems of pantomime and dance are combined with symbolic hand gestures, facial expressions, and body movements to tell a story (Crystal, 1987). Some of these dances have survived for thousands of years and communicate traditions and ideas from the past to every new generation. Similarly, opera combines singing, costumes, movement, and other modes of communication. Some people enjoy going to the opera even if they don't understand the words of the songs because they can understand the story through the universal language of gestures, facial expressions, and vocal intonations.

Body Language

Body language is a form of nonverbal communication. Through posture, facial expressions, eye contact, and hand gestures, we can express our feelings, emotions, and attitudes. Waving a forefinger back and forth can say "You are wrong." Holding someone's gaze for a number of moments can indicate "I know you" or "I am interested in you." Leaning forward during a conversation can mean "I am involved in what you are saying." Some body language is universal. For example, certain facial expressions or gestures signify pain, fear, and joy in every culture. However, other expressions may have different meanings in different cultures. Nodding one's head up and down, for instance, means "yes" in the United States and Europe but may mean "no" in other cultures (Beier, 1990).

In some cultures, touching is a very important part of communication. Touching can involve a wide variety of activities: embracing, holding hands, kissing, linking arms, nudging, patting, shaking hands, and slapping, just to name a few. Tactile activities express basic social interactions such as gratitude, greeting, leave taking, sexual interest, aggression, congratulation, and affection. Some societies are more tolerant of touching than others. Northern Europeans and Indians, for example, tend to avoid touching, while Arabs and Latin Americans tend to favor it. In a study of couples sitting together in cafés, it was found that Puerto Ricans touched each other 180 times an hour while Londoners never touched at all (Crystal, 1987). This does not mean that Puerto Ricans are more affectionate than Londoners, just that in British culture communication is less tactile.

There is a science of "visible speech" called *eurhythmy*, in which the body symbolically interprets the sounds of language. Each sound that a person can articulate is reflected by a body movement. The sound *a*, for example, means astonishment and wonder and is shown by raising the arms over one's head as if holding a giant ball. The sound *u* means something is chilling and is expressed by pressing the arms and legs together. Sound, movement, and meaning come together in this intricate system of body language.

Written and Spoken Language

There are between 4,000 and 5,000 languages spoken around the world. The following are the twelve principal languages and the number of speakers (native plus non-native):

Mandarin	930,000,000
English	463,000,000
Hindi	400,000,000
Spanish	371,000,000
Russian	291,000,000
Arabic	214,000,000
Bengali	192,000,000
Portuguese	179,000,000
Malay-Indonesian	152,000,000
Japanese	126,000,000
French	124,000,000
German	120,000,000

(derived from Hoffman, 1993)

David Crystal (1987) has explained that all languages are "equal in the sense that there is nothing intrinsically limiting, demeaning, or handicapping about any of them" (p. 6). No one language is necessarily easier or more difficult to learn or speak than another—even the languages of primitive societies have complex grammatical rules.

Because every language meets the social and psychological needs of its speakers, the study of languages can provide you with valuable insights into human nature and society

(Crystal 1987). That's because a society's intellectual heritage and cultural traditions are directly shaped by the society's language. If you become fluent in another language, you will be able to read great books in the original language of the author and meet the great minds of another culture on their *own* terms. You will learn how other people think, and then you will truly understand another culture and appreciate its values. Ultimately, your own heritage will be enriched because you will see it from an outside perspective. If your native language is English, or if you are in the process of learning English, you will discover that it has borrowed from many other languages.

There is as of yet no such thing as an international language. Through the Middle Ages, Latin was the language of education in western Europe. From the 17th to the 20th century, French was the international language of diplomacy. Today there are more Chinese speakers than any other, but the complexity of the Chinese writing system discourages its use. English has assumed special status internationally, though it is still not a world language. Attempts have been made over the years to design an artificial language–a new, simplified language that combines elements of natural languages–to serve as an international language. The artificial language Esperanto, invented in 1887 expressly as an international language, has millions of speakers worldwide and is sometimes used at international conferences. However, the United Nations has yet to grant Esperanto international status.

Children's Development of Language and Speech

The age at which children develop language varies greatly. Generally speaking, however, we can safely say that the earliest communication begins with social interactions between the caregiver and the baby. For example, the caregiver may play peek-

---

Spotlight on Diversity

I am Japanese, and my husband works for a large American company. When I first arrived in the United States, the wives of my husband's co-workers gave a luncheon to welcome me. I was horrified when several of them greeted me by saying "I hate you." I cried as soon as I got home and told my husband I was sorry. Obviously I had done something terribly rude at the luncheon, but I didn't know what.

After several days of worry and thinking that I could never go out again in America, I told my one American friend what had happened. She said that I had misunderstood. The women were paying me a compliment. She told me, "American women often say things like 'You're so thin, I hate you,' or 'You look beautiful, I hate you.' It means they envy you." I was relieved, but I also understood that it takes more than fluency in another language to be able to communicate.

—Myshio Y., Nashville, TN

a-boo with the baby, point to and name objects, make facial expressions, and so on.

During the first half-dozen months, babies typically experiment with vocalizing simple sounds. This "cooing" gradually becomes a string of babbling, and at about age one the child may put different syllables together and may have learned to "answer" when spoken to.

Between ten and eighteen months, children usually say their first words. At this stage they often echo what they hear without understanding the word or mispronounce a word and therefore remain misunderstood. At about a year and a half, they typically make their first two-word combinations, such as "more juice."

At two years, children begin to effectively communicate with simple sentences and a vocabulary of several hundred words. After age two, the child's vocabulary and grasp of the language continues to grow. However, because the development of language varies so greatly from child to child, it is often difficult to properly diagnose communication disorders at an early age.

Speech and Language Disorders

Several million people in the world are unable to communicate effectively with others because of speech or language problems. The National Institute of Health estimates that over fourteen million Americans alone experience such difficulties (Voice Foundation, 1994). The problem is magnified immeasurably because anyone who tries to communicate with a person with a speech or language disorder may also experience difficulties. Speech and language disorders inevitably draw attention to themselves, and the awareness itself may inhibit communication. The challenge, then, is to overcome this barrier, not to create yet a further problem with communication. With information and understanding, we can avoid this pitfall.

Speech and language disorders are actually quite different. An individual with a speech disability usually has some level of difficulty in communicating because of such characteristics as an incorrect pronunciation of words or parts of words, or a lack of fluency when saying words or phrases.

While the person with a speech disorder may have problems expressing him or herself, the person with a language disability may have either an expressive or a receptive difficulty. When an individual has an expressive language problem, that person is able to correctly produce the sounds necessary for speech but the words themselves may be used incorrectly or illogically. A person who has a receptive disorder has no known hearing difficulties and usually has knowledge of the meaning of words. However, the individual may have difficulty comprehending what has been correctly heard.

Some other common communication problems are:

aphasia: This condition is usually caused by brain damage and characterized by labored speech and an inability to choose the right words.

dyslexia: This is an inability to read and spell correctly, despite normal intelligence. Frequently, letters become reversed or out of order.

illiteracy: The inability to read and write is called *illiteracy*. One in five Americans is functionally illiterate, meaning they do not have the reading or writing skills required to function effectively in society. Often illiteracy is the result of another disorder such as vision impairment, hearing impairment, or dyslexia.

vocal problems: Raspy, hoarse, nasal, breathy, weak, or abnormally loud voices may make someone difficult to understand. Disorders of vocal expression are usually due to an anatomical abnormality in the vocal tract, such as the formation of nodules or polyps.

articulation problems: A difficulty with pronunciation or a lisp is an articulation problem. People with articulation problems may experience anxiety and embarrassment, which interferes with communication.

fluency disorders (stuttering): This disorder of fluency affects one's ability to control the rhythm and timing of speech. Stuttering often involves a repetition of sounds, syllables, words, or phrases. Though people who stutter may speak with difficulty, this has nothing to do with their intelligence. People who stutter frequently experience anxiety and embarrassment, and communication is invariably affected.

cleft lip and palate: A cleft lip is a congenital splitting of the upper lip. A cleft palate is a congenital fissure along the middle of the palate. Both conditions may affect the development of speech, but not in all cases.

laryngeal abnormalities: Malignant growths in the throat may require surgical removal of the larynx. Persons who have undergone an laryngectomy must learn to speak by vibrating their esophagus or by using an artificial larynx which, when placed against the neck while they are talking, emits a speech substitute which is often characterized as having a "buzzing" sound.

muteness: This is the inability to speak, due either to a physical abnormality or to emotional stress (as when someone "loses her voice").

Stereotypes of Persons with Communication Disorders

The following stereotypes of people with communication disorders are *not* true:

- People with communication disorders tend to also be mentally retarded
- Stuttering is an indication of an extremely high IQ
- Articulation disorders are easy to correct
- A person with a cleft palate always has difficulty speaking
- People with communication disorders have emotional disorders as well
- A language disorder by definition means difficulty with speech

Issues Persons with Communication Disorders May Face

- Ridicule from others
- Classroom problems
- Finding support
- Finding role models and mentors
- Relationships
- Labeling
- Finding the "right" type of treatment
- Finding acceptance
- Getting a job that accepts or is willing to recognize communication challenges
- Others considering them either less or more intelligent

Support Services

Local chapters of service organizations such as the American Speech-Language-Hearing Association, may be able to provide information on communication disorders and educational programs. Speech pathologists in private practice and in hospitals may be able to provide information on scientific research and methods of treatment. Speech pathologists and local organizations also may be able to refer an individual to a support group which meets regularly.

Language differences. It is sometimes necessary to be patient and understanding when speaking with someone from another country. It may help your patience to imagine yourself speaking someone else's native tongue. It is difficult to hear and speak a foreign language, and people from other countries are not always proficient in English. They may not be used to making the foreign sounds of our language. Mistakes in pronunciation or grammar do not mean that they are uneducated or unintelligent. Such mistakes just mean that they are in the process of learning another language. If you speak slowly and clearly, it will help others to understand you. However, raising the volume of your voice will not accomplish anything.

Illiteracy. Offer help without making any judgement about the person's inability to read and write. Give clear, simple directions or draw a map showing landmarks. As with other disabilities, do not assume illiteracy means low intelligence. Be sensitive to feelings of embarrassment.

Fluency and articulation disorders. Try not to allow a stutter or a lisp to dominate your attention. You may end up missing what the person is saying and embarrassing him or her at the same time. Just as with a non-native speaker, remember that hesitant speech does not indicate slowness of thought. Be patient and relaxed, and listen carefully rather than attempting to speak for the other person.

Eye contact. Different cultures have different customs about eye contact. Some societies favor prolonged eye contact, while others find prolonged eye contact to be rude or threatening. If you notice that someone from another culture is either averting her eyes or holding them on yours for too long, keep in mind that she may be following different rules of etiquette. Generally, it is best to try to find a middle ground if you are unsure. Body language expert Julius Fast recommends that you break eye contact frequently as you talk or listen. Look down to the side and then back (Fast, 1994).

Hand gestures. As with eye contact, hand gestures are closely linked to culture. Some people use few hand gestures (such as the Japanese) and may seem stiff or standoffish to one who uses sweeping, expressive gestures (such as the Italians). Again, different rules of behavior may apply. Before making generalizations about any individual, try observing for a while.

Personal space. We may feel uncomfortable when strangers invade our "body space." However, how one measures the comfort zone depends upon one's culture. The normal social interaction distance can vary significantly among peoples. Be aware if the person is instinctively inching closer to you or farther away, and try to accommodate his comfort zone. As with eye contact, when you are unsure, try a middle ground.

Summary

Communication allows the people of the world to share in the experience of being alive. It gives us the opportunity to grow and to evolve individually and collectively. "Communication is the back and forth of telling and listening and responding, so you know you are not alone" (Brandenberg, 1993, p. 3). We communicate in many ways, through our speech, our body language, and our written language. Our ability to communicate effectively may break down when we meet someone who has a physical impairment which creates a difficulty in speech or language, or when we are ignorant about the ways we can choose to send and receive information.

References

Brandenberg, A. (1993). *Communication*. New York: Greenwillow Books.

Beier, E. (1990). Body language. *Encyclopedia Americana* (International edition, vol. 4, pp. 131-32). Danbury, CT: Grolier.

Crystal, D. (1987). *The Cambridge encyclopedia of language*. Cambridge: Cambridge University Press.

Fast, J. (1994). *Body language in the workplace*. New York: Penguin Books.

Gerbner, G. (1990). Communication. *Encyclopedia Americana* (International edition, vol. 7, pp. 423-24). Danbury, CT: Grolier.

Hoffman, M. (1993). *The world almanac and book of facts 1994*. Mahwah, NJ: Funk and Wagnalls.

Voice Foundation. (1995). *The voice foundation*. Philadelphia: The Voice Foundation.

Suggested Readings

Axtell, R. E. (1992). *Do's and taboos around the world* (2nd ed.) New York: Wiley.
This is an overview of intercultural communication and etiquette that helps you to avoid using offending or misleading gestures, body language, or phrases.

Berger, G. (1981). *Speech and language disorders.* New York: Franklin-Watts.
This is a readable explanation of the facts and fallacies of communication disorders.

Illich, I. & Sanders, B. (1988). *The alphabetization of the popular mind.* San Francisco: North Point Press.
This is an historical discussion of the development of written language and an exploration of how language alters our world view, our sense of self, and our sense of community.

Ong, W. J. (1982). *Orality and literacy.* New York: Routledge.
This book is a fascinating survey of primary oral cultures (those with no written language) and the societal effects of writing, print, and electronic technology.

Exploration

Individual Activities:

1. Imagine that you are illiterate or are encountering an unknown language. How do you feel when confronted with the following message on a bottle?

$$\Pi\theta\chi\lambda\delta\lambda\Sigma: \ \Omega\zeta\delta\varpi\zeta\lambda! \ \Psi\zeta \ \lambda\zeta\beta \ \Psi\chi\delta\lambda\eta!$$

Now decipher the message using the key below:

$$\theta \ \omega \ \Delta \ \Psi \ \Phi \ \psi \ \Sigma \ \alpha \ \delta \ \phi \ \eta \ \varphi \ \kappa \ \lambda \ \zeta \ \Omega \ \xi \ \chi \ \varpi \ \beta \ \mu \ \Theta \ \Pi \ \sigma \ \vartheta \ \Xi$$
$$a \ b \ c \ d \ e \ f \ g \ h \ i \ j \ k \ l \ m \ n \ o \ p \ q \ r \ s \ t \ u \ v \ w \ x \ y \ z$$

Write your reactions below:

_____

_____

_____

_____

_____

_____

2. At lunch today, observe the body language of the people around you. Can you tell if someone is intrigued, or bored, or excited by a conversation? Do they touch each other, and if so, where and how often? Characterize their proximity to one another and thereby determine how well acquainted they are. Write your observations below:

_____

_____

_____

_____

_____

Group Activities:

1. a. Non-verbal visual communication serves a variety of functions. Facial signals are particularly versatile in responding to the speaker. As a group, complete the following list of facial expressions:

fear _____

happiness _____

anger _____

_____

_____

_____

_____

_____

_____

_____

_____

_____

b. Certain body behaviors are used especially for ritual or official occasions. Complete the following list of ritual body language:

kneeling _____

bowing _____

_____

_____

_____

_____

_____

_____

2. Every language serves its speakers effectively. The Eskimos, for example, have numerous words for *snow,* but these would be totally unnecessary for the people of Egypt. As a group, come up with some words or concepts that are familiar to most Americans but that probably do not exist in another language like Chinese, Navaho, or Swahili.

Notes

Reaction Paper 12.1

Recall a situation in which you were unable to effectively communicate with someone. What was the problem and how did you (or could you have) overcome it?

Reaction Paper 12.2

Over the generations, our society has passed down bits of folk wisdom which we sometimes call "old sayings." We often hear these proverbs from our grandparents. For example, "Absence makes the heart grow fonder." What are your favorite old sayings, and how do they help to express and preserve your culture?

Notes

Chapter 13

Behavior and Personality

Introduction

Inappropriate behavior violates an unwritten social contract about how people should interact. We also find the aberrant behavior inherently fascinating. A personality different from society's expected norms tests the tolerance of society. The severity of behavior and personality patterns can be judged by the level of inappropriate behavior/personality, the persistence of the behavior/personality pattern, and the effect on social functioning.

Mental illness is commonly associated with behavior and personality disorders. Mental illness refers to chronic or transient conditions of an emotional/personality disorder that significantly interrupt the functioning of an individual. Other terms for mental illness include emotional disorders, emotionally disturbance, and psychiatric illness. Edgar Allan Poe, Charles Darwin, and Vincent van Gogh are several notable individuals with documented behavior and personality disorders.

This chapter will highlight various common characteristics and definitions, describe some common behaviors and personalities, and provide appropriate techniques to interact with someone with a behavior or personality disorder.

Common Characteristics

We all have emotional outbursts, show signs of fear and anger, and are hostile and aggressive at times. However, persons displaying actions beyond the normal outbursts, causing continual and serious disturbances and continually frustrating those around him or her are considered to have behavior and personality disorders. Persons with emotional or behavioral problems "...may be severely antisocial, aggressive, and disruptive; they may be socially rejected, isolated, withdrawn, and nonresponsive; they may show signs of severe anxiety or depression or exhibit psychotic behavior, they may vacillate between extremes of withdrawal and aggression; and they nearly always have serious academic problems in addition to their social and emotional difficulties" (Kauffman, Lloyd, Baker & Riedel, 1995, p. 224). Approximately 10 percent of children and adolescents have emotional or behavioral problems that impede their social development and require treatment if these students are to function adequately in society (Kauffman, 1993).

Many persons with behavior and personality disorders are involved with drugs, gangs, or are homeless. In a quest to balance the need for medication, persons with a personality disorder will often try to self-medicate instead of seeking proper medical assistance. In a similar way, the person may seek to belong by joining or forming a gang. A gang is a group, often associated with a territory or "turf" that shares a common identity, and delineates membership through common clothing, symbols, and insignia (Clay & Aquila, 1994). These behaviors are not seen as normal by society and often lead to self-destructive behaviors and homelessness. Although many mental health programs do offer assistance, the person is often unaware how to access assistance or could be too proud to seek support.

Philosophy or conceptual orientation may differ from support program to program. Kauffman, Lloyd, Baker & Riedel (1995) indicated that the most effective programs share the following characteristics:

- Systematic data-based interventions
- Continuous assessment and monitoring of progress
- Treatment matched carefully and specifically to the nature and severity of problems
- Multi-component treatment
- Provisions for frequent-guided practice of academic and social skills
- Programming for transfer and maintenance
- Commitment to sustained intervention

Programs like "Alcoholics Anonymous" allow the person an opportunity to share feelings and frustrations in a non-threatening environment. Additionally, people learn to help themselves. Support programs should be carefully selected based on the characteristics and severity of the behaviors.

Characteristics that consistently appear in definitions of behavior disorders and personality differences include:

- Inappropriateness of the behavior when compared to the expected behavior
- Degree of severity or intensity of the behavior
- Frequency of occurrence of the behavior
- Duration of time that the disorder exists
- Response to normally available interventions
- Effects of the behavior on the individual's performance, personal satisfaction, and interactions with others
- A tendency to develop physical symptoms of fears associated with personal problems
- Difficulty learning what cannot be explained by intellectual, sensory, or health factors

- Difficulty building or maintaining satisfactory interpersonal relationships with others
- A general pervasive mood of unhappiness or depression

Definitions

One of the most respected classification systems of behavior and personality is provided by the American Psychiatric Association (APA) in their guide, "Diagnostic and Statistical Manual" (1994). The current manual describes abnormal behavioral patterns in terms of clear-cut symptoms (such as anxiety or depression), recurring patterns of disturbed lifestyles, and personality disorders. Specific disorders of development, physical disorders, severity of life stresses before the disorder appears, and the highest level of adaptive functioning prior to appearance are also outlined. Some of the most common behavior and personality difficulties are discussed in the following sections.

Psychoses and Schizophrenia

The most disabling disorders related to behavior are the psychoses. Asked to describe a person who is psychotic, lay persons might use the inappropriate words *mad* or *insane*. Society often perceives the bizarre behavior that people with psychotic difficulties exhibit as insanity. Psychologists characterize a psychotic breakdown as a radical change in consciousness, perception, thinking, and social behavior. The experience is sometimes mystifying to family, friends, and even the person involved.

Schizophrenic psychoses are a major mental health problem worldwide. Schizophrenia, which affects about one percent of every nation's population and occurs equally in males and females, should not be confused with multiple personality disorders. Persons with schizophrenia display disturbances in thinking patterns that cause them to act and speak strangely. Some of the patterns include:

- Peculiar thinking, such as a belief that another's thoughts are inserted into the affected person's mind
- Thought broadcasting, such as a belief that the affected person's thoughts are directly sent to the external world
- Delusions of being controlled, such as feeling that an external force is directing the affected person's life
- Hallucinations, such as experiencing a voice that comments on behavior or thought
- Social withdrawal, to seemingly be out of contact with the world around them

Obsessive-Compulsive Disorder

Compulsive actions are repetitive acts one feels compelled to perform without understanding why. If you have ever locked a door, and returned later to confirm the door is locked because you think it might be unlocked, then you have some insight into the relationship between an obsessive thought and a compulsive action. Compulsions are intentional behaviors usually performed in an attempt to reduce anxiety.

Obsession is an intrusive thought. These are unwanted, persistent thoughts, ideas or worries that repeatedly besiege a person's mind (Slater, 1995). An example of an obsessive person is one who insists that you should not go shopping because you will be shot, or one who counts the cracks on the floor during walks. Persons who are obsessive usually appear to be very rigid, very comfortable with sameness and order, and resist change and spontaneity.

Common treatments for Obsessive-Compulsive Disorder are medication and behavior modification. The goal is to treat the disorder quickly before self injury occurs. Perhaps the most famous fictional sufferer of compulsive ritual was Lady Macbeth, washing her hands over and over after she and her husband had murdered the King of Scotland (Rapoport, 1989).

Depression

Persons may be depressed if they display a sad mood, have a persistently sad facial expression, and demonstrate many of the following symptoms nearly every day for a minimum of two weeks (Rosenberg, 1995):

- A poor appetite
- Significant weight loss
- Increased appetite or significant weight gain
- Insomnia or sleeping too long
- Motor restlessness
- Inability to function
- Lack of activity
- Loss of interest or pleasure in usual activities
- Signs of apathy

Depression is seen in all economic groups, social classes, and all races and has been documented in many cultures throughout the world. Studies involving twins have shown that depression can be inherited (Rosenberg, 1995).

Bipolar Depression

The primary characteristic of bipolar depression is high-to-low mood swings. Other characteristics include risk-taking, impulsivity, reckless spending, and a high distractibility. At times, the person is fun loving and enjoyable in social settings, and at other times the person is depressed and moody. A majority of persons with bipolar depression are also manic depressive.

Manic depressive symptoms include sadness, hopelessness, feeling worthless, constantly sleeping yet having no energy, and an occasional desire to be dead. The essential feature of a manic episode is a sustained elevated or expansive mood, or predominant irritability. An episode may begin suddenly and varies in length from days to a few months.

Individuals with bipolar depression may also have relatives who have depression, Tourette's Syndrome, Attention Deficit Disorder, and/or Obsessive Compulsive Disorder, since these disorders appear to be related genetically as well as in symptomology (Rosenberg, Skiba, LeBlanc, Rosenberg, Ossowski & Wolford, 1995).

The mood swing pattern varies from individual to individual. The person may display a significant change in values, attitude, compliance, friends, attire, and/or priorities. Many persons with bipolar depression have attempted suicide at least once. Usually, a diagnosis is not made until the mid-teen years. Several famous people have been diagnosed with bipolar depression. These include Abraham Lincoln, Theodore Roosevelt, and Winston Churchill.

Attention Deficit Disorder and Attention Deficit Hyperactivity Disorder

Attention Deficit Disorder (ADD) is the inability to focus on a task for a sustained period of time, along with the tendency to act impulsively. Individuals with ADD may also exhibit hyperactivity (ADHD). The differences between persons with ADD and with Learning Disabilities (LD) are not entirely clear, since the characteristics overlap. As with LD, there is disagreement about the causes of ADD.

Proper diagnosis of ADD/ADHD is crucial. There are problems which can mimic ADD/ADHD behaviors and symptoms based on allergies, food intolerances, hypothyroidism, depression, anxiety, manic-depressive illness, auditory processing problems, learning disabilities, poor parenting, inappropriate teaching methods, disorganized environment, excessive stress, inappropriate school placement, or situational adjustments (e.g. death, divorce). Stimulant medications are frequently used to assist with control of behavior.

Characteristics of ADD/ADHD include:

- Inattention/distractibility
- Impulsivity
- Activity-level problems (overactivity, underactivity)
- Non-compliance
- Attention-getting behavior
- Immaturity
- Poor achievement
- Cognitive and visual-motor problems
- Emotional difficulties
- Poor peer relations
- Family interaction problems

Spotlight on Diversity

When my daughter was in the fourth grade, she became a special education student in the public school system. A psychologist had diagnosed her as "mildly depressed." She was experiencing a great deal of school-related stress, mostly involving being picked on by other children, and I believe that she did show some signs of depression.

When I requested that she receive some special assistance in school, our nightmare began. My daughter was diagnosed by a school psychologist as "emotionally handicapped" with a "written language disability." Without my consent, she was placed back in the third grade, although she had completed the grade successfully. My child began to label herself as a failure. Her written language skills steadily decreased, and she changed from being an excellent writer to a poor one.

The greatest tragedy has been the way teachers and others in the school system have treated her since her diagnosis. On the playground one day, a classmate tried to force my daughter to do something she did not want to do. In an attempt to gain freedom from her grasp, my daughter made a motion to bite the girl. However, the school's report of the incident, which was placed in my daughter's cumulative school record, reflected that my daughter had bitten a classmate. The report did not even mention what the other child was attempting to force my daughter to do. When I questioned the teacher who had reported the incident, I was told that the other child was "normal" and her behavior was "hardly serious."

Although an isolated incident, my daughter's dilemma is a perfect example of the struggle that is involved in being different in our society.

—Jan Lee P., Gainesville, FL

Autism

Autism is a developmental disability affecting verbal and nonverbal communication and social interaction. First identified in 1943 by Leo Kanner, autism is a severely incapacitating, developmental disability that usually appears during the first three years of life. Brain and/or biochemical dysfunction before, during, or after birth could be the cause. One out of every 2,500 children has autism. It is primarily a disorder of two-way social interaction and communication. Autism is four times more common in boys than girls, and is rarely found in more than one child in a family.

Typical characteristics of autism include abnormal ways of relating to people, objects, and events, little imaginative play, use of toys and objects in an unconventional manner, abnormal responses to sensory stimulation, impaired social and communication skills, avoidance of eye contact, unusually high or low activity levels, insistence that the environment and routine remain unchanged, repetitive movements such as rocking and spinning, head banging, skin picking, hand twisting, and developmental delays and differences.

Tourette's Syndrome

Tourette's Syndrome is an inherited condition that may be exhibited along with attention deficit disorder, bipolar depression, and obsessive compulsive disorder. Tourette's Syndrome is a neurological disorder involving involuntary, sudden, rapid, recurrent, nonrhythmic motor movements or vocalizations. Commonly observed characteristics include blinking, nose twitching, and cursing. The popular media has highly publicized the often slight and rapid head movements, called tics, that persons with Tourette's Syndrome typically experience. Tics can occur anywhere in the body and can be mild and repetitive.

Professionals who work with persons with Tourette's Syndrome generally recommend an intensive behavior management program, including warnings, time outs, isolation, removal of privilege, and rewards for appropriate behavior.

Phobic Disorders

A person with a phobic disorder will often recognize that the fear is unreasonable but also will feel helpless to control the subsequent avoidance behavior. We all have some phobias, such as fear of heights, certain animals, flying, or public speaking. When a fear drastically interferes with everyday life then a phobia is present. Phobic disorders are defined as the persistent and recurring fear of a specific object, activity, or situation that is avoided at all costs.

Eating Disorders

Anorexia nervosa is the most well-known eating disorder. Ninety percent of the persons with anorexia nervosa are adolescent, middle- and upper-class women. Symptoms include weight loss leading to body weight 25 percent below average, a distorted body image, and fear of weight gain or of loss of control over food intake. The cause of anorexia nervosa is not known. Many researchers prefer a primary psychiatric origin, but no single psychiatric hypothesis satisfactorily explains all cases. Characteristically, the person comes from a family whose members are highly goal and achievement oriented. They commonly have destructive or inadequate interpersonal relationships, exhibit perfectionist behaviors, and have obsessional personality characteristics.

Bulimia nervosa is the episodic uncontrolled ingestion of large quantities of food followed by purging (self-induced vomiting, diuretics, or cathartics), strict dieting, or vigorous exercise. Like anorexia nervosa, bulimia nervosa is predominantly a disorder of young, middle- and upper-class women. Characteristics are similar, but bulimia nervosa is more difficult to detect.

Overeating, due to psychological or physiological reasons, may also be considered an eating disorder. Be cautious, however, not to conclude that an individual who is very thin or heavy has an eating disorder; most individuals who are very thin or heavy are naturally their size and weight.

Substance Abuse and Dependence

Tobacco, cocoa, alcohol, poppies, wild mushrooms, and hemp (cannabis) have provided people with a means of celebration, escape, pleasure, and relaxation throughout history. However, recent, more powerful, and sophisticated substances have been added to the supply of mind-altering substances. A person with a compelling desire (but not necessarily a physical need) to use a chemical substance and not stop, or reduce frequency or dosage, has a psychological dependence. That person believes the substance is necessary for continued functioning. An individual may also develop a physical dependence or be considered physically addicted to any of the mentioned substances as well as to other prescription drugs such as nasal sprays, stimulants, and depressants. Several classic treatment techniques are used, including social skills training, relaxation training, self-management skills, and operant conditioning.

Suicide

Persons with behavioral and personality disabilities often are at-risk for attempting suicide. It is important for you to know the warning signs. The following have been adapted from the San Diego Crisis Team pamphlet (1995):

Threats. Often feelings of possible suicide are mentioned to others. Take threats of suicide seriously.

Depression. Feelings of sadness, hopelessness, and a sense of loss are common before suicide.

Withdrawal. Suicidal people may pull away from family, friends, and others close to them.

Behavior changes. Sudden changes such as irritability, aggressiveness, or changes in eating and sleeping habits can signal problems.

Making final arrangements. A suicidal person may give away valued possessions, prepare a will, or write a suicide note in preparation. The person may purchase weapons or stockpile medications.

Lack of interest in future. Suicidal people may act without care for the future or make statements such as, "Life is not worth living."

Each year, 30,000 Americans take their own lives. Suicide occurs in all age groups and all socioeconomic populations, regardless of gender. College students are known to be at high risk for suicide. The important thing to remember is that persons who are considering suicide can be helped by these San Diego Crisis Team suggestions:

Ask. Do not be afraid to ask directly: "Have you been thinking of killing yourself?" It can be a relief for the suicidal person to discuss his or her feelings. The more talking, the better. You are not contributing new ideas into the person's thinking.

Listen. Let the person express his or her feelings and concerns. Do not worry about saying the right thing, just listen.

Show you care. Tell the person you care and want to help. Take active steps to ensure the person is safe. Remove weapons or pills and remain close by. Tell people close to the person. It does no good to keep the secret and lose the person.

Get help. Ensure that a suicidal person gets in contact with a professional counselor or other helping person trained to assist. Call the Suicide Crisis Helpline listed in the telephone Yellow Pages. A crisis counselor can help decide the best way to control a situation and give referrals to other resources.

Labels are Difficult to Discard

Critics of psychiatric classification systems argue that negative expectations generated by the labels can become self-fulfilling prophecies and drastically limit a person's chances for full reintegration into society. This is seen in the classic Rosenhan study (1973). Over a period of three years, Rosenhan arranged for a number of average people to be admitted to several psychiatric hospitals in the United States. All pseudo-patients were diagnosed as psychotic. Most of the imposters were diagnosed with schizophrenia; one was labelled manic-depressive. Once the label was assigned, essentially normal behavior was judged quite differently. Even at the time of discharge, most patients were diagnosed "schizophrenia-in remission," implying that they remained schizophrenic, but did not show signs of the disorder at the time of release

This study has a powerful message for all of us. We often label to receive funding or for decisions on programming or school placements. The crucial task is to assist the person to control aberrant behaviors and to display socially acceptable personality characteristics.

Support Services

Behavior therapy is a valuable, relatively inexpensive treatment for most of the topics covered in this chapter. The person is taught to focus on specific behaviors and to systematically lessen the targeted behavior. Persons often need external motivation, which can include contingency contracting and/or a menu of diverse tangible rewards.

Psychiatric treatments include medicine, psychotherapy, psychoanalysis, and group and individual counseling. The psychiatrist, a person who has been trained in both physical and psychological illness, can diagnose the symptoms and prescribe the appropriate psychiatric treatment. A psychologist, trained in a variety of non-medical intervention strategies, may provide excellent therapy options. Other professionals, such as behavior specialists, art therapists, and music therapists, also offer excellent therapeutic interventions.

Support groups can be a critical part of coping with behavior and personality differences. Groups are available for the person with the disability as well as family members and friends.

Interactions

Engage the person in a reinforcement program allowing him or her to set the positive and negative contingencies. Ensure focused behaviors are documented clearly and concisely. Token economies, contingency contracts, and behavior therapies are beneficial. Set up a similar program at home, school, or the job site.

Ignore inappropriate behavior. Unless the behavior could endanger the safety of those in close proximity, ignore inappropriate behavior.

Be consistent with discipline and supervision techniques. Provide a structure for every opportunity and be consistent with the discipline and supervision techniques you utilize. Set firm limits and reinforce the limits.

When an important rule is violated, the assigned consequence should follow as soon as possible. There should be no second or third "chances." There should be no debate at the time of violation. Be consistent when the person tests the limits.

Encourage counseling. Group and/or private counseling is highly recommended for persons with behavior and personality disorders.

Watch for signs of confrontation. Attempt to proactivly redirect and defuse the situation early. Appear calm and relaxed. Keep the pitch and volume of your voice down.

When there is no alternative to confrontation, make statements instead of questions. An example of a statement is, "I am waiting for you to get control or yourself." When talking to the person, avoid sarcasm or humiliation.

Do not convey that the person is being interrogated or challenged. This will only anger the person and increase the behaviors. Do not give commands or make demands. Talk *with* the person.

Avoid power struggles. Many persons with behavior and/or personality disabilities have been in a subordinate position all their lives and have learned to manipulate exceeding well. By being consistent and restating expectations, it will become clear to the person that you are serious.

Determine whether the person is testing you. Is the situation a true crisis? Always leave the person an avenue of escape.

Try reflection and redirection. Reflection lets the person know you are aware, and by redirection the person is provided a face-saving alternative.

State expectations in positive terms. Use "walk with me" instead of "come back here," or "please be quiet" instead of "shut up" or "stop yelling."

Offer options. Do not assume the person can't make decisions. Most people know what is appropriate and generally want approval.

Use cognitive and/or behavior therapy. Cognitive therapy attempts to help persons understand and overcome negative conditions that maintain a depressive episode. Automatic thoughts that cause the behavior or personality altering disorder are identified and the person is taught to recognize conditions and observations of distorted reality. Behavior therapy attempts to restore adequate positive experiences by changing the type and variety of activities and interaction.

Do not argue. The more you argue, the more likely you are to escalate the behavior. Remember, the person may display negative tenacity and provoke you to argue. Give the person the needed personal space. The rewards will be far greater than if you provoke an argument.

Summary

Behavior and personality are viewed on a continuum ranging from effective functioning to severe personality disorganization. In this chapter, we explored some of the categories related to personality and behavior and suggested several interactions that will help you look past the label and seek assistance and support for the person.

References

American Psychiatric Association. (1994). *Diagnostic and Statistical Manual of Mental Disorders (4th ed.) Revised.* Washington, DC: American Psychiatric Press.

Clay, D. A. & Aquila, F. D. (1994). Gangs and Americas schools. *Phi Delta Kappan, 76*(1), 65-69.

Kauffman, J. M. (1993). *Characteristics of emotional and behavioral disorders of children and youth*, 5th ed. Columbus, OH: Merrill/Macmillan.

Kauffman, J., M., Lloyd, J. W., Baker, J., & Riedel, T. (1995). Inclusion of all students with emotional or behavioral disorders? Let's think again. *Phi Delta Kappan, 76*(7), 542-546.

Mertens, G. C. (1964). *An operant approach to self-control for alcoholics.* Paper presented at the American Psychological Association, September, 1964.

Rapoport, J. L. (1989). *The boy who couldn't stop washing.* New York: E.P. Dutton.

Rosenberg, B. A. (1995). *Depression in children.* Philadelphia: Cornerstone Psychiatry Associates.

Rosenberg, B. A., Skiba, W. E., LeBlanc, R. M., Rosenberg, M. L., Ossowski, S., & Wolford, A. Z. (1995). *General symptom of bipolar disorder.* Philadelphia: Cornerstone Psychiatry Associates.

Rosenhan, D. L. (1973). On Being Sane in Insane Places, *Science, 179,* 250-58.

Slater, J. K. (1995). *Obsessive compulsive disorder in children.* Milford, CN: National Association of School Psychologists position paper.

Suggested Readings

Dorris, M. (1990). *The broken chord*. Los Angeles: Harper Perennial.
In this book, after struggling for many years over his adopted son's disabilities, a father discovers Fetal Alcohol Syndrome (FAS), and writes to educate others on this very preventable syndrome.

Duke, P. & Hochman, G. (1992). *A brilliant madness: Living with manic depressive illness*. New York: Bantom Books.
In this book, Patty Duke joins with medical reporter Gloria Hockman to explain the powerful, paradoxical and destructive manic depressive illness.

Elliott, M. & Meltsner, S. (1991). *The perfectionist predicament: How to stop driving yourself and other people crazy*. New York: W. Morrow.
Provided in this book are helpful ideas for working with a person who is a perfectionist.

Gehret, J. (1991). *Eagle eyes: A child's view of attention deficit disorder*. Fairport, NY: Verbal Images Press.
This book presents a picture of living with ADD from the point of view of a child who lives with the disorder.

Guetzloe, E. D. (1989). *Youth suicide: What the educator should know*. Reston, VA: The Council for Exceptional Children.
This book provides information on issues, statistics, risk factors, intervention, assessment of suicide potential and counseling of persons who may be suicidal.

Moss, R. (1990). *Why Johnny can't concentrate*. New York: Bantam Books.
This is a great text for helping families with children who are diagnosed with ADD.

Exploration

Individual Activities

1. Positive reinforcement is often used to control or modify the behavior of people with emotional disturbances. List 10 reinforcements which would be appropriate to use with children, and 10 for adults.

Children

_____   _____
_____   _____
_____   _____
_____   _____
_____   _____

Adults

_____   _____
_____   _____
_____   _____
_____   _____
_____   _____

2. Find out how others perceive emotional or behavioral disturbance by asking five of your friends for a definition. Write their definitions below. Rate each definition's accuracy (A, B, C, D, or F).

Definition   Rating

_____   _____
_____   _____
_____   _____
_____   _____
_____   _____

Group Activities

1. There has been conversation regarding the opening of a center for people with behavior and personality disturbances in your neighborhood. Form groups of 4-5 people and discuss the pros and cons of the center and its location. Then present your group's ideas to the entire class.

Reactions:

_____

_____

_____

_____

_____

_____

_____

_____

_____

2. With your same group of 4-5 people, develop a list of terms which have been used to label people with personality or behavioral disorders. Identify those terms which are positive and those which are negative.

Reactions:

_____

_____

_____

_____

_____

_____

_____

_____

_____

Reation Paper 13.1

Assume that you have just been told by a psychologist that your child has a behavior disorder. How would you react to the diagnosis? How would you feel? What would you tell others?

Reaction Paper 13.2

Assume that you are a camp counselor and you notice that Alex, one of your campers, is always isolated from the others. This troubles you and you decide to appoint Alex as your helper. This attention aggravates him and sends him into a frenzy of kicking, biting, and yelling. Alex may have a behavior disorder. How would you deal with the situation? What could you do to calm him down? How would you avoid future problems?

Notes

Chapter 14

Sensory Differences

Introduction

We use our senses—hearing, sight, smell, touch, and taste—to gather the information which we require to function safely and effectively in the world. Author and lecturer Helen Keller rejoiced in sensory experience. She wrote at length about life's abundant aromas, tastes, touches, and feelings. The fact that she could neither see nor hear did not diminish her zest for the sensory world. She was able to enjoy music by placing her hands on a radio, to read literature in Braille, to communicate with her friends through sign language, and to write down her wisdom and experiences. As Helen Keller demonstrated by expressing her ideas and emotions, people with hearing or vision impairments do not think differently than other people. Nor do they necessarily lead impoverished lives. The purpose of this chapter is to examine the broad range of hearing and vision impairments and suggest methods for fuller and more enjoyable communication with those individuals.

The Culture of Blindness and Deafness

Hearing is the sense we use primarily in the development of language and speech. Since speech is the means by which we communicate with others, it is a fundamental factor in all social interactions. Hearing facilitates learning, and through hearing and speech we pass on our cultural values and our heritage. Vision, too, is important for assimilating our culture. We read printed words in books, watch the moving images in films, and study the intricate details in paintings. As with any culture, deaf and blind cultures celebrate their ancestors, heroes, victims, survivors, and trailblazers.

The culture of deafness is quite rich. From the ancient Greek historian Herodotus to the French novelist Guy de Maupassant, people have written eloquently about their own deafness or the deafness of friends and loved ones (Ackerman, 1990). Brian Grant's anthology *The Quiet Ear* compiles writings about deafness that span many different eras and cultures, and the play *Children of a Lesser God,* by Mark Medoff, has been made into a powerful movie. The German composer Ludwig van Beethoven, who became totally deaf at age 46, wrote his greatest music during his later years.

Just as with deafness, blindness has not hindered the productivity of some of our great cultural figures. The Argentine poet and story writer Jorge Luis Borges, many of whose works have been translated into English, was blind. Joseph Pulitzer, the prominent journalist, publisher, and congressman, went blind at the age of 40 but continued his various activities during the remaining 24 years of his life. James Thurber, the well-known magazine writer, dramatist, and cartoonist, lost the sight of one eye in a boyhood accident and the sight of the other as an adult. And the Greek poet Homer, author of the famous epics *The Iliad* and *The Odyssey*, was blind.

Section I

Hearing

What exactly does *hearing* mean? To a porpoise, hearing is a kind of sonar, like a bat's, that brings back three-dimensional images more like sights than sounds. A porpoise can "hear" all sorts of details about a shark–its size, texture, motion, direction, and distance. If you go to a rock concert, you may *feel* the pulsing rhythm vibrating in your chest cavity. What hearing entails often depends upon the hearer and the context. Our range of hearing also depends upon which tools we use to extend it. A stethoscope allows us to hear someone's heart beating. Loudspeakers make it possible to hear an orator in a large auditorium. With a telephone we can hear someone in another part of the world. A radio telescope allows us to hear the distant echoes of outer space. And a hearing aid amplifies the volume of the sounds around us.

Of all the senses, hearing offers perhaps the greatest potential for information because of its flexibility. While taste, touch, vision, and to a lesser extent smell require our proximity to the source, hearing potentially offers information about objects and events when all other senses are useless. For instance, we may hear a siren in the dark outside from our bedroom and be able to tell that there is an emergency or a fire nearby. We may be able to judge the distance and direction, and even determine if the siren is from a fire truck or police car, fairly accurately by using our sense of hearing.

Nobody can escape the world of sound. As sensory expert Diane Ackerman observed, even if we don't hear the outside world, we hear the throbbings and buzzings and whooshings of our own bodies. Many who are legally deaf can hear gunfire, low-flying airplanes, jackhammers, motorcycles, thunder, and other loud noises. Hearing disabilities don't protect us from ear distress, either, since we use our ears for more than just hearing. Our ears help us keep balance and equilibrium and tell the brain how our head moves (Ackerman, 1990).

Hearing Impairment

Our ability to hear is the result of a complex sequence of events. The outer ear collects sound waves and channels them through the auditory canal. The eardrum conducts sound waves through three tiny bones in the middle ear. The third bone is connected to the inner ear, which houses the cochlea. Here highly specialized cells translate vibrations into nerve impulses that are sent directly to the brain.

Estimates of hearing loss in the United States go as high as 28 million people, or 11 percent of the total population (Toufexis, 1991). Our range of hearing can be affected by a variety of circumstances. Factors present before, during, or after birth can disrupt the hearing process. Childhood ear infections, loud concerts, gunshots, fireworks, and loud noises at work all have the potential to reduce one's hearing acuity. Even the natural process of aging gradually reduces our ability to hear high frequencies.

There is no single phenomenon of "deafness," but rather a wide spectrum of hearing loss, from mild impairment to total deafness. We use the term *hearing impaired* to refer to all individuals who have a hearing impairment, regardless of its severity. A hearing loss is reported in decibels (dB) and is generally categorized as:

- mild (27-40 dB)
- moderate (41-55 dB)
- moderately severe (56-70 dB)
- severe (71-90 dB)
- profound (91+ dB)

A person with mild hearing loss may experience difficulty with faint or distant speech. A moderate loss makes speech beyond five feet difficult to understand. A person with severe loss is unlikely to hear a loud voice if it is more than one or two feet away, though he or she may be able to

Spotlight on Diversity

My oldest child, Juanita, was born with normal hearing. Today, she cannot hear a single word, but she lives an independent and fulfilled life. At the age of seven Juanita developed spinal meningitis, which resulted in a severe hearing loss in both ears. Her teachers, mother, and I all worked closely with her to retain the speech that she had acquired prior to the loss of hearing.

Juanita spent the rest of her elementary school years in a special program for children with hearing impairments. As an adolescent, she graduated with honors from the neighborhood high school. She decided to continue her education at the university level, earning an undergraduate degree in international relations and then completing law school.

Now Juanita is an attorney specializing in intellectual property. She actively volunteers for local charitable organizations and spends her leisure time doing freelance photography, collecting stamps, and rollerblading.

—Rodriguez M., Chula Vista, CA

distinguish between different environmental sounds. Finally, a person with profound loss may be able to hear only very loud environmental sounds.

Common terms relating to hearing loss include:

deaf: This is a hearing loss so severe that it generally is not helped by amplification. An individual with total deafness must rely upon vision as the primary means for developing communication.

hard of hearing: This refers to a hearing loss that does not prohibit the development of speech and language skills, with or without amplification.

prelingual hearing impairment: A hearing impairment that occurs either at birth or before speech and language skills have been acquired is called "prelingual." An individual with prelingual loss may have difficulty mastering language and speech.

postlingual hearing loss: A hearing impairment that occurs after speech and language skills have been acquired is called "postlingual." An individual with postlingual loss may have no difficulty with speech and language.

conductive loss: This is a hearing impairment that is located in the outer or middle ear. With proper amplification, sounds will be heard without distortion.

sensorineural loss: This hearing impairment is located in the inner ear or along the auditory nerve to the brain. Even with amplification, sensitivity to sounds is reduced and/or distorted.

tinnitus: This refers to a range of noises in the ear (typically a ringing or hissing) that can disrupt hearing.

unilateral loss: This is a hearing impairment in only one ear.

bilateral loss: This is a hearing impairment in both ears.

People with hearing impairments communicate through speech, lip or speech reading, or sign language. Depending upon the severity of hearing loss, one may use hearing aids to amplify sounds or have an electronic cochlear implant which aids the individual by stimulating nerve endings when sound is perceived. Obviously, hearing loss increases the challenges a person faces in daily living, but it does not necessarily prevent one from enjoying life or attaining his or her goals.

Stereotypes of Persons who have Hearing Impairments

The following stereotypes and expectations of people with hearing impairments are *not* true:

- People with profound deafness cannot learn to speak
- People with hearing impairments are not as challenged as those with visual impairments
- All people with hearing impairments can read lips
- The inability to hear is a sure sign of aging and/or senility
- People who use sign language simply gesture to one another in a very limited form of communication
- People with hearing impairments are usually also mentally retarded

Issues that Persons with Hearing Impairments May Face

- Comprehension and production of the English language
- Academic achievement
- Social isolation
- Separate or regular education
- Finding good auditory training
- Restrictions on the choice of job due to perceived limitations
- Adaptable equipment
- Finding support
- Finding role models and mentors
- Dealing with other people's discomfort
- Feelings regarding the need for assistance
- Independent living

Support Services

Telecommunication devices (TDDs), resembling small typewriters, can be hooked up to telephones to allow people who are hearing impaired to carry on a conversation. Captioned films and close-captioned television offer subtitled dialogue. Signaling devices, using vibrations or flickering lights, can alert people with hearing impairments when the doorbell rings, the alarm clock goes off, or the baby cries. Telephone companies also offer "Relay Services" which allow an individual with a hearing impairment to engage in communication with a hearing individual in a manner equivalent to those individuals who are able to use standard voice telephone services. Relay Services utilize employees who use TDDs the same way an interpreter would.

Sign language classes are frequently included in community education programs offered by high schools, community colleges, and universities. Police and fire departments often train in basic sign language to be better prepared to communicate in any situation. Sign language interpreter services are typically offered in places of worship and at public events. Interpreters are also on-call 24 hours a day in many communities to assist in emergencies such as accidents and arrests.

Interactions

Learn sign language. If you are skilled in some basic signs, you'll be able to communicate more comfortably and fully.

A light touch on the arm is appropriate to get someone's attention. To avoid possible offense, do not touch other parts of the body and do not wave your hand in an exaggerated fashion.

Make sure the hearing impaired individual can see your face clearly. Avoid turning away, moving around excessively, or obstructing your mouth.

Speak in moderate tones. Raising your voice or exaggerating your speech may only distort your facial expressions and make you more difficult to understand.

If you are not understood, rephrase rather than repeat what you said. Rephrasing your thoughts may make your point more clear, and the person will have a second chance to understand you.

If you are in a group, speak one at a time. Too many people talking at once can be confusing to anyone, with a hearing impairment or not.

If you are communicating through an interpreter, speak directly to the person with the hearing impairment. Keep in mind with whom you are talking. The interpreter is just there to interpret.

Section II

Vision

   In the absence of light, everyone is blind. Photons of light bounce randomly off the objects around us, but it is the millions of rods and cones in the human retina that capture the light and send it through the optic nerve to the brain. Then the brain translates the photons into meaningful vision. Through the visual process, we observe the world around us and assimilate knowledge. We rely upon our eyes to direct us through our environment, to inform us through the written word, and to give us pleasure. But eyesight isn't the only means by which we can perceive the world.

   What do you see when you walk into a room? An old friend? A boring co-worker? A beautiful landscape painting? An expensive vase? Much of what we "see" is wholly subjective. Our eyes do not technically "see" an old friend, but rather the figure of a person. We "see" the relationship in our minds. Whether the painting is beautiful or not, and whether the co-worker is boring or not, are also opinions we form in our minds (Chopra, 1991). What we see with our eyes is certainly important, but visual information is clearly only one part of observation. A person with no eyesight might touch your face and "recognize" that you are her friend or think that you resemble someone else. Blindness and visual impairment affect *how* information is obtained, but not necessarily *what* information is obtained.

   Though blindness conjures up images of total darkness in the minds of the general public, only a small number of people are totally blind. Even people who have been totally blind since birth are greatly affected by light, Ackerman noted, because light influences us in many subtle ways. "It affects our moods, it rallies our hormones, it triggers our circadian rhythms [biological cycles recurring at 24-hour intervals]" (1990, p. 249).

Visual Impairments

   We extend our field of vision in all sorts of ways, using glasses, contact lenses, magnifying glasses, telescopes, cameras, binoculars, microscopes, X-rays, and magnetic resonance imagers, just to name a few. Some people must augment their vision due to a physical problem with their eyes. At least twenty percent of the population has some visual problems (Reynolds and Birch, 1982), but most of these cases can be corrected to the extent that the problem is not serious. It is estimated that approximately 1,440,000 individuals of all ages have visual impairments that are significant enough to limit their activities (LaPlante, 1991). The figure of one-tenth of one percent of the population is frequently cited for the prevalence of those people legally blind.

   The term *visually impaired* describes a wide range of people with partial or complete loss of sight. Visual impairment may be either present at birth or acquired later through injury to the eye or brain. Visual disability may be due to:

- refractive problems (farsightedness, nearsightedness, blurred vision, cataracts)
- muscle disorders (uncontrolled rapid eye movements, crossed eyes)
- receptive problems (damage to the retina and optic nerve).

Visual impairment is classified into three general categories: profound, severe, and moderate. With profound visual disability, one's performance of the most basic visual tasks may be very difficult. With severe visual disability, extra time and energy are needed to perform visual tasks. With moderate visual disability, visual tasks may be performed with the use of special aids and lighting.

Other potentially confusing terms are used to specify various levels of visual impairment. A brief overview of these terms follows:

blindness: A person who is totally without the sense of vision or has only light perception is considered to be blind. Such a person must learn primarily through touch and hearing.

legal blindness: Visual acuity of 20/200 or worse in the best eye with correction is considered to be legal blindness. This means that an individual can read at 20 feet what a person with normal vision can read at 200 feet.

tunnel vision: This describes to field of vision limited at its widest angle to 20 degrees or less. A normal field of vision is generally measured on a horizontal arc of 160 to 180 degrees. A person with severe tunnel vision is considered to be blind.

partially sighted: People who are partially sighted have a visual acuity greater than 20/200 but less than 20/70 in the best eye after correction. People who are partially sighted are able to use their vision as a primary source of learning.

low vision: People with low vision have limitations in distance vision but are able to see objects and materials within a few inches or feet.

residual vision: Any usable remaining vision is called "residual vision." For example, if an individual can detect only light, he or she can use that ability to an advantage.

The fact that a person has a visual impairment tells us nothing about what he or she is like, what he or she can do, or even how much he or she can see. Blindness is not debilitating. The general public's attitudes and prejudices are more likely to be a handicap than the visual disability itself.

Spotlight on Diversity

Kirk was ready with the safety rope which could keep me from falling off the steep incline of the Eagle.

I reached forward to the weathered rock which showed none of its beauty to me; I was almost totally blind. I became completely absorbed in searching for the next handhold, the next foothold. The incline was sharp; soon I was nearly perpendicular to the ground. Kirk shouted encouragement from above. I was somewhere in the middle of my climb, distant from everyone.

That is how I'd felt as a little girl with the first signs of retinal deterioration. I was the only child who had to wheel around a print-enlarging machine from class to class, the only sixth-grader who had to leave home for a blind school, the only one who had to learn Braille in high school, the only blind student at my tiny college, and later the only blind high school teacher in my school district. When the remainder of my vision had started disappearing in December of 1993, I felt fully isolated.

My mind snapped back to the present. Suddenly, I froze. I was 70 feet above the ground, clinging to the side of the Eagle, and I couldn't move. I was far from safety, my hands gripping a thin crack, my right toes balancing on a one-inch rock protrusion.

My foot began to slip. I clawed wildly, searching for some outcropping which could hold me. Nothing! I could not sustain my balance anymore. I screamed as I fell, imagining crashing down dozens of unyielding rock.

Silence. I lay stunned against the rock. Then, I felt a one-inch rock protrusion pressing against my ankle. I was only two inches below my previous resting point. I had been caught by the safety rope.

"Great job, Kath!" Kirk shouted from above. Were falls okay? Was it really okay to stumble and struggle and search—and slip?

I ran my left hand along the granite, almost immediately finding a 3-inch crack which would serve as a perfect handhold and after that a foothold. Because of the slightly altered position resulting from my slip, I'd located a new ledge, a promising route up the Eagle.

Later, sitting at the top of the Eagle next to Kirk, I seemed to hear the wind whisper, "You did this, so you can do anything." I realized I never had to fear being alone or falling again, for new supports would always be found with the simple stretching out of my hand.

At that moment, my blindness mattered not a bit. I could see again the unfailing safety ropes of courage and inner strength. I soared—without wings but renewed hope—high up on the Eagle.

—*Kathy N, West Lafayette, IN*

Stereotypes of Persons who have Visual Impairments

The following stereotypes of people with visual impairments are *not* true:

- All people who are blind have superior musical talents
- People with visual impairments automatically develop heightened senses of smell, touch, hearing, and taste
- People with visual impairments are able to detect obstacles with a "sixth sense"
- People who are legally blind have no functional vision at all
- People with visual impairments cannot go out without assistance

Issues that Persons with Visual Impairments May Face

- Accessibility
- Adaptable equipment
- Finding support
- Finding proper optical care
- Self-esteem
- Relationship and marriage issues
- Transportation and mobility
- Labeling
- Finding role models and mentors
- Dealing with other people's discomfort
- Restrictions on choice of job due to perceived limitations
- Feelings regarding the need for assistance
- Independent living

Support Services

People with visual disabilities use various types of adapted equipment to assist them at work, school, and throughout daily life. Some are quite ordinary, such as black felt tip markers that produce darker print, adjustable lamps to increase the amount of light and adjust its direction, large-type books, bifocals, contact lenses, magnifiers, tape recorders, friends, and guide dogs. More sophisticated technological aids include computers with speech output and enhanced screen images, Braille printers, and optical scanners and readers.

The local Division of Blind Services offers a wide range of information, from how to receive mobility training , how to obtain a guide dog, and where to find Braille newspapers or reader services. Public Radio, in many communities, also provides reader services by reading new books and the daily newspaper each day.

Interactions

Speak first and identify yourself. Let the person know who you are before he or she has to ask.

Use the person's first name. Using the person's first name will make it clear who is being addressed.

Use a normal tone and volume of voice. People with visual impairments do not necessarily have trouble hearing, so speak naturally.

Be precise when describing something. Provide a reference point, such as "next to the door you came in" or "to your immediate left, about shoulder level."

Give tactile clues. Be aware that the person may rely on other senses to provide information. You can help to provide tactile clues: "Joan, let me take your hand and show you the skirt I just made."

Don't assume that help is needed. Ask if you can help, and then follow the lead of the person.

Summary

It is impossible to make generalizations about people with hearing or vision disabilities. Few people have perfect hearing or perfect vision. People with sensory impairments experience the same feelings and emotions as everyone else. They also have the same potential for fulfilling their dreams and living dynamic, interesting lives.

References

Ackerman, D. (1990). *A natural history of the senses.* New York: Random House.

Chopra, D. (1991). *Unconditional life.* New York: Bantam Books.

LaPlante, M. P. (1991). The demographics of disability. In J. West (Ed.), *The Americans with Disabilities Act: From policy to practice* (pp. 55-80). New York: Milbank Memorial Fund.

Reynolds, M. C. & Birch, J. W. (1982). *Teaching exceptional children in all America's schools.* Reston, VA: Council for Exceptional Children.

Toufexis, A. (1991, August 5). Now hear this—If you can. *Time,* pp. 50-51.

Suggested Readings

Baldwin, S.C. (1993). *Pictures in the air: The story of the National Theatre of the Deaf.* Washington DC: Galludet University Press.
This book offers a window into the fascinating history of the theatre for the deaf and the individuals who helped to shape it.

Bienvenu, M. J. & Colonomos, B. (1993). *An introduction to deaf culture: Rules of social interaction.* Burtonsville, MD: Sign Media.
This is a fascinating exploration of the complex world of deaf culture.

Brady, F. B. (1994). *A singular view: The art of seeing with one eye.* Annapolis, MD: Frank B. Brady.
This book is a first-person account of living with monocular vision and finding ways to improve daily life.

Cohen, L. H. (1994). *Train go sorry: Inside a deaf world.* Boston: Houghton Mifflin.
This book is an intriguing look at the students and social condition of the Lexington School for the Deaf.

Keller, H. (1956). *The story of my life.* Boston: Houghton Mifflin.
In this fascinating autobiography, Keller describes the joy of learning to speak her first word.

Koestler, F. A. (1976). *The unseen minority: A social history of blindness in America.* New York: McKay.
This book traces the little-known history of individuals with visual disabilities in America.

Krebs, B. M. (1987). *Braille in Brief.* Louisville: American Printing House for the Blind.
This is an elementary guide to learning Braille. Includes charts of Braille characters and contractions.

Preston, P. M. (1994). *Mother father deaf: Living between sound and silence.* Cambridge: Harvard University Press.
This book is an account of growing up hearing but having two parents who cannot hear. A compelling examination of how deafness affects family relations.

Notes

Exploration

Individual Activities

1. Watch an entire prime-time television program, either comedy or drama, with the sound off. Were you able to follow the show? What things proved helpful to your understanding? What things contributed to your confusion? Write your reactions below:

_____

_____

_____

_____

_____

_____

_____

_____

_____

_____

2. Blindfold yourself upon getting out of bed in the morning, then do everything you normally do to get ready for the day, including taking a shower and getting dressed. (Be careful!)

List three things that you found difficult, frustrating, or even frightening.

_____

_____

_____

List three things you were able to do which surprised you.

_____

_____

_____

Group Activities

1. Using only gestures and movements, help the members of your group guess the movie, book, or famous person you are describing.

Reactions:

_____

_____

_____

_____

_____

_____

2. Have your group divide into threes to participate in simulated community interactions with vision impairments. Assign roles:

> Person #1: individual with vision impairment
> Person #2: friend of person #1
> Person #3: community worker

Scene One: fast food restaurant. Individual with vision impairment orders food and may have questions about selection, size of portions, etc.
Scene Two: asking for directions. Individual with vision impairment asks someone at the front desk for directions to a room on the third floor.

Discuss the communication between community worker and friend, bypassing the individual with vision impairment. Discuss the precision of the language that the worker uses. Examine the role of the friend as an intermediary.

Reactions:

_____

_____

_____

_____

_____

_____

Reaction Paper 14.1

Should sign language be a required course? What would you think if your school required sign language fluency for graduation?

Reaction Paper 14.2

If you had to choose being blind from birth or acquiring blindness later in life, what would you decide, and why?

Notes

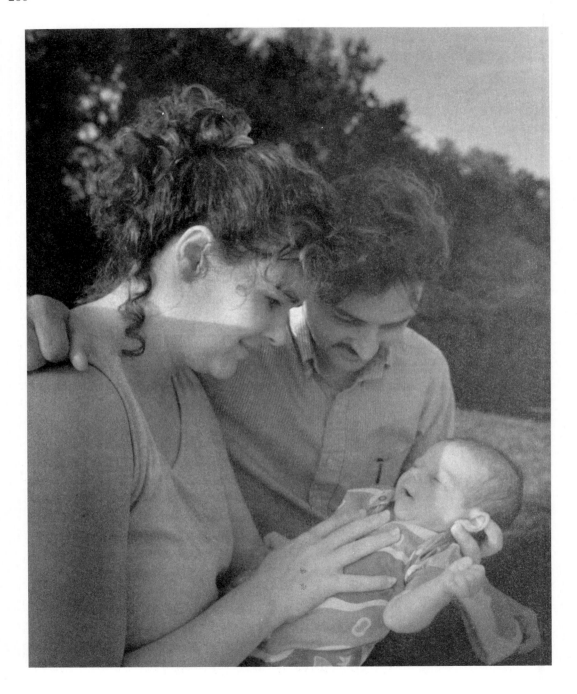

Chapter 15

Family Perspectives

Introduction

As we have become more educated about the human experience, we have learned that no American family is "typical." We realize that American families are diverse. In order to foster integration within a community, we need to normalize environments which nurture and provide for larger numbers of participatory citizens. Because of social changes, families spend far less time together and are seldom together during the work day. Television and video games have changed the way families interact. The amount of time young children spend alone or with substitute caregivers has increased significantly since the 1960's. Also, the make-up of the nuclear family has changed. In 1994, only 51 percent of all youths lived with both biological parents, 24 percent lived in one-parent families, and 21 percent lived in stepfamilies (New York Times, 1994).

Currently, the most significant adults in a child's life may be grandparents, aunts, uncles, siblings, or even neighbors, rather than parents. Primary caregivers and extended family members may fill the traditional role of parents. Families can range from extremely successful (i.e. all members of the family are reasonably satisfied with the character of the family) to extremely unsuccessful. This chapter will discuss the culture of the family, define sociological terms to delineate family, and provide information on family violence and child abuse.

The Culture of the Family

Families differ in composition, size, structure, resources, religion, education, wealth, attitudes, and cultural background. Families vary so widely, with so many categories, that we must conclude every family is unique. No "formula" for examining families exists. Child-rearing is only one of many family functions. From birth to death, the family unit is responsible for providing basic necessities, such as shelter, food, friendship, love, attention, and a sense of worth and dignity.

Opinions vary as to the efficacy and value of the family as a social system (Karge, 1988). However, we know that people find it hard to exist without their own or a surrogate family. Staff members in group residences and institutions usually attempt to simulate a family group small enough to enable intimate personal relationships. The family is a child's most important psychological field. Ideally, it is a haven, a source of attachments, of identity, and of identification throughout life (Benedek, 1990).

The Nuclear Family

A father, mother, and two children living together in a home is the traditional image of the nuclear family. However, for many children, the nuclear circle may include only one parent. More and more children are living in single-parent homes. Benson (1988) believes the changes in family structures from the traditional to reconstituted/blended families, one-parent homes, or extended families are not digressions from the ideal but rather are attempts to adapt family life to a rapidly changing society.

The Extended Family

When we limit the discussion to the immediate family, we exclude an important source of support potentially available to parents and children. An extended, multigenerational family can provide layers of support. In some situations grandparents, aunts, uncles, and cousins live in the same community. In other situations, several generations actually live together. Occasionally, this living arrangement is necessary, as when families provide care for elderly parents and/or relatives, for instance. In 1990, the average adult could expect to spend nine years coping with an aging parent who was dependent in some manner. Today, an average of 18 years of some level of care is required (Kolata, 1992).

Many cultural traditions foster the idea of the extended family. In Asian, Indian, Latin, and numerous other cultures, parents, grandparents, great-grandparents, children, grandchildren, and in-laws all live under a common roof. They support each other, love each other, plan together, and share the process of living cooperatively. This was true of Western culture until the second half of this last century and is still true of some families.

Step Families

More than two parents may influence their children when the original family members have remarried. The blended family may include children from both marriages. Approximately one out of five children is a stepchild (Turnbull & Turnbull, 1990). This is not a new experience for American families. In colonial days, because of higher parent death rates, a higher proportion of children were reared in stepfamilies than today.

Circle of Friends

   Our lives overlap with those of many other people. We have an inner circle of relatives, bonded at birth or by family ties. A second circle includes close friends. Third, we have acquaintances whom we know casually but who play no significant role in our lives. Finally, we all know people who are paid to be in our lives, such as our teachers, doctors, and employers. Below is a diagram of the circle layers.

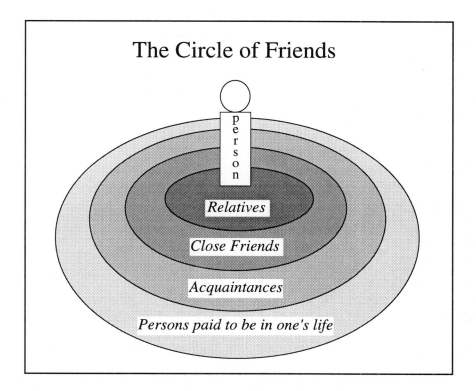

   At their best, families provide us nurturance and give us a sense of self and of place. But friends help us reach past our families and inspire us to explore a broader world and to interact with other people. Our quality of life depends upon the satisfaction we feel with our lives and our social relationships.
   This satisfaction is enhanced by friendships. Friendships grow out of proximity, shared experiences, and mutual interests. Friends are made across generations, age groups, ethnicitites, political persuasions, and social classes. Friendships allow us to appreciate the diverse nature of other individuals and to enjoy sharing our lives with each other.

Family Size

Turnbull and Turnbull's (1990) research on families suggests that the larger the family, the less distressed the members are by the presence of a family member with an exceptionality. The hypothesis is that larger families have more people to assist the individual with special needs. Further, positive adaptation to a child's exceptionality appears to be better in two-parent families than in single-parent homes.

Socioeconomic Status of the Family

We usually assume that families in higher socioeconomic levels have more resources available to assist with raising children, particularly those with special needs. Indeed, the ability to pay for services is an important factor. However, the equation is not that simple. The higher socioeconomic status of the family does not guarantee better parenting or a better family structure. Families of lower socioeconomic status have resources and have extensive support and care networks. For those who live in real poverty, the daily responsibilities of survival often take precedence over care concerns. There may be less time for fostering education and limited opportunities to avail themselves of community resources.

Separation and Divorce

Separation and/or divorce are frequently difficult situations for families. The divorce rate has increased, with almost 55 percent of marriages ending in divorce. Often, children feel responsible for parental breakups. The child frequently perceives a parent's exit as a departure from him or her personally. The physical departure and continuing absence of the parent are psychologically comparable to a death and frequently evoke similar responses of disbelief, isolation, and denial. Frequent shuttling from one parent to another, and the imbalance of familiar structure can be frustrating and may cause the child to behave inappropriately. Some children become frightened by their unstable family situations.

Latchkey Kids

More and more children spend time at home alone. Ysseldyke & Algozzine (1995) stated that 14 percent of eighth-graders surveyed in 1991 reported they were usually home after school for longer than three hours without adult supervision. With the necessity of dual-worker or dual-career families, and lack of funding to finance appropriate childcare, numerous children are given house keys and told to stay home, do their homework, make themselves a snack, and wait for the parent to arrive.

Family Violence

In history, some societies sanctioned, or at least tolerated, violence and abuse in order to maintain family order. Traditional Anglo-American law permitted corporal punishment when a man "disciplined" his spouse and his children. Until recently, much of what we now call child abuse was a standard parental disciplinary prerogative. Americans founded the Societies for the Prevention of Cruelty to Animals before we extended the same protections to our children.

Furthermore, violence in the family was a hidden crime, overlooked by law enforcement, the medical profession, churches, schools, and other institutions. The "battered child syndrome" was first described in a 1960's medical journal (Kempe, 1962), and spouse beating emerged in public awareness during the 1970's. Yet family violence continues as an enormous social problem with millions of victims each year.

The Reverend Jesse Jackson has called on youths to break the code of silence about drugs and guns in schools and has provided strong leadership for a victim-led movement to stop violence. Empowering youth to speak out and become actively involved in reclaiming lives, schools, and communities, is one way to stop family violence (Children's Defense Fund, 1994). Perhaps if we teach about the problem while children are young, they will be able to avoid violence in their own families.

Child Abuse

Child abuse is often thought to be family related. Abuse occurs in all groups and subgroups of our culture. Child abuse is any physical or verbal injury suffered by a child as a result of cruel or inhumane treatment or of neglect. It may be a result of malicious acts by any adult who is responsible for the care and supervision of a minor. It may include sexual abuse, whether physical injuries are sustained or not. Reports of abuse and neglect have tripled since 1980. About half of the reports indicate neglect. In 1994, the Children's Defense Fund reported 2.7 million children were abused in 1993. Terms commonly associated with child abuse are:

Physical abuse. Physical abuse includes physical harm, sexual abuse, exploitation (excessive responsibilities placed on the young), malnourishment, lack of essential medical care including necessary prosthetics such as eyeglasses and hearing aids, or improper hygiene.

Emotional abuse. Emotional abuse includes denial of normal experiences which produce feelings of being loved, wanted, secure, and worthy. Examples of emotional abuse and emotional neglect include rejection (overt or through indifference), verbal degradation, and abandonment.

The abusers. The abusers are not demons but rather ordinary people unable to cope with their life circumstances or their own emotional or psychological problems. Circumstances which could lead to abuse include:

- Marital discord
- Alcoholism
- Drug addiction
- Immature parents
- Criminal environment
- Illiteracy
- Family values in conflict with societal values

Identifying abuse. The signs of child abuse and neglect are not always easily observed. One sign might not necessarily indicate abuse, but several should alert you to possible problems. According to the *Child Abuse Hotline*, one should suspect abuse if a child:

- Is overly compliant
- Is withdrawn and passive
- Is uncommunicative
- Has an unexplained injury
- Is dirty, smells, has bad teeth, missing hair or lice
- Is unusually fearful
- Is thin, emaciated, and constantly tired, showing possible evidence of malnutrition and dehydration

If you suspect child abuse, you must call the Department of Public Welfare-Child Protective Services Division in your state. Consult the Yellow Pages for these numbers. You can file a confidential report, and in most states an investigation is initiated within 24 hours of the report.

Accepting a Family Member Who is Different

When a family includes a member who fits some category of exceptionality, the family may face additional challenges or frustrations. One member may exhibit mental illness, may choose a different religion, may have a different sexual orientation, or may be born with disabilities. However, there are many common threads that connect family members as they learn to accept diversity and eventually benefit from it.

Turnbull & Turnbull (1990) explained that the process of accepting an exceptional family member is similar to that of accepting the death of a loved one. However, if long-term planning, empowerment and advocacy, community integration, and financial planning are taken into consideration, the grief can be turned into something positive. Feelings of grief may arise in times of stress. Families may grieve for the child they have and for the child that might have been. They may grieve for relationships that are permanently changed. Or they may grieve for themselves and for some imagined ideal life. The process may include any of the following emotions: shock, depression, isolation, denial, guilt, shame, anger, fear, uncertainty, and acceptance.

No family can be without diversity because every individual is unique. When the members of the family realize this fact, they tend to embrace differences and to view them as enriching opportunities for growth rather than as challenges or problems. However, it is often the case that some members of a family feel strongly about their traditional religion, ethnicity, politics, or lifestyle. These individuals may go through a process of adjustment and acceptance which can best be aided by education.

The reason that diversity is a positive aspect of society is that fear of the unfamiliar inhibits the exchange of ideas and the cooperation which promotes enlightenment and the advance of humankind. The experience of diversity among those whom we love best motivates us to give up our fear and to move forward. Therefore, all of society benefits from our familial feeling.

Support Systems

Support groups consisting of parents and family members with similar situations are usually the most successful at procuring information and obtaining assistance. Parents and family members discover that they are not alone, receive concrete information, share fears and roadblocks, and give each other the benefit of their insights (Lessen, 1991).

294
Summary

There is no such thing as a "typical" family. Every family is a unique mix of personalities, values, cultural heritages, expectations, behaviors, and communication styles. The individual members of a family are so interrelated that any experience affecting one member will affect all. As families educate themselves about human diversity, individual members discover how each person's difference enhances and empowers the whole.

References

Benedek, T. (1990). The family as a psychologic field. In E. J. Anthony & T. Benedek (Eds.), *Parenthood: Its psychology and psychopathology.* Boston: Little, Brown, Co.

Benson, H. (1988). The changing American family and students at risk. *Behavior in Our Schools, 3,* 7-12.

Children's Defense Fund (1994). The State of America's Children Yearbook. Washington DC: Author.

Karge, B. D. (1988). *Handicapped Awareness Training Manual.* Boy Scout Council of America.

Kolata, G. (1992). Strong family aid to elderly is found, *Progress in Alzheimer's Disease Research, 1*(1), 4.

Kemp, C. H. (1962). The battered child syndrom. *Journal of the American Medical Association*, 181(3) , 12-24.

Lessen, E. (1991). *Exceptional Persons in Society.* Needham, MA: Simon and Schuster.

New York Times, (1994, August 30), *Step-families in todays world.* A-9.

Turnbull, A. P. & Turnbull, H. R. (1990). *Families, professionals, and exceptionality: A special partnership.* Columbus, OH: Merrill.

Ysseldyke, J. E. & Algozzine, B. (1995). *Special education: A practical approach for teachers.* (3rd ed.) Boston: Houghton Mifflin.

Suggested Readings

Anderson, W., Chitwood, S., & Hayden, D. (1990). *Negotiating the special education maze: A guide for parents and teachers.* Rockville, MD: Woodbine House.
This is a practical, step-by-step guide to assist parents and teachers in advocating for children with disabilities.

Hite, S. (1994). *The Hite report on the family: Growing up under patriarchy.* New York: Grove Press.
This book analyzes the changing shape of family life and seeks to legitimize the infinite ways that people live as "families," whether as single parents, same-sex partners, in traditional family groups, or alone.

Louv, R. (1990). *Childhood's future.* New York: Anchor Books.
This is a penetrating look at American children and their families.

Perske, R. & Perske, M. (198?). *Circle of friends.* Nashville: Abdingdon Press.

Powell, T.H. & Ogle, P.A. (1985). *Brothers and sisters: A special part of exceptional families.* Baltimore: Paul H. Brooks.
This booklet suggests techniques and services that will help siblings of children with disabilities better understand the feelings and circumstances which surround the experience of growing up with a brother or sister with an exceptionality.

Rose, H. W. (1987). *Something's wrong with my child.* Springfield, IL: Charles C. Thomas.
This is a personal account of a mother's experience living with a child with a disability.

Weston, K. (1991). *Families we choose.* NY: Columbia University Press.
This book examines the subject of lesbian and gay kinships.

Notes

Exploration

Individual Activities

1. Draw your own diagram of your circle of friends and family. Who are the most important people around you and how do they function in your life?

2. Each person in a family plays more than one role and participates in more than one relationship. For instance, you may be a mother, a sister, a sister-in-law, a daughter, a wife, a cousin, a peace-maker, and a friend all at the same time. How many roles do you play in your family, and what is expected of you in each role?

_____

_____

_____

_____

_____

_____

Group Activities

Divide yourselves into groups of 4 or 5 students. This is your new family! Choose a mom, dad, brothers, and sisters. Now choose one of the scenarios below.

Scenario A: Your sister Julie is not with you at this time. She has run away from home because she felt different from the rest of the family and didn't know how to explain her feelings. Discuss your feelings about Julie's situation. What will you say to her if/when you see her again?

Reactions:

_____

_____

_____

_____

_____

_____

Scenario B: The mom and dad have different political viewpoints and are 20 years apart in age. One of the children is married to someone of a different race. Another of the children has chosen a religion different from the parents'. One grandparent has either a disability, a different sexual orientation, or speaks a different language. The family is spending time together over a holiday. Imagine that you are all at the dinner table and one of you starts talking about the ties that bind the family together. What do you all have in common that keeps you so close?

Reactions:

_____

_____

_____

_____

_____

_____

Reaction Paper 15.1

Child abuse is often thought to be family related. Explain the meaning of physical and emotional abuse. Suggest possible reasons why reports of abuse and neglect have tripled in the last decade.

Reaction Paper 15.2

The family unit is responsible for providing basic necessities. What basic necessities do your family or circle of friends provide for you? How is your family or circle of friends a source of attachments, identity, and identification for you?

Notes

Chapter 16

Educational Perspectives

Introduction

E ducation provides children with the capability to become productive, independent members of society. Education, a civil right,is more than learning academics. It is the process of training and developing the knowledge and skills to enable individuals to live up to their potential. Regardless of religion, sexual orientation, language, ethnicity, size, socioeconomic status, or race, most persons are educated in general education programs in the mainstream of society. If you are a parent or a neighbor of a person who fits into a category of human exceptionality, or if you are a person who is interested in teaching or a related profession, this chapter will help you to become aware that all children, regardless of language differences, race, or any other aspect of diversity, deserve a non-discriminatory individualized education.

Modern Risk Factors in Students' Lives

Most educational experts tend to agree that home life and parental involvement are crucial to a child's achievement in school. However, teachers are finding that an increasing number of their pupils do not have a supportive home life, either living in broken homes or in homes in which both parents work and have little time for the needs of their children. As Landes (1994) observed, some teachers are overwhelmed with obligations to provide emotional support and values to children to who do not receive them from their parents. "In some classrooms, the need to teach children the basic skills of living (brushing one's teeth, for example) has supplanted academic instruction" (p.102).

In addition to lack of parental involvement, other modern risk factors affecting students' academic success (adapted from Landes, 1994) include:

* Home alone more than three hours on weekdays
* Involvement in pregnancy
* Use of alcohol or drugs by student and/or family
* Physical or sexual abuse

- Excessive absences
- Failure of courses
- Low self-esteem
- Sickness or death of parent
- Parent's loss of job
- Death of friend or sibling
- Illness
- Parent's negative attitude
- Limited English proficiency
- Broken home
- Move frequently
- Change school frequently
- Parents divorced recently

Students with two or more risk factors are twice as likely to be in the lowest academic achievement quartile and are over six times as likely to think that they will not finish high school (Landes, 1994). Clearly, the daily problems that children are confronted with outside of school directly affect their academic performance. Interventions must begin in the home—one family at a time—if we ever hope to see a significant reduction of such problems in the classroom.

Current Controversial Issues in Education

As our society continues to embrace diversity, our schools often find themselves in delicate positions as they struggle to bring multicultural perspectives and experiences to the classroom. In the past, school curricula centered on the cultural aspects of Western civilization, to the exclusion of other cultures and languages. Histories are now being rewritten from a global perspective to include ethnic groups that had previously been excluded. Curriculua are constantly being revised to include the interests of more categories of diversity. Yet even as our schools attempt to stay abreast of current trends, they frequently come under fire by groups of parents who disgree about how to teach certain controversial subjects. These controversial issues include:

- Ethnic history and literature
- Sexual orientation
- Sex education
- AIDS education
- Values

- Basic skills of living
- Gender studies
- Minority studies
- Observance of religious holidays
- School prayer
- Learning styles of different ethnic groups
- Bias in standardized testing
- Bilingual education
- Inclusion

Though the issues themselves will change over time, our educational system will no doubt continue to find itself in the firing line as our society redefines its attitudes about cultural pluralism and our schools seek to reform their goals and objectives concerning human diversity.

Education Models

There are three general systems of schooling in the United States: public, private/parochial, and alternative. Each system offers its own unique benefits.

Public school. The vast majority of students in the United States attend public schools, which are regulated and funded by state, local, and federal governments. Curricula is designed and chosen which seeks to meet the needs of individual children within a sturucture which recognizes and respects diverse cultural, social, academic, physical, and language differences. Parents choose public schooling for socio-economic reasons—it is supported by tax dollars—and also for the excellent programs and facilities public schools frequently offer which may not be feasible for private schools with smaller student populations and more limited budgets. Another reason parents may prefer public schooling is that it offers social interaction with a broader range of students and allows for the experience of learning within an environment which is more likely to be composed of persons who are diverse.

Private/Parochial schools. Private and parochial schools may also receive some government funds, but they are primarily tuition-driven. They also have to meet state standards for curriculum, but their individual philosophies and goals are focused on a particular point of view. This perspective is religious in the case of parochial and church schools, and philosophical in the case of many other private schools. For example, for the past half-century throughout the United States and Europe, Montessori schools have flourished. These are small private schools based on the educational philosophy of an Italian educator named

Maria Montessori. She developed her teaching methods for children with disabilities, but as her books were widely read around the world, people began to apply her ideas in all classrooms. Other private schools stress more traditional teaching methods and use such models as the old Latin schools.

Though private and parochial schools are largely privately funded, many seek to make their student body more diverse by offering scholarships to disadvantaged students. Free, universal schooling is at the core of our requirement as a democratic society to have an educated citizenry. However, we are enriched by the diversity of avenues to education, and parochial and private schools serve the important function of preserving and fostering diverse and distinct cultural and religious points of view.

Alternative schools. The reasons people have for choosing an alternative method of schooling for their children are as varied as the individuals involved. Thousands of parents in every state choose to teach their children at home. Some of them are interested in meeting the special physical, emotional, or academic needs their children may have. Many families find that the flexibility of home schooling allows for family travel, intensive study, and other educational experiences which traditional schooling inhibits. Home schoolers have many gifted students among their ranks, who may use their control over scheduling to devote time to music, art, or special academic interests. Many children with physical disabilities or health issues also profit from the individualized environment and one-to-one instruction which home schooling can provide.

Home schooling has a long tradition in America. All of the founding fathers of our country, including George Washington, John Adams, and Thomas Jefferson, were taught at home. In more recent times, Supreme Court Justice Sandra Day O'Connor was taught at home as well. Since home schooling has been legal in most states for over 20 years now, there are statistics showing that students typically achieve at about two grade levels above average, that they are generally socially active, and that a high percentage goes on to successfully complete college.

Special Education

Occasionally, persons with disabilities need specialized education. Of the 43 million Americans with disabilities, nearly 20 million are children. Special education is the critical element to children with disabilities. Special education is specialized education designed to meet the needs of the individual child. Special education refers to an individually planned, carefully monitored arrangement of physical settings, special equipment, and materials. Specialized teaching procedures and other interventions help exceptional children achieve personal self-sufficiency and academic success.

Special Education Legislation

Schools are the communities where many children spend much of their most formative years. Beginning in preschool, children with disabilities need to be immersed in classrooms that reflect the real world in which they live. The school must mirror a society that is ready to embrace all children, regardless of abilities or disabilities, so they can be educated together and learn to value one another as unique individuals. The classroom is a place to meet daily with peers who are appropriate role models, learn academic skills, and participate in activities to assist the mind in growth and development.

Special education in the United States has a long history. For many students with special needs, access to programs has been slow in coming. However, advocacy and litigation have brought major changes to our schools. Schools have progressed from full exclusion of special needs students to full inclusion into the regular classroom. The schools have gone to a unified system based on the philosophy that all students are expected to achieve, and there must be a unified or core curriculum that all students have a right to access. Schools are becoming sensitive to the fact that students have more needs in common (in terms of knowledge and skills required for productive lives) than they have differences. Equity and equality must be insured for all students.

Many recent laws have been passed ensuring students with disabilities have the best possible education at the elementary, secondary, and postsecondary levels. The Rehabilitation Act of 1973 and the Individuals with Disabilities Education Act (IDEA) of 1990 are among the federal statutes affecting special education and establishing rights to empower parents, teachers, and students. These laws are not pro-parent/anti-teacher, or vice-versa. Each is supportive of good educational practices. In 1990, equal rights for all Americans with disabilities received the strongest support in our nation's history when Congress passed, and President Bush signed, the Americans with Disabilities Act (ADA), Public Law 101-336. A discussion of the ADA was presented in Chapter Three.

The Rehabilitation Act of 1973

The Rehabilitation Act of 1973 (Public Law 93-112) is a major piece of federal legislation which prohibits discrimination against persons with disabilities. Under Section 504 of the Act, a person with a disability who meets the academic and technical standards requisite to admission or participation in the education program or activity is entitled to participate without discrimination in programs or activities receiving or benefiting from federal assistance. Basically, it is a civil rights act which protects the civil and constitutional rights of persons with disabilities. According to Section 504, a person is considered *handicapped* if he or she:

- has a physical or mental impairment which substantially limits one or more major activities,
- has a record of such an impairment, or
- is regarded as having such an impairment.

In addition to school-age children who are eligible for special education services, this includes persons with communicable diseases, temporary handicapping conditions, attention deficit disorder, behavior disorders, chronic asthma, severe allergies, physical handicaps and diabetes. The 1986 amendments to the Rehabilitation Act of 1973 added another protection for persons with disabilities with Section 508, by requiring access to electronic equipment for individuals with disabilities.

Students with documented disabilities are entitled to receive approved modifications, accommodations, or auxiliary aids enabling them to participate in, and benefit from, all educational programs and activities. For example, Section 504 mandates reasonable accommodation for students with learning disabilities via such methods as audio textbooks, alternative testing arrangements, and sign language interpreters for students who are deaf.

Adapting the educational environment to allow all students with disabilities the same access to educational activities already available to nondisabled students is mandated by law. Accommodations include modifying educational practices when such practices would limit or prohibited the student with a disability from participating in an educational activity.

Several of the most common accommodations include:

Extended time. Some students with disabilities require additional time to accomplish required tasks and successfully take exams. Class time may be too restrictive for them to display their competence.

Tapes, audio and video. These tapes can serve as alternatives to written assignments. This can be of tremendous assistance to students with writing disabilities (dysgraphia) and those with physical disabilities that inhibit their ability to write.

Note taking services. These services can be provided for writing and manual manipulation in classroom and related academic or job activities.

Taping lectures. These tapes can be an alternative method to using a scribe. This provides an accurate and complete record of the course content for the student.

Transcription services. Braille and large print materials can be provided if not available from original source material.

Text on tape. Taped books can be obtained from public service agencies and some private social service agencies for persons who are blind or learning disabled.

Reader services. Reader services can coordinate and provide access to information required for equitable academic participation if this access is not available in other suitable modes.

Interpreter service. The service can include manual and oral interpreting for persons with hearing impairments.

Assessments. Diagnostic assessment, including both individual and group assessment, can determine a student's functional, educational, or employment level, or can verify specific disabilities.

High tech equipment. Enlargers for reading material can enlarge printed documents.

Adaptive equipment. Some equipment may require adapting to fit the physical needs of students with physical limitations. There are also specialized computers providing services required by some types of disabilities such as voice output and spell checking.

Assistive technology. An assistive technology device is "any item, piece of equipment or product system, whether acquired commercially off the shelf, modified, or customized, that is used to increase, maintain, or improve functional capabilities of individuals with disabilities" [IDEA, 20 U.S.C. Chapter 33, Section 1401 (25)].

An example of low assistive technology might be a device for holding a pencil to assist with writing. Other examples may be positions for seating in the classroom so the student may participate more effectively or adapted utensils to enhance the student's ability to feed him or herself.

Assistive technology devices also include long white canes, adapted puzzles, trays, chair inserts, electronic switches, and velcro attachments on equipment or clothing. High-level assistive technology could be such things as communication boards, electronic communication devices, speech synthesizers, powered wheelchairs, and electronic image sensors which provide information through vibrations. Schools may access funding sources such as Medicaid, Maternal and Child Health, Vocational Rehabilitation, and private insurance in order to defray the costs of providing assistive technology devices and services.

Litigation Prior to the Individuals with Disabilities Education Act

It is difficult to select several cases as the beginning of the trend extending civil and educational rights and privileges to all people. However, the following five cases appear to be catalysts.

In the case of Brown v. Board of Education of Topeka Kansas (1954), Brown successfully argued that "separate educational facilities are inherently unequal." The school district justified the segregation in schools by stating the resources provided at Brown's school were equal to other area schools so Brown had an equal educational opportunity. The Supreme Court rejected that assertion. In the written decision, the Court established two principles that have been used by those seeking educational equality for persons with disabilities. Those principles are "all people have a right to an equal educational opportunity" and "separate is not equal." Furthermore, the opinion stated "Education is the very foundation of good citizenship. Today it is a principle instrument in awakening the child to cultural values, in preparing him or her for later professional training, and in helping him or her to adjust normally to the environment. In these days, it is doubtful that any child may reasonably be expected to succeed in life if denied the opportunity of an education. Such an opportunity, where the state has undertaken to provide it, is a right which must be made available to all on equal terms." Brown v. Board of Education paved the way for a variety of lawsuits challenging the right of schools to exclude students based on a handicapping condition.

Two major court cases radically affected educational opportunities for individuals with mental retardation. The Pennsylvania Association for Retarded Children (PARC) brought suit against the Commonwealth of Pennsylvania (1972) for claiming the state denied access to education for children with mental retardation. Educational equality for children with mental retardation was broadened to include all children with disabilities in the case of Mills v. Board of Education of the District of Columbia (1972). The court further held that to deny educational opportunity to children with handicaps is a violation of due process and equal protection clauses of the Fourteenth Amendment to the Constitution.

In both cases, the federal courts ordered school authorities to provide a free, appropriate public education to students with disabilities within the same schools and programs as students without disabilities and to put in place procedural safeguards so students could challenge schools that do not support the courts' order (Turnbull, Turnbull, Shank & Leal, 1995). A series of landmark court decisions followed these two cases which established rights of parents to a fair and orderly process in determining if a student is disabled, and the determination of the type of special services that should be provided.

Larry P. v. Riles (1972) was a class action suit where the plaintiffs contended that testing instruments used to assess the students were discriminatory when used to place and maintain minority children in classes for students with special needs. This case was filed on behalf of six African American elementary school-aged children in San Francisco. The argument was the children were not mentally retarded but were victims of tests that failed to account for their ethnic background. In 1972, a preliminary injunction was issued stating that African American children could not be placed in classes for students who were mentally retarded on the basis of traditionally administered IQ tests. Embedded in the case was the mandate to assess African American children with testing instruments that would take into account their cultural background. The schools were required to ensure that the distribution of African American children in special education classes for students with retardation be proportional to the number of African American children in the total population. In 1979, on appeal of Larry P., the court again ruled in favor of the plaintiffs while holding the defendants had placed a disproportionate number of African American students in classes for mental retardation.

Diana v. State Board of Education (1970) also took place in California. The plaintiffs maintained that nine Mexican American children had been denied equal educational opportunity by being placed in classes for children who were educable mentally retarded on the basis of culturally biased intelligence tests. Additionally, because Spanish was their native language, it was argued that discrimination had occurred because the children were tested in English and those tests had been standardized on children whose first language was English. As a result of this case, education officials must test children in their native or primary language.

Cultural bias in assessment leads to inaccurate results based on cultural background. Norm-referenced measurement procedures, i.e. test employing norm data, language patterns, content and/or knowledge based on the cultural majority, are highly vulnerable to assessment bias. These procedures were challenged in both the Larry P. v. Riles and Diana v. State Board of Education cases. These two widely publicized court cases challenge educators to find assessment instruments that are equitable.

The Education for All Handicapped Children Act, Public Law 94-142. is legislation passed by the United States Congress and signed into law by President Gerald R. Ford in November of 1975. Public Law 94-142 has had significant impact upon the education of children and youth with disabilities. The law mandates the provision of free, appropriate public education for each individual with a disability. Implementation of the law began in 1978. Public Law 94-142 essentially has four major purposes, including:

- to guarantee the availability of special education programing to children and youth with disabilities who require it
- to assure fairness and appropriateness in decision making about providing special education to children with disabilities
- to establish clear management and auditing requirements and procedures regarding special education at all levels of government
- to financially assist the efforts of state and local government through the use of federal funds

In 1992, The National Institute on Disability and Rehabilitation Research reported that for the 1988-89 school year, a total of 4,190,515 children in the United States and insular areas, ages 6-21, were provided special education services under Public Law 94-142. Public Law 94-142 established six fundamental policies which have endured.

The Six Fundamental Policies of Public Law 94-142

Zero reject. Specially designed, free instruction will be available to all children with disabilities and no one (zero) can be rejected. "Free" means the education and related services will be provided at no cost to the person or to his or her parents or guardian. If a public education agency decides that a public or private residential program is appropriate, this type of placement (including nonmedical care and room and board) shall be provided at no cost.

Nondiscriminatory evaluation. Appropriately designed evaluation procedures must be followed. Each child must be tested in his or her native language (including such primary communication modes as Braille and sign language) and each must receive an individualized plan based on the results of the testing. The child cannot be placed in a program based upon a single assessment or the judgment of a single individual.

Due process. States must guarantee procedural safeguard mechanisms for children and their parents. For example, parents must have an opportunity to examine all relevant records. Prior written notice to parents and parental consent is required when any action respecting special education is proposed. Children and parents have the right to a formal, due process hearing if desired.

Parental participation. Parents must be involved in shared decision making and must provide consent to assessments and placements in special education services. Information about the child and family must remain confidential.

Least Restrictive Environment (LRE). Children and youth with disabilities must be educated with children who do not have disabilities to the "maximum extent appropriate." The LRE principle recognizes that a continuum of services and placements must be available to meet the child's needs.

Individualized Education Plan (IEP). The IEP is the management tool used to monitor the maximum LRE and therefore shall be applied within the framework of meeting the "unique needs" of each child.

The Individuals with Disabilities Education Act

The Individuals with Disabilities Education Act (Public Law 101-476), the education equivalent to the Americans with Disabilities Act of 1990, reauthorized and expanded the Education for All Handicapped Children Act of 1975 (Public Law 94-142). The Education for All Handicapped Children Act mandated a free and appropriate education for all children with disabilities. The Individuals with Disabilities Education Act was designed to update and reevaluate the original features of Public Law 94-142.

Additionally, IDEA provides federal funds to assist state and local agencies in educating children with disabilities from birth to age 22. Under IDEA, children with disabilities are defined as children with: mental retardation, hearing impairments, deafness, blindness, speech or language impairments, visual impairments, serious emotional disturbance, orthopedic impairments, other health impaired (including attention deficit hyperactivity disorder), autism, traumatic brain injury, children with multiple disabilities, and children with specific learning disabilities, who require special educational and related services. The following section will explain how children are assessed for special education services.

Assessment cycle

How do educators determine if a child has a need for special education? How is a child initially assessed? Regardless of your location in the United States, the assessment cycle (based on IDEA) is similar. The following six steps outline the process.

Recognition/intervention. Children with severe and/or physical disabilities are often diagnosed at birth (for example, a child born with cerebral palsy). However, for the many children who have academic and/or social difficulties, the disability might not be diagnosed until school age. Usually, a teacher recognizes a student having difficulty and tries several intervention ideas prior to referral to the special education assessment team. The interventions could be as simple as moving a child to the front of the room, or as complex as teaching specific mnemonic strategies to help the child remember content. The teacher should document at least two interventions before assuming the interventions are not working and referring the student to special education. During the recognition stage, a teacher normally notes some surface clues or signals that something could be wrong.

Referral to special education. If the student's needs are not met after the teacher attempts several modifications of the curriculum and/or behavior plans and the student still is not improving, it is critical the student be referred to special education. The referral must be made in writing. Teachers, parents and even the child himself may make a referral. Once a referral is made, the assessment cycle begins. The parents are sent a locally generated permission-to-test form and are provided several weeks to respond in writing. Once parents grant permission, the student must be tested within 50 days. Usually, a school-wide team is established to determine assessment instruments and observations.

Assessment procedures. During assessment procedures, a determination is made about student needs and the nature and extent of any special education and related services required. Assessments may be given by psychologists, medical doctors, teachers, or other professionals deemed appropriate by the team.

Many different professional disciplines offer services related to specific areas of expertise. A multidisciplinary assessment team could consist of an administrator, adaptive physical education specialist, art therapist, audiologist, general education teacher, language pathologist, music therapist, nutritionist, occupational therapist, ophthalmologist, parents, physician, physical therapist, psychologist, rehabilitation counselor, school nurse, social worker, speech therapist, and/or a therapeutic recreation therapist. Usually the assessment includes achievement, intelligence, social, academic, behavior, language, and psychomotor areas. It is common to use both standardized and nonstandardized tests as well as observation reports and parent questionnaires.

Individualized Education Plan. The IEP is a locally generated written document designed by a team of persons interested in programming the child for success in school. Once the assessments have been completed, a team meeting is scheduled. The participants at the IEP meeting must minimally include:

- The school representative who will provide or supervise the provision of special education
- Child's teacher or teachers
- Parent(s) or guardian(s)
- The child (when appropriate)
- Other individuals at the discretion of parents/committee

The team of experts contribute interdependently to each child's individualized program. Nationwide, IEP forms contain several standard elements:

- The child's present level of educational performance
- A statement of annual goals and short-term objectives
- Related services
- Percent of time in general education
- Beginning and ending dates for special education services
- An annual evaluation plan

Beginning no later than age 16, Individualized Education Plans must include a statement of the "transition services" the student will need before leaving the school setting based on a post-school timetable. Transition services promote the student's movement from school to post-school activities (including post-secondary education, vocational training, integrated employment, independent living, or community participation) and must include instruction, community experiences, development of employment, and other post-school living objectives. In some cases, acquisition of daily living skills and functional vocational evaluation are requirements in the transition services.

Placement. What types of services are available and what setting is most suitable for the child? IDEA requires that "to the maximum extent appropriate, children with disabilities...are educated with children who are not disabled, and that special classes, separate schooling, or other removal of children with disabilities from the regular environment occurs only when the nature or severity of the disability is such that education in regular classes with the use of supplementary aids and services cannot be attained satisfactorily." This requirement has deep seated roots in the special education literature. The principle of normalization is a philosophical principle which came to us from the Scandinavian countries. Normalization means making available to the person with disabilities patterns and conditions of everyday life which are as close as possible to the norms of the mainstream of society (Nirje, 1969). Today, there are many options for placement. The chart below provides an overview of available services. More restrictive services are listed at the bottom of the chart. The services progress toward the top, which represents full inclusion in society.

Continuum of services
- full day general education classes
- full day general education classes with consultation services for the teacher
- general education classes with support from special education staff
- general education classes with peer or cross-age tutor
- general education class with part-day resource or itinerant services
- part day placement in special day class and mainstreaming into general education class
- full-day placement in special class and social integration with general school population
- full-day placement in special class
- private school
- residential facility
- homebound
- hospital setting

All placement support services are provided within the general education program. The placement should be done after deciding that the student can benefit from placement. The decision is made during consultation with both the general and special education teachers and the members of the IEP team.

It is critical that all eligible individuals be permitted to participate in non-academic and extracurricular activities as well as academic classes in the general education setting. Students should be removed from the general education environment only when to remain is determined to be detriment to the child. The goal is to place the child in the Least Restrictive Environment where learning can take place.

If you volunteer in school sites, several terms will become commonplace:

Mainstreaming occurs when a child with special needs spends some time in classes designed for general education students and taught by general education teachers. Usually the child spends time in a special education class but moves to a general education class for some of the curricula, such as physical education, art, and music. The special education teacher remains responsible for placement in the general education classroom and the goals and objectives on the IEP.

Integration refers to the participation of students with disabilities in regular school programs with instructional support from the special education teacher. Occasionally, the student is "pulled out of" the general education class for some specialized services. The responsibility for student learning is shared between the general education and special education services.

Inclusion of students with disabilities means involvement in all aspects of school life alongside peers who do not have disabilities. Involvement should be at the same ratio as that which occurs in the community; this is referred to as "natural proportion." Usually, students spend the entire day in the general education class. Instructional modifications and/or specialized tools and techniques to succeed educationally and socially are provided in the general education classroom through the collaboration of general education and special education services. Students attend their neighborhood school with children their same age.

Student and program evaluation. The student's progress should be evaluated at least annually. The IEP must include plans to show how the evaluation should be accomplished, who will conduct it, and what assessment instruments and criteria will be used.

Instructional Strategies for Students with Disabilities

Regardless of whether the work is with general education or special education, good teaching is good teaching (McCabe, Mortorff, Karge & Lasky, 1993). There are many proven strategies that are very helpful for students with special needs. These strategies may include (but are not limited to) direct instruction, peer tutoring, inquiry approaches, questioning approaches, cross-age tutoring, total physical response, syntactics, problem solving, brainstorming, concept attainment, cooperative learning, and/or group discussion. Interested readers can refer to *Effective Instruction for Students with Learning Difficulties* by Cegelka & Berdine (1995).

Early Intervention Services for Infants and Toddlers with Disabilities

Just as IDEA provides a framework for free appropriate public education for school-aged children, Public Law 99-457 provides a framework for assisting states in developing and implementing a comprehensive, coordinated, and multidisciplinary program of early intervention services for families and children with disabilities from birth to age two.

There are several important differences between the educational provisions of IDEA and Public Law 99-457. Instead of focusing on special education and related services, the term *early intervention services* is used. Early intervention services include (but are not limited to) family training, counseling, and home visits; special instruction; speech pathology and audiology; occupational therapy; physical therapy; psychological services; case management services; medical services for diagnostic or evaluation purposes; early identification; screening; assessment services; and the health services necessary to enable the infant or toddler to benefit from other early intervention services. Case management services are specifically included as an early intervention service to assist families to obtain any other services that may be required. The case manager is responsible for assisting with the assessment process, including the compilation of the team, designation of services, and family support.

The definition of disabilities is conceptualized somewhat differently in Public Law 99-457. States can include infants and toddlers who are "at risk" or have substantial developmental delays in the definition. The philosophy is that early intervention will prevent and/or assist with other difficulties developing later in life.

"Individuals from birth to age two, inclusive, who need early intervention services because they (1) are experiencing developmental delays in cognitive development, physical development, language and speech development, psychosocial development, or self help skills or (2) have a diagnosed physical or mental condition which has a high probability of resulting in developmental delay" (Public Law 99-457, sec. 672).

Finally, Public Law 99-457 differs from IDEA in that early intervention services focus on *both* the child and the family, whereas the child alone is addressed in IDEA. Under Public Law 99-457, the team develops an Individualized Family Service Plan (IFSP) instead of an IEP.

Summary

All education, whether public, private/parochial, alternative, or special, should be designed to meet the needs of the individual child. Special education refers to an individually planned, carefully monitored arrangement of physical settings, special equipment and materials, teaching procedures, and other interventions designed to help exceptional children achieve personal self-sufficiency and academic success. This education is carefully designed by a team via the assessment process. An IEP must be designed to program the student for success with *individualization*. The unique individual needs must be assessed and placement and services must be based accordingly. When a student with a disability receives an appropriate education (as required by IDEA), the student has a better chance of progressing to a postsecondary education, entering the work force, and becoming a full tax-paying member of society.

References

Brown v. Board of Education of Topeka, 347 United States 483, 74 S. Ct 686 (1954).

Cegelka, P. T. & Berdine, W. H. (1995). *Effective instruction for students with learning difficulties*. Boston: Allyn and Bacon.

Diana v. State Board of Education. C-70-37 R.F.P., (N.D. California, Jan. 7, 1970).

Landes, A. (Ed.). (1994). *Minorities: A changing role in America*. Wylie, TX: Information Plus.

Larry P. v. Riles. 343 F. Supp. 1306 (N.D. California 1972); 343 F. Supp. 1306, 502 F. 2d 963 (N.D. California 1979).

McCabe, M., Mortorff, S. A., Karge, B. D., & Lasky, B. (1993). Support: The road to success for beginning special education teachers. *Intervention in School and Clinic, 28*(5), 288-293.

Mills v. Board of Education of the District of Columbia, 348 F. Supp. 866 (D.D.C. 1972).

Pennsylvania Association for Retarded Children (PARC) v. Commonwealth of Pennsylvania, 343 F. Supp. 279 (E.D. Pa. 1972).

Nirje, B. (1969). The normalization principle and its human management implications. In R. B. Kugel & W. Wolfensberger, (Eds.), *Changing patterns in residential services for the mentally retarded*, pp.179-88. Washington, DC: President's Committee on Mental Retardation.

Turnbull, A. P., Turnbull, H. R., Shank, M. & Leal, D. (1995). *Exceptional lives: Special education in todays schools*. Columbus, OH: Prentice Hall.

Suggested Readings

Driedger, D. (1989). *The last civil rights movement*. New York: St. Martin's Press. *This book traces the history of the Disabled People's International.*

Cook, R. E., Tessier, A. & Armbruster, V. B. (1987). *Adapting early childhood curricula for children with special needs*. (2nd Ed.) Columbus, OH: Merrill. *This book provides reader with excellent information on early childhood special education and ways to adapt education to meet the specific needs of young children.*

Cegelka, P. T. & Berdine, W. H. (1995). *Effective instruction for students with learning difficulties*. Boston: Allyn and Bacon. *This provides detailed descriptions for how to program students for success in the educational environment by using effective teaching strategies.*

Public Law 94-142, the Education for All Handicapped Children Act of 1975. Public Law 101-476, the Individuals with Disabilities Education Act of 1990. You can obtain a copy of the laws by writing to your United States senator or congressional representative. The laws are very interesting reading!

Rogers, J. (1994). *Inclusion: Moving beyond our fears*. Bloomington, In: Phi Delta Kappa. *This volume is a compilation of 22 research based articles and professional opinion on one of America's most immediate and least understood educational problems.*

Notes

Exploration

Individual Activities

1. Develop a list of those things that are special about special education.

_____

_____

_____

_____

_____

_____

2. Develop a list of opportunities that alternative schooling might allow a student to pursue.

_____

_____

_____

_____

_____

_____

Group Activities

1. Make arrangements so your class can visit and observe special education classes in your local school district. While observing, look for the aspects you listed as being special about special education.

Reactions:

_____

_____

_____

_____

_____

_____

2. Arrange for a panel of teachers with different types of students to visit your class. Ask the panel to discuss some of their experiences with student risk factors.

Reactions:

_____

_____

_____

_____

_____

_____

Reaction Paper 16.1

Assume that you are a political leader and you have to make a decision whether to support or oppose a bill to give additional money to special education. How would you vote and why?

Reaction Paper 16.2

An important part of special education is inclusion. How do you feel about this idea? How does inclusion benefit students with disabilities? How does it benefit other individuals? What are your concerns about inclusion?

Chapter 17

Human Diversity in Society

A Vision of Possibilities

Although it appears that people have generally become more understanding of human differences over the past several decades and we have attempted to institutionalize respect for human difference through legislation, it is still common for individuals to fear and ridicule those who are different. For instance, someone may be critical of a person with a visible disability who eats in a restaurant. Another person may be concerned about a group living home for people who are diverse being established in his or her neighborhood. Prejudice against a co-worker because of race, gender, or sexual orientation is something many of us hear expressed on a regular basis. Myths and negative attitudes about human diversity still exist, and will exist until we change them, one person at a time. The easiest person to change is the one you see when you look in the mirror. We hope that this course has been a good beginning for you.

There has been progress toward establishing equal rights for diverse people. However, that does not mean that everyone who interacts with them will be kind, considerate, or comfortable. Part of the problem is that children learn certain attitudes from their parents and from other adults and peers in society. Now you are in a position to alter those attitudes for yourself and others. You are equipped with information and can help to insure that society makes additional progress beyond the laws which have assisted diverse people.

Wouldn't you prefer to live in a society where people don't stare at others who are different? Where everyone, regardless of race, ethnic, or religious background, gender, sexual orientation, age, intellectual ability, nationality, socioeconomic level, size, or shape is treated with respect? Where people are evaluated on the basis of their skills and their personality, not on the basis of the labels which have been imposed upon them? When that happens, the society is richer in every way because we all have the opportunity to contribute to the fullest extent of our capacity. You have the ability now to influence others so that fair treatment is afforded to everyone.

This final chapter will help you to develop strategies for assisting others in dealing with diverse individuals. Remember that you are educated now. By taking this course, you have prepared yourself to be a leader of others, and others will follow your example since they know you have had an opportunity to study and consider these issues. Each of the sections in this chapter offers you ideas and encouragement as you reconsider your own attitudes and begin to change society. It will be a wonderful and exciting experience to grow in understanding as you help others to do the same!

Your Comfort Level

Each chapter has stressed the importance of being comfortable when you interact with people who are different. Comfort logically follows the reduction of fear as you dispel myths, correct misinformation, and develop knowledge and understanding. Some steps toward becoming more comfortable around people who are different are listed below.

Make a firm personal decision to be comfortable when you interact with anyone different from you. Often, merely having the *intention* to be comfortable will help you to actually feel comfortable. You might begin your day with an affirmation such as this: "Today I hope to meet someone different from me so that I can discover an underlying similarity."

Continue to learn more about human diversity. Consider taking additional courses. Classes which offer skills such as sign language will make it possible for you to easily converse with people who use that form of communication and will make you a more expressive person. Showing an interest in the problems of any special interest group, whether it is a senior citizens' organization, a women's rights group, a local AIDS service organization, or a club for international students, will broaden your perspective and allow you to participate more fully in the world. At your college or in your neighborhood you should be able to find many opportunities for interacting with different types of people.

When you make friends with people who are different, don't be afraid to talk to them about their exeptionality. Ask the questions you want to ask. Raise the issues you want to raise. Openness and honesty is the key to friendship, and it is important to treat people who are different the same way you treat anyone else. Remember that the most important lesson you have learned is that individuals are unique. They are not defined by labels.

Assist different types of people through volunteer organizations. This will offer you another opportunity to get to know people with differences. Literacy programs exist in every community, as do programs for economically disadvantaged people, and nearly every other category of exceptionality. Such organizations or agencies will welcome your assistance and will usually have a variety of projects or activities from which you can choose. An annotated listing of organizations dealing with human diversity is included at the end of this book.

Include diverse people among your acquaintances and friends. Don't be afraid to invite someone different to social functions. Remember that differences are not contagious, and even if they were, you and every other person alive is exceptional in some way, in some context. Some of your friends may not be comfortable with your new acquaintance. Their response may be due to their ignorance, and you can use that as an opportunity to help them see your perspective.

Just be yourself around people who are different. If you are false, they will recognize it. Don't worry about your mood—we all have good and bad days. Don't adjust your vocabulary. Consider the feelings of others as you always do, letting your new knowledge and sensitivity enhance your natural good manners.

Community Impact

Now, or in the future, you may be in the position of having significant influence upon your community. You may belong to civic, religious, and professional organizations. Perhaps you will be a city commissioner, a state legislator, or the President of the United States. You may be a leader in business or industry and have responsibility for hiring or influencing the careers of others. What wonderful opportunities you may have to make a positive impact upon our society.

As a member of a civic, religious, or professional group, you certainly can set an example for others regarding interactions with diverse people. Some individuals with exceptionalities may need your sponsorship to facilitate their membership, or they may need special accommodations for access in order to participate fully.

For instance, if your group is presenting a special speaker and opening the meeting to the public, be sure to hire a sign language interpreter and let that be known in your publicity so that those needing that service will be motivated to attend. Obvious requirements for location such as wheelchair ramps may be overlooked by those unaccustomed to thinking inclusively. You can point out these considerations.

If you become active in politics, you will have many chances to significantly influence the funding of programs, the establishment of procedures for service development and provision, and the design of laws which directly affect diverse people. At the local, state, and federal level, as an active politician or simply as a voter, you should follow two simple rules. The first is that people who are different deserve every opportunity to lead the normal lives they desire. The second is that they should not be merely tolerated or accepted, but respected as full and important members of the community.

Careers With Diverse People

Before closing your study of human diversity you might consider your future. A possible career path could be in one of the professions dealing with people who are different. Such fields as psychology, sociology, anthropology, political science, counseling, medicine, special education, music therapy, speech and language therapy, sheltered workshop management, sign language interpreting, and many others offer challenging careers which let you make meaningful contributions to your fellow women and men. If you think you might be interested, a good way to begin is to visit some professionals in the area of your choice to explore the possibilities and ask advice on some courses of study.

A Final Self-Check

Now that you are educated and informed about human diversity, here is a test of your new attitudes and ability to respect and assist those who are considered different. Imagine this situation:

You are being wheeled into a hospital emergency room. You have sustained a life-threatening injury. Your life depends upon the ability of the lone doctor on duty. Which *one* of the following labels do you want that doctor to have?

Male   Female   Christian   Jewish   Homosexual   Heterosexual

Slim   Tall   Heavy   Short   Wealthy   Disabled   Caucasion   Hindu

Black   Hispanic   Old   Young   Foreign   Poor   Muslim   Expert

If you value your life, more than likely your answer was "Expert." It is doubtful that you would refuse treatment and choose to die if the doctor had any of the other labels coupled with "expert." Since that is true, we know that you, and most everyone else, can ignore labels when it suits our needs. If you can choose to ignore them at all times and in all situations, looking only at the abilities of the person involved, then you have learned to treat individuals with the respect they deserve. When old habits of thinking and fears based on prejudice and ignorance creep in, it is a handy reminder to ask yourself, "If I were in that hospital emergency room and this person were the only doctor on duty, would I want this person to save my life?" Every time you say "yes," you save your own humanity and make the world a much better place.

The Next Step

Your study of human diversity is at a close. The next step you take is up to you. We hope that this text has inspired you to continue discovering more about differences among people. We are confident that you are now equipped to make a difference in the lives of people with whom you come in contact. We are also confident that you can set an example in your community. As you strive to learn more about human diversity, we hope that you continue to see the underlying unity among all peoples while at the same time you respect individual uniqueness. The human race has a long way to go before universal understanding becomes the norm, but the only way we'll ever reach that goal is by changing one person at a time, starting with ourselves. If, after this course, you have a better understanding of human diversity and an attitude of respect for persons who are diverse, you have taken a big step toward the goal.

Suggested Readings

Famighetti, R (1994). *The world almanac and book of facts.* Mahwah, NJ: Funk and Wagnalls.
This is a global-scale source of important facts on economics, employment, arts, media, people, national affairs, and vital statistics.

Gerbner, G. (1990). Communication. *Encyclopedia Americana* (International edition, vol. 7, pp. 423-24). Danbury, CT: Grolier.
This is an insightful overview of the diverse ways in which humans exchange information.

Hirsch, E. D., Kett, J. F., & Trefil, J. (1988). *The Dictionary of Cultural Literacy.* Boston: Houghton Mifflin Co.
This is an essential quick reference for facts and terminology relating to world literature, philosophy, religion, art, history, politics, geography, anthropology, sociology, psychology, science, mathematics, medicine, and technology.

336

Jampolsky, G. G. (1990). *Love is the answer: Creating positive relationships.* New York: Bantam.
This is a guide to improving interpersonal relationships, love, and peace of mind.

Keyes, K. (1990). *The living love way.* San Francisco: New Dimensions Foundation.
This book discusses the importance of transforming conflict in one's daily life and expressing love wherever and whenever possible. The discussion also provides insights about the possibilities of world peace.

Kronenwetter, M. (1993). *Prejudice in America: Causes and cures.* New York: Franklin Watts.
This book traces the origins of prejudice in America and suggests practical solutions to the far-reaching problem.

Exploration

Individual Activities

1. What are some things that you have done in the past in regard to diverse people that will be different in your future? List five things.

_____

_____

_____

_____

_____

2. List six things that you have learned during this course that have assisted you in improving your comfort level with human diversity.

_____

_____

_____

_____

_____

_____

Group Activities

1. In a few years all of you are going to hold important positions in your communities. Get together in small groups and discuss what you will do to make your community a better place for *all* people. Present these actions to your entire class.

Reactions:

_____

_____

_____

_____

_____

_____

2. Invite a panel of diverse individuals and parents of diverse people to your class. Discuss and evaluate the suggestions regarding the improvement of your comfort level which were given in the chapter.

Reactions:

_____

_____

_____

_____

_____

_____

Reaction Paper 17.1

In the summary of the chapter you were asked about labels and an emergency room doctor who could save your life. What label did you choose? Why?

Notes

Appendix A

Sign Language

Artwork by Robert Stiff, B.S.

Sign languages are complex communication systems that incorporate hand movement combinations, facial espressions, and body language to express whole words, thoughts, and concepts rather than spell them out one letter at a time. Sign languages are not merely systems of gestures. They are true languages with their own complicated grammar and rules of handshape, hand location, movement, facial espression, and body language.

Sign language can be both highly concise and highly poetic. With just one handshape—the thumb and little finger stretched out and the first finger pointing forward—a person can make an airplane take off, experience turbulence and engine trouble, circle an airport, and come in for a bumpy landing. One can sign that entire sentence in a fraction of the time it would take to say it aloud (Walker, 1986).

There is no universal sign language. Sign languages differ from one another just as spoken languages differ around the world. American Sign Language (ASL) is one of the most commonly used, featuring approximately 6,000 signs. ASL is popular because it has a long history of use and is easy to master. Though this sign language is called "American," it is not English and is in fact more similar to Chinese because its signs represent concepts rather than single words (Hardman, Drew, Egan, & Wolf, 1993).

As opposed to sign languages, sign systems use manual gestures which attempt to create visual equivalents of spoken language. Finger spelling is a sign system that uses all 26 letters of the alphabet to spell out individual words. Finger spelling frequently supplements sign languages. For example, when there is no sign for a particular word using ASL, a person may resort to finger spelling. A number of sign systems are used in the United States: Seeing Exact English, Linguistics of Visual English, and Signed Exact English.

Knowing sign language will enable you to communicate with people with hearing impairments who use sign language as their means of communication. Another important reason to learn sign language is that it will enrich all your other modes of expression. Just as learning another language increases your vocabulary and helps you to understand the way other people think and communicate, so too will learning sign language enrich your life.

As an introduction to signing, you will find drawings of finger spelling on the following pages. Practice these with a friend or in a mirror. While practicing, say the word (not the letters) as you finger spell. Practice the letters in random order so that you master them individually rather than depend upon the sequence.

After you learn finger spelling, try your hand at learning some common sign language words which are presented in this chapter. Then practice these words with a friend.

References

Hardman, M., Drew, C., Egan, M., & Wold, B. (1993). *Human exceptionality: Society, school, and family.* Boston: Allyn and Bacon.

Walker, L. A. (1986). *A loss for words: The story of deafness in a family.* New York: Harper and Row.

Suggested Readings

Bornstein, H., Saulnier, K., & Hamilton, L. (1983). *The comprehensive signed English dictionary.* Washington, D.C.: Kendall Green.

Costello, E. (1983). *Signing: How to speak with your hands.* New York: Bantam.

Riekehof, L. (1987). *The joy of signing.* Springfield, MO: Gospel.

Sternberg, M. (1990). *American sign language: A concise dictionary.* New York: Harper and Row.

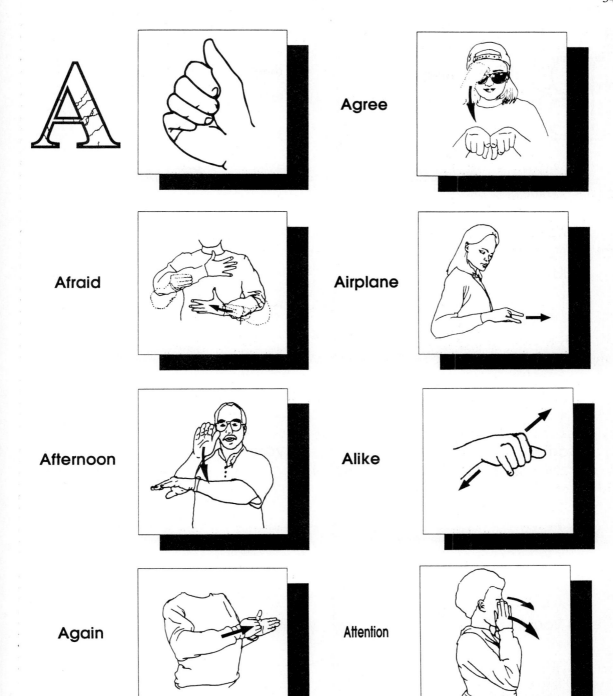

A

Agree

Afraid

Airplane

Afternoon

Alike

Again

Attention

B

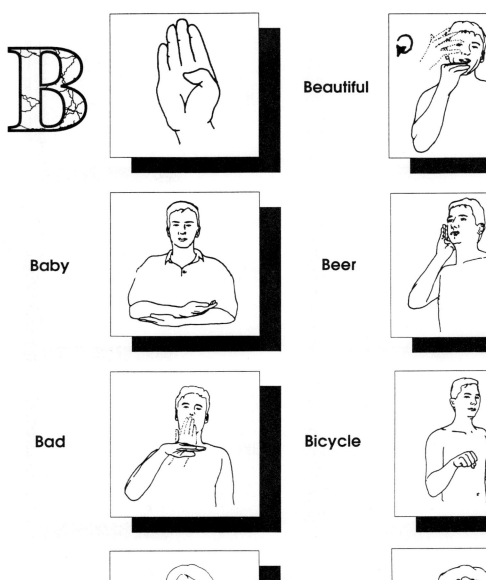

Beautiful

Baby

Beer

Bad

Bicycle

Bath Room

Blind

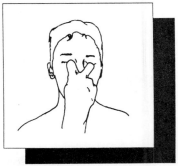

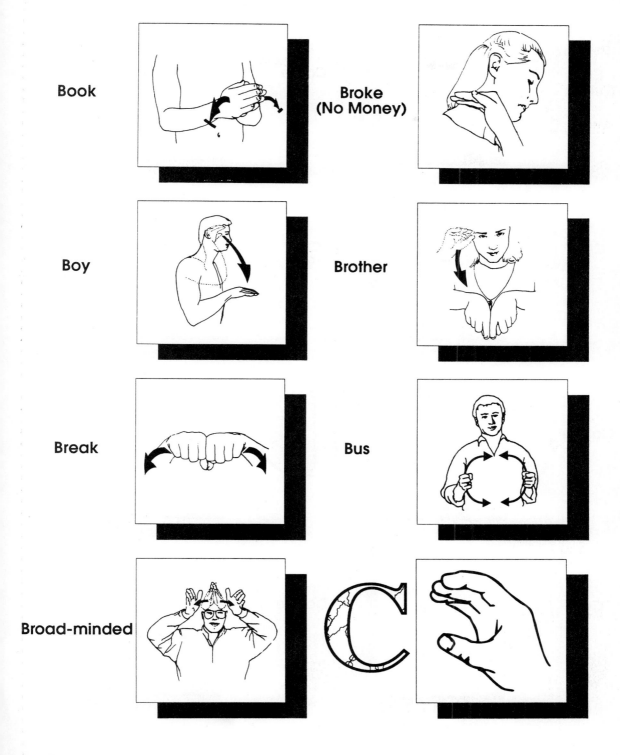

Book

Broke
(No Money)

Boy

Brother

Break

Bus

Broad-minded

C

350

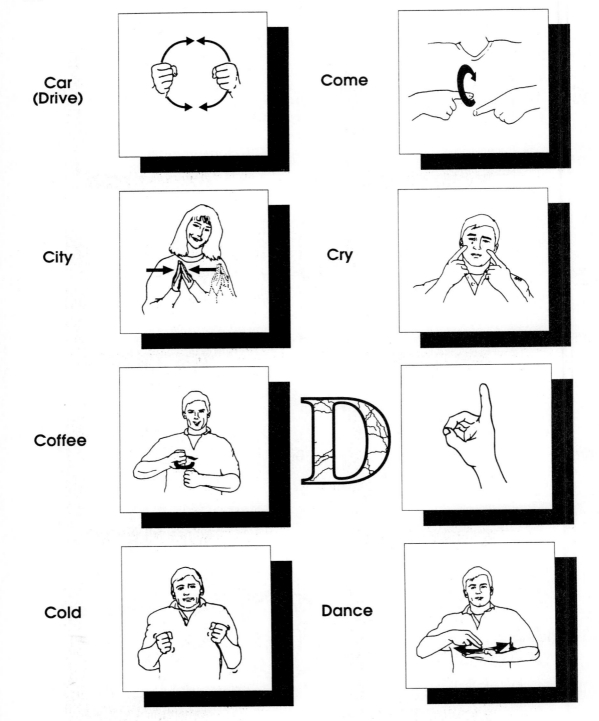

Car
(Drive)

Come

City

Cry

Coffee

Cold

Dance

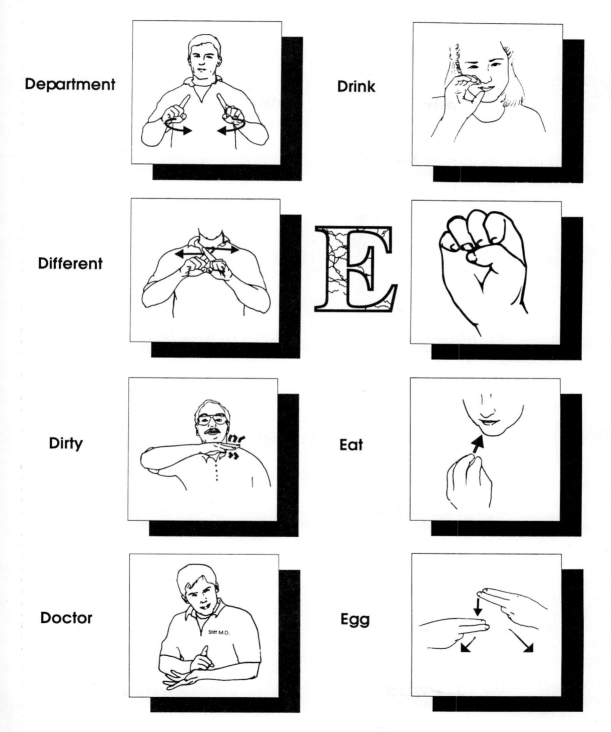

Department

Drink

Different

E

Dirty

Eat

Doctor

Stiff M.D.

Egg

Embarrass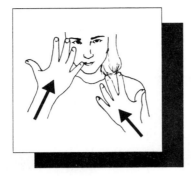

Father

Experience

Feel

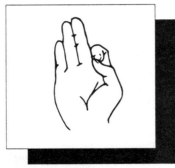

Female

Family

Fine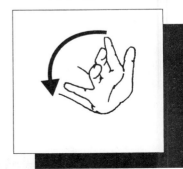

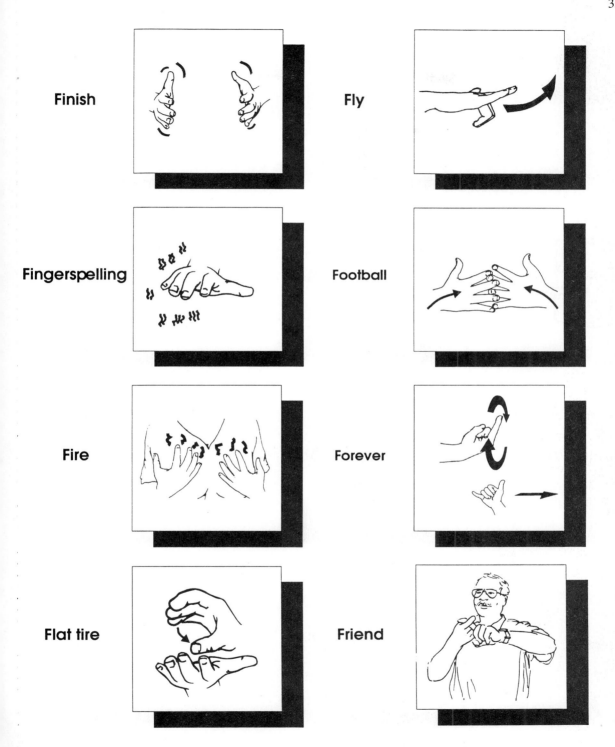

Finish

Fly

Fingerspelling

Football

Fire

Forever

Flat tire

Friend

Future

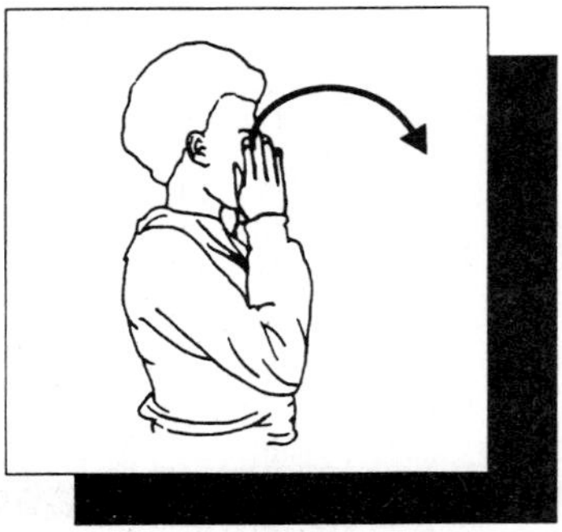

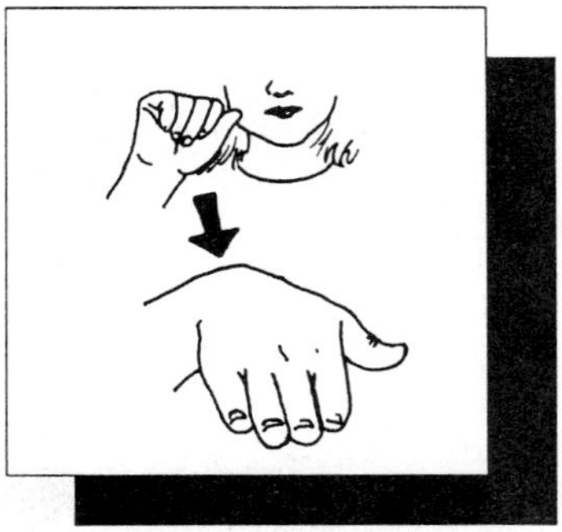

Give

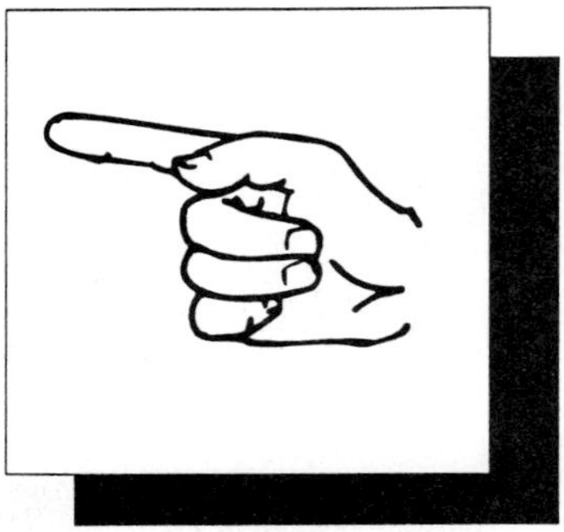

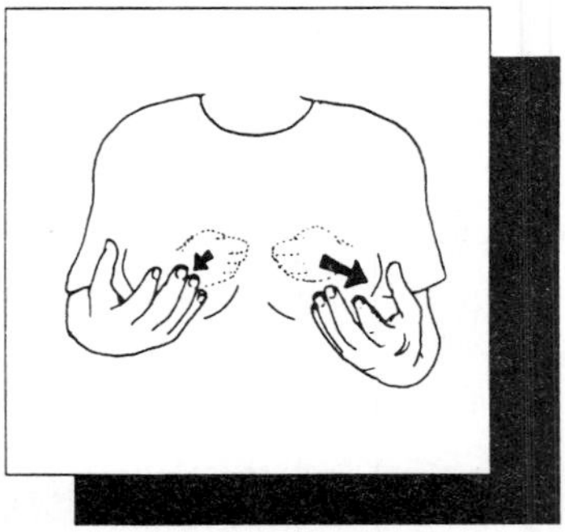

G

Go

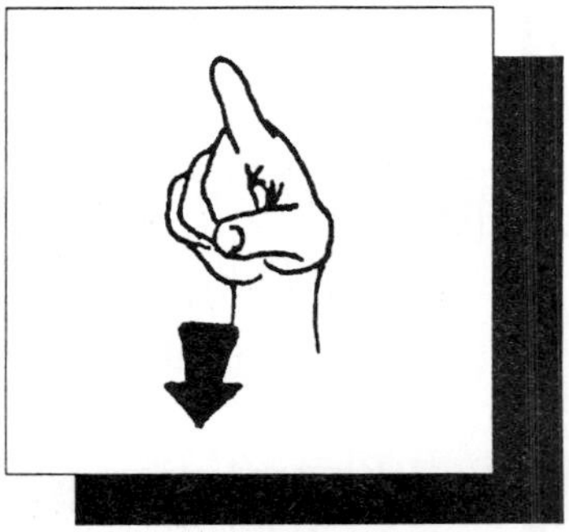

Gentleman

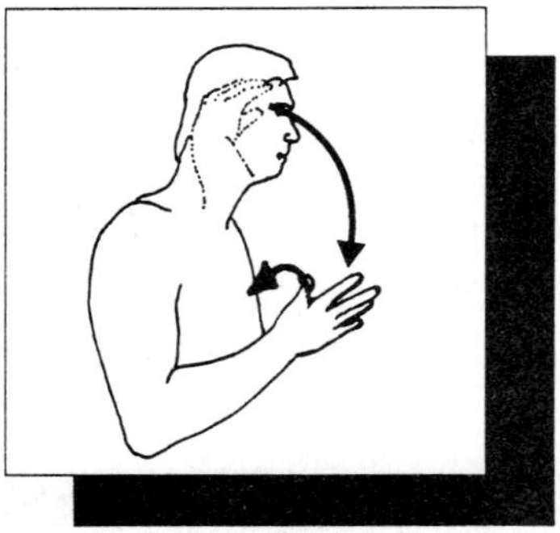

Golf

Girl

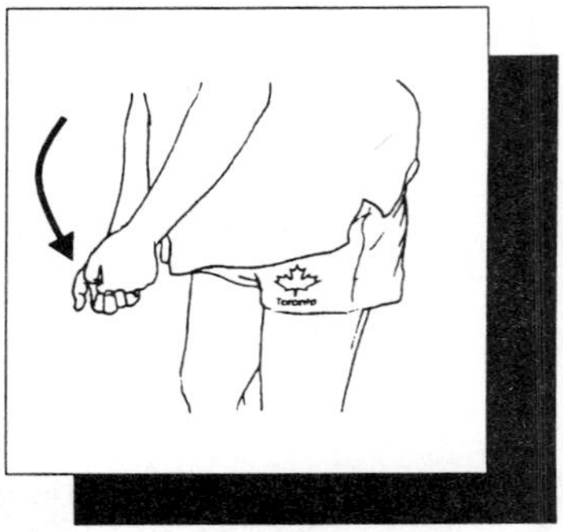

Good

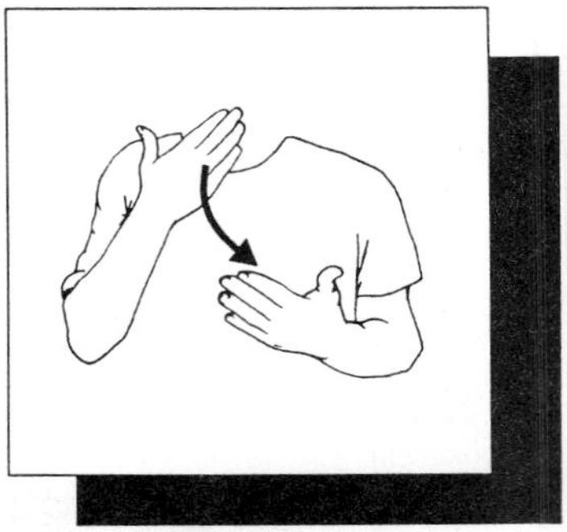

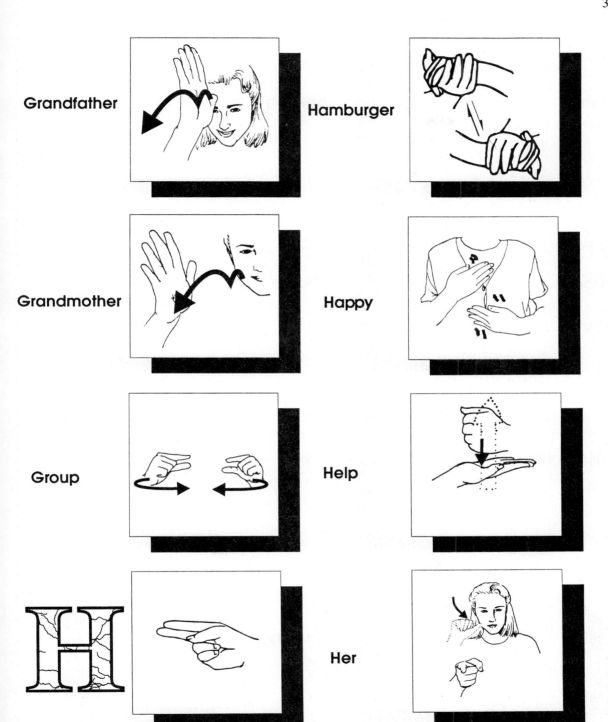

Grandfather

Hamburger

Grandmother

Happy

Group

Help

H

Her

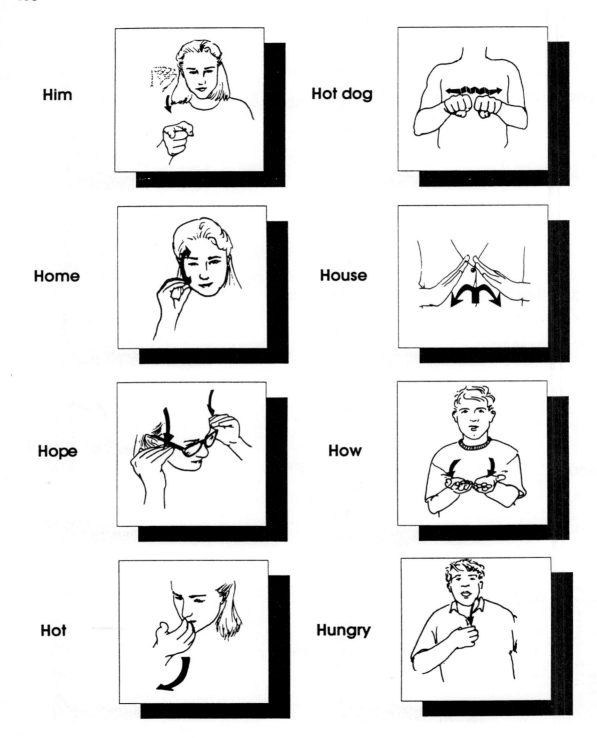

Him

Hot dog

Home

House

Hope

How

Hot

Hungry

Husband

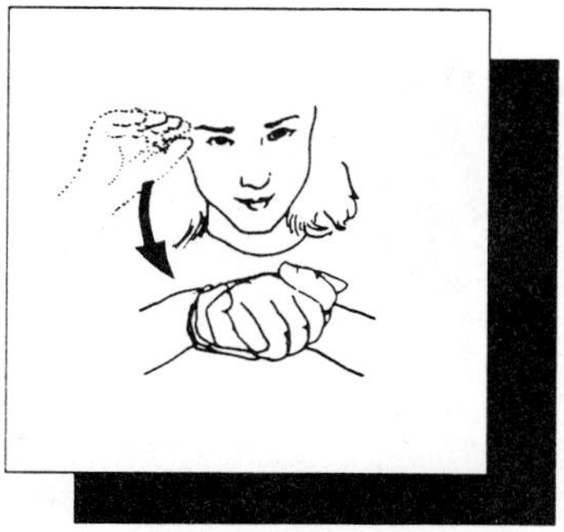

Kiss

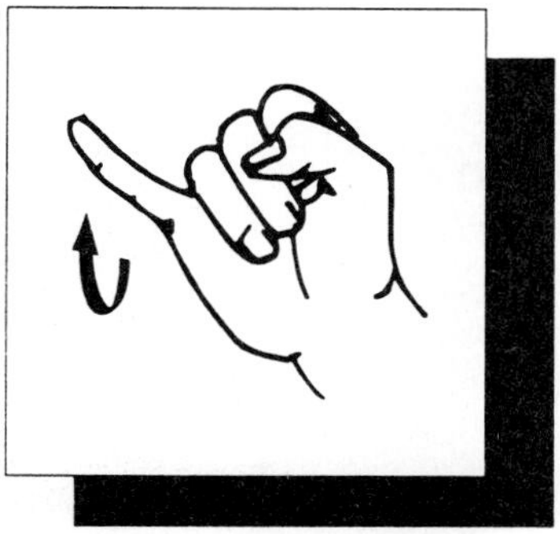

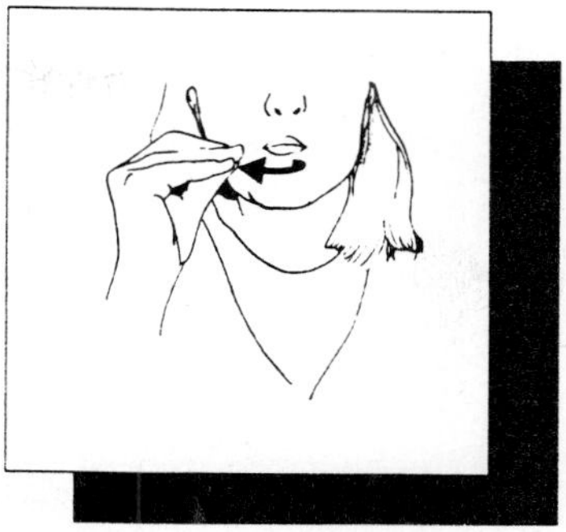

I

Know

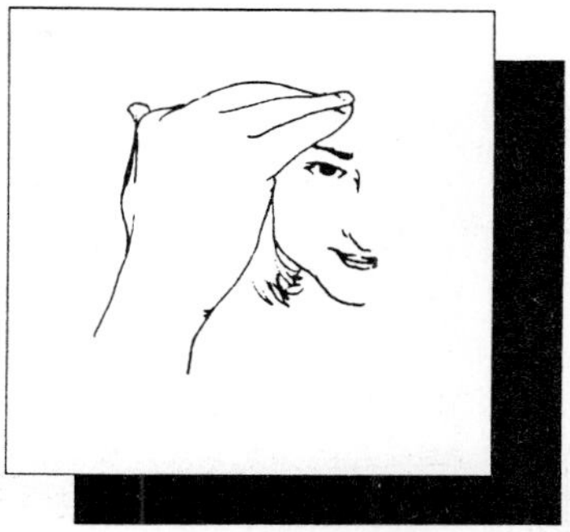

J

L

K

Lady (Woman)

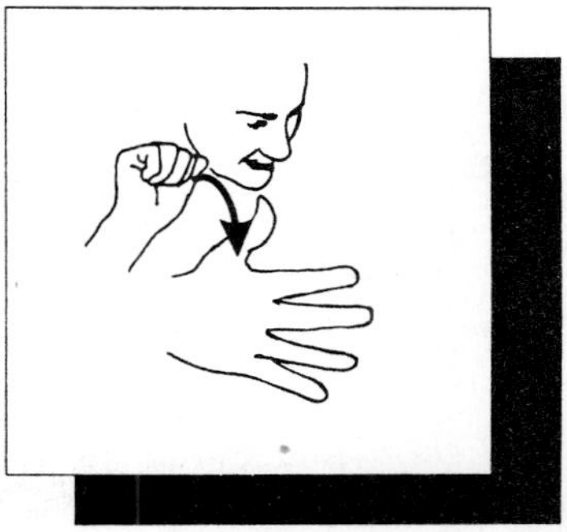

358

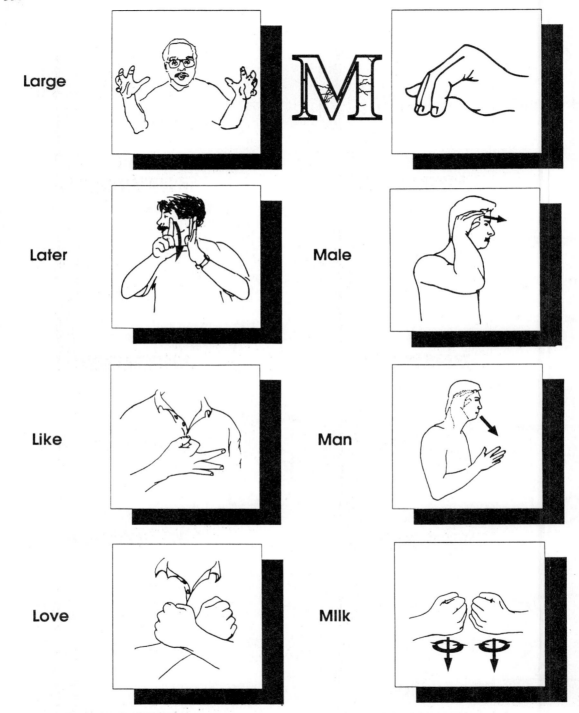

Large

Later

Like

Love

M

Male

Man

Milk

Mine

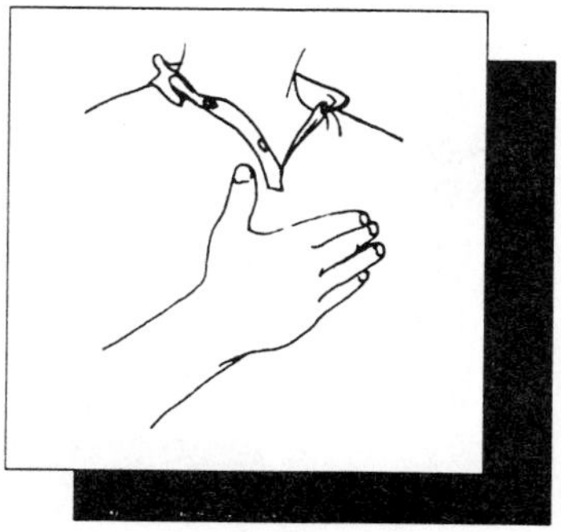

N

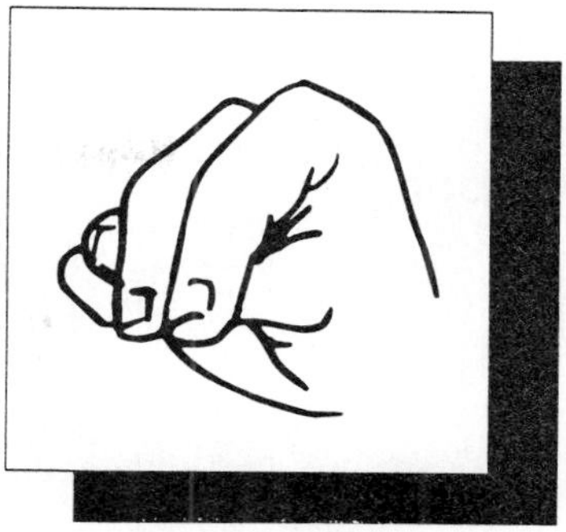

Morning

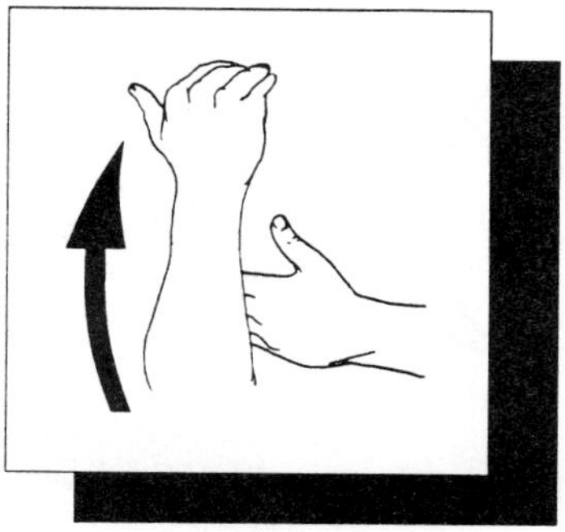

Name

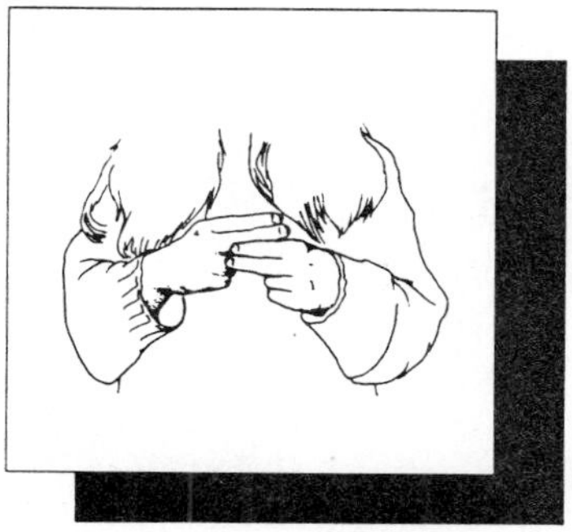

Mother

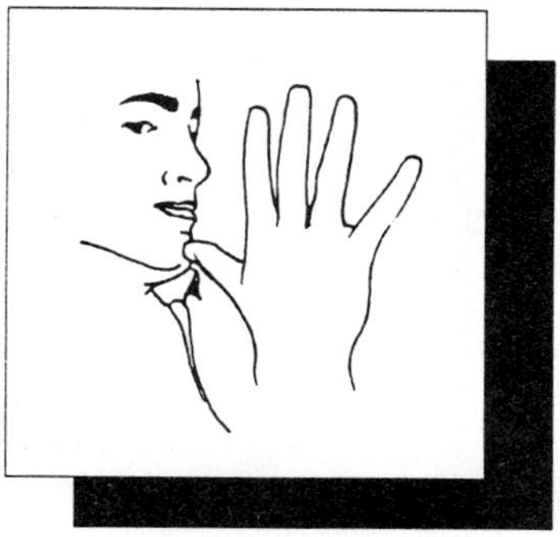

Narrow-minded

Music

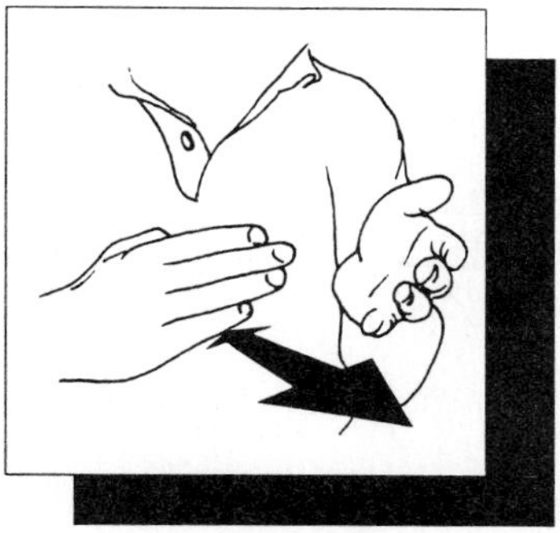

Necessary
(Need)

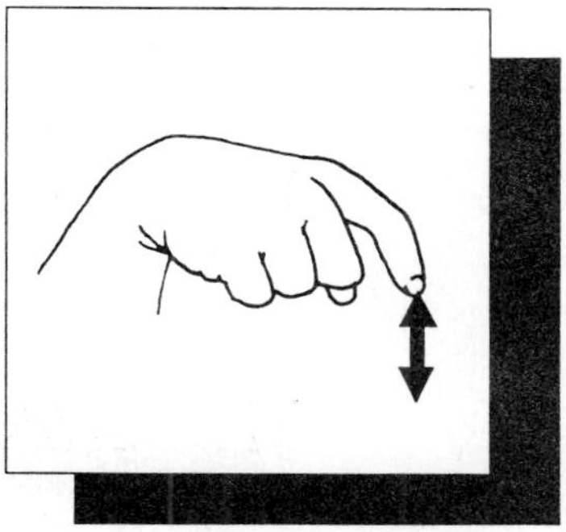

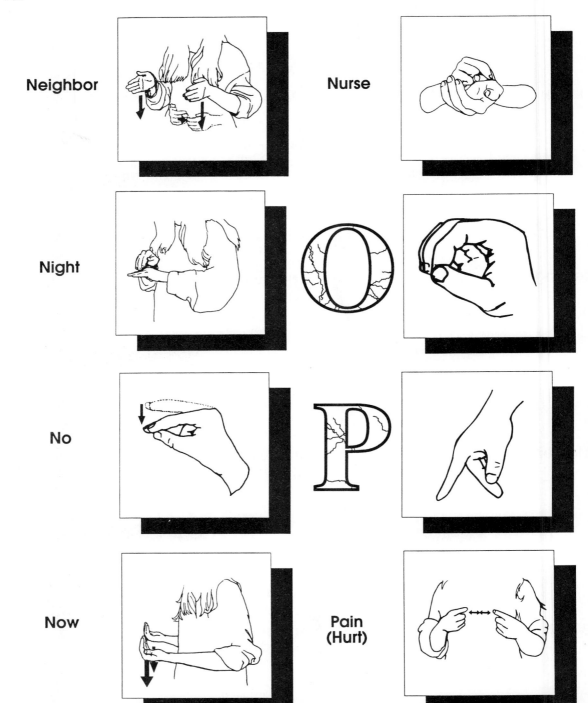

Neighbor

Nurse

Night

O

No

P

Now

Pain (Hurt)

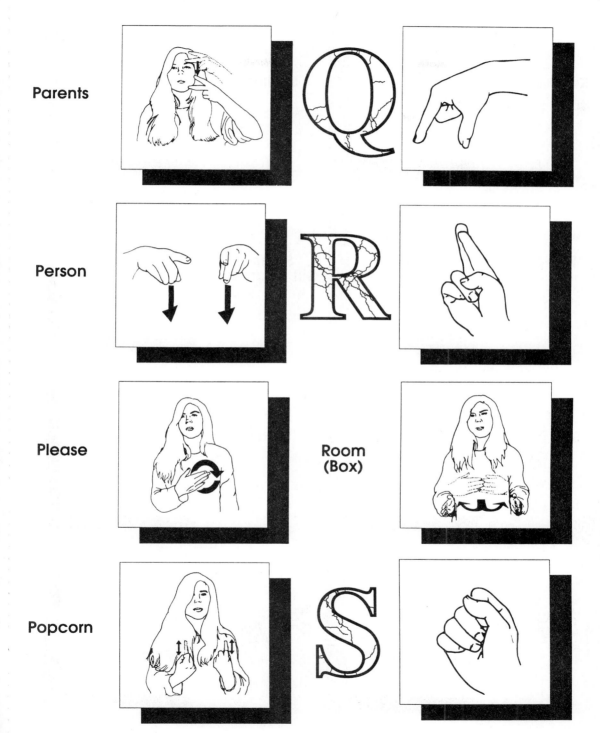

Parents

Person

Please

Room (Box)

Popcorn

362

School
(Two Claps)

Similar

See

Sister
(Girl + Same)

Sick

Small

Sign
(Sign-Language)

Soda
(Soda Pop)

Sorry

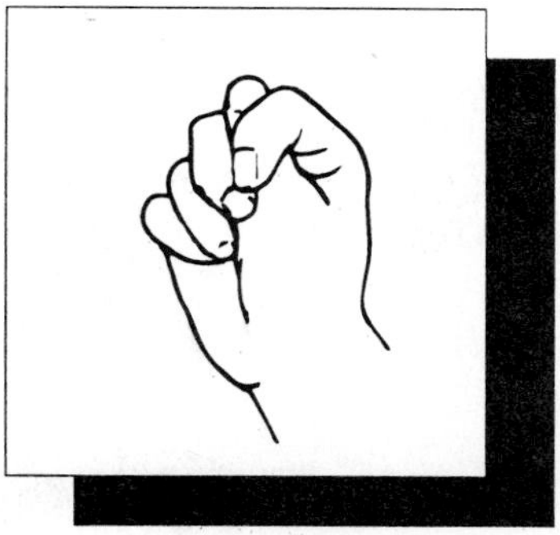

Take

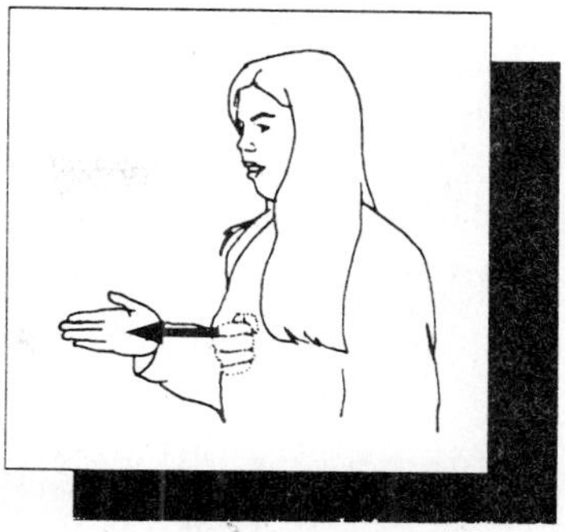

Spaghetti

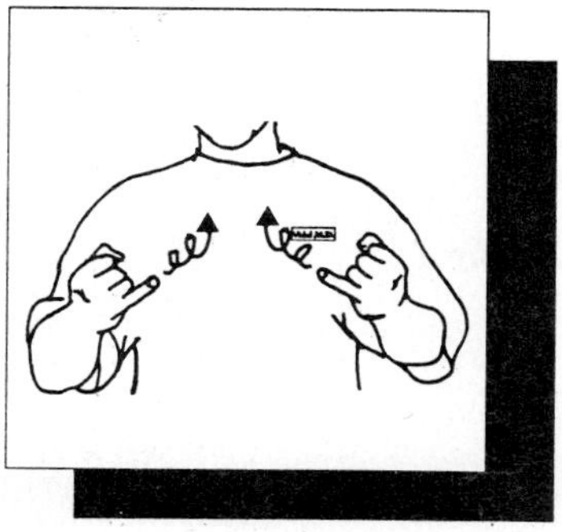

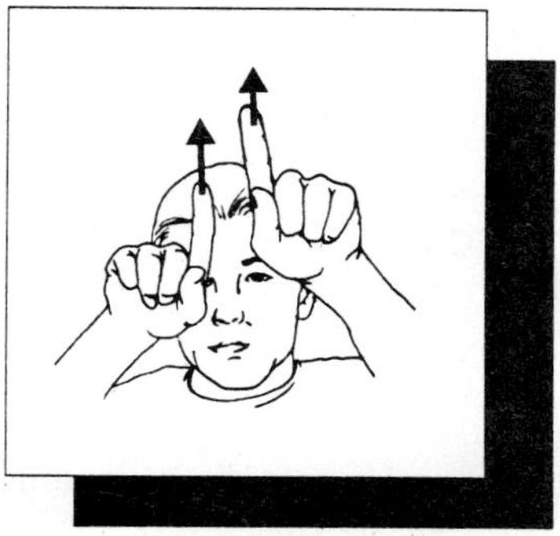

Talk

Star

Tea

T

Team

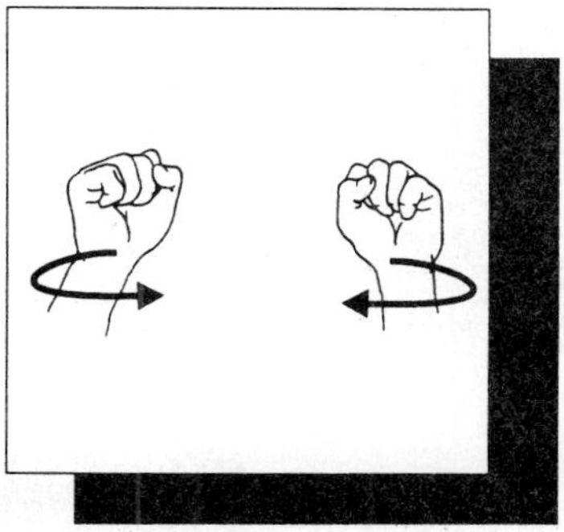

Tell (Speak)

Those

Thank you

Today

Think

Tomorrow

Thirsty

Town

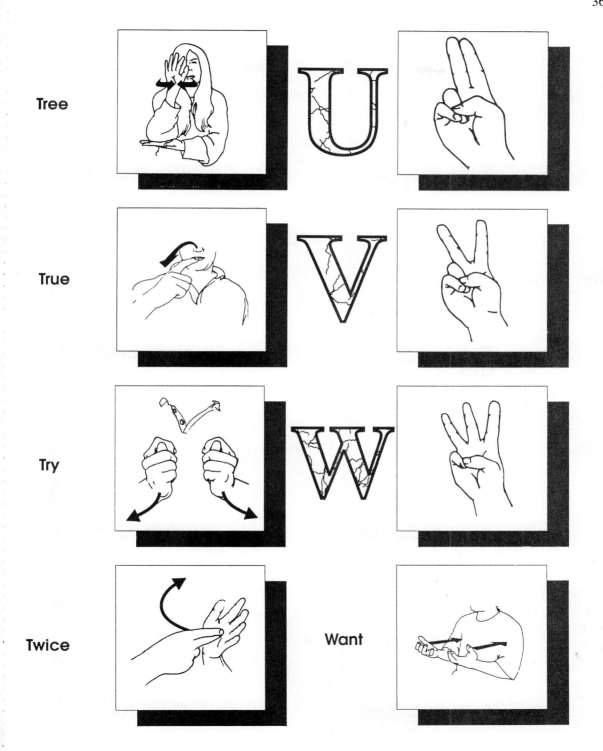

Tree

True

Try

Twice

Want

We

When (2)

Week

Where

What

Whiskey

When (1)

Who

Why

With

Wife

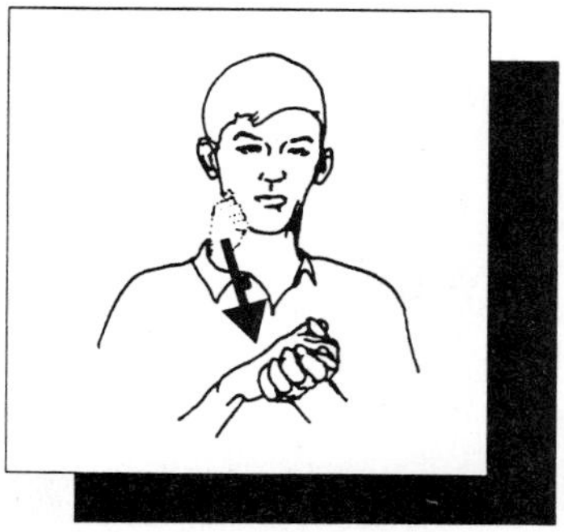

Word

Wine

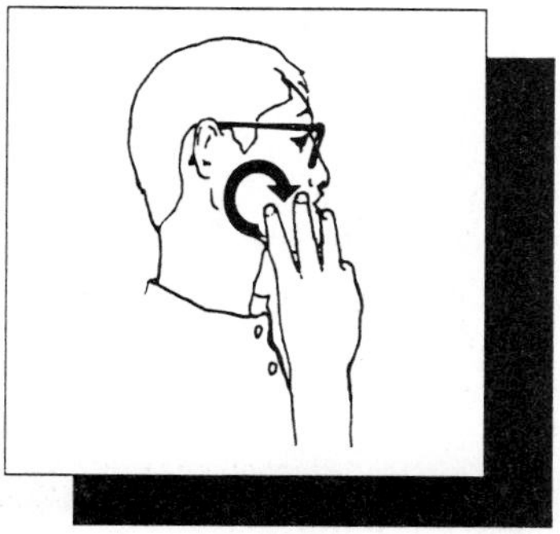

Work

Wisdom

X

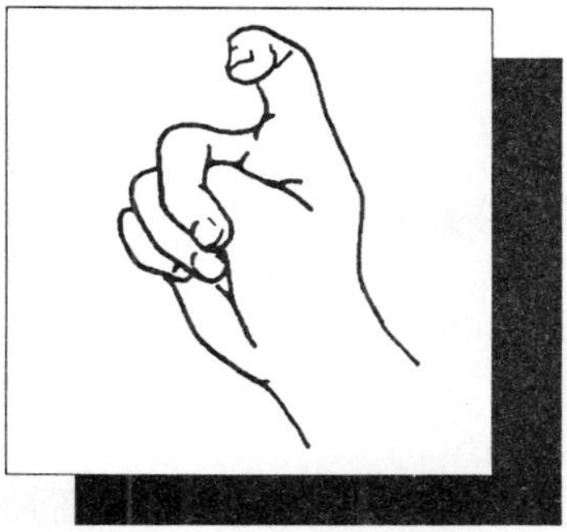

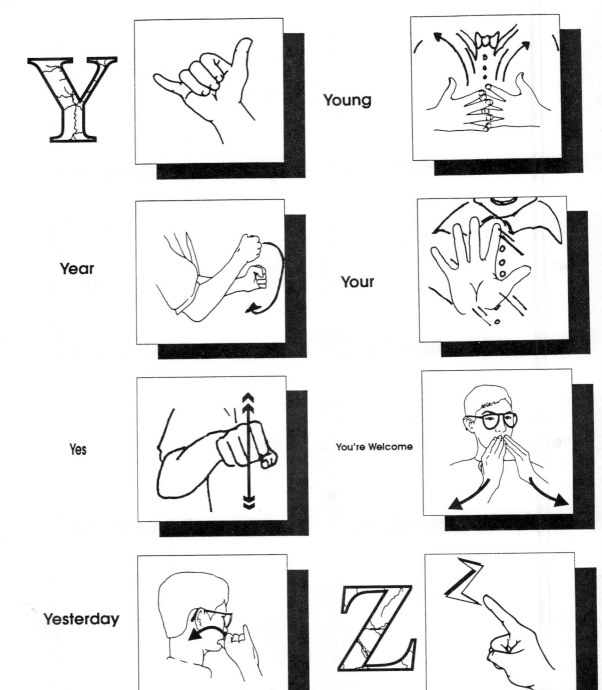

Y

Young

Year

Your

Yes

You're Welcome

Yesterday

Z

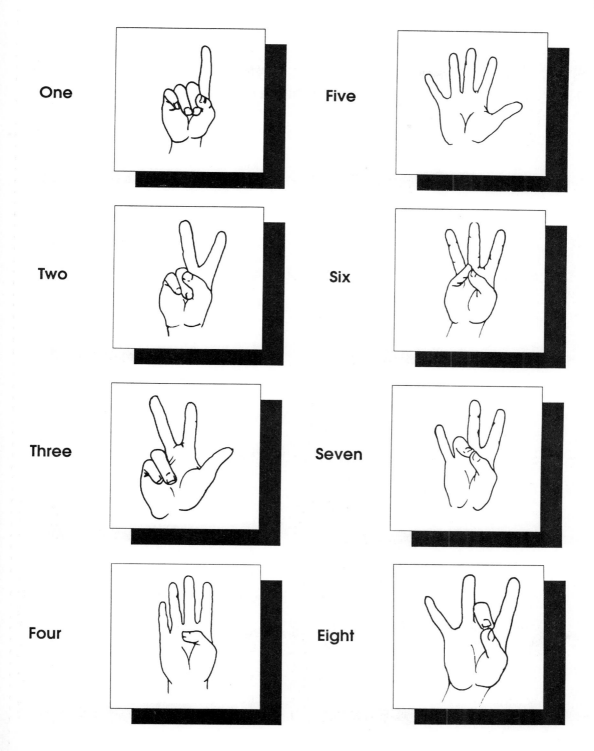

One

Five

Two

Six

Three

Seven

Four

Eight

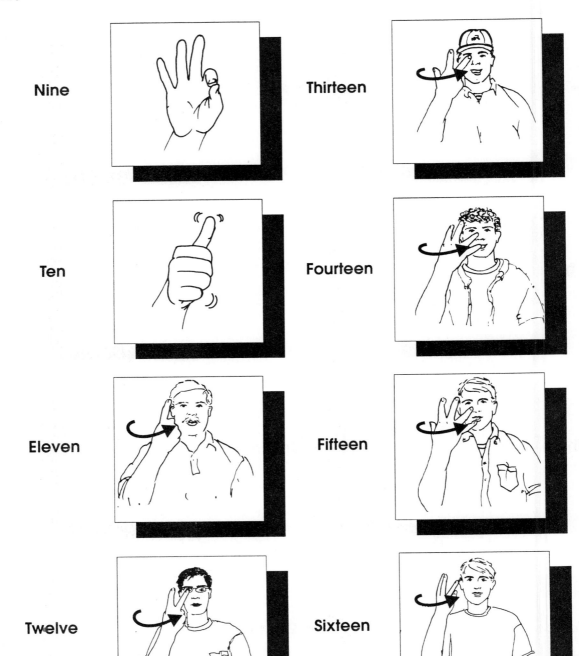

Nine

Ten

Eleven

Twelve

Thirteen

Fourteen

Fifteen

Sixteen

Seventeen

Twenty-One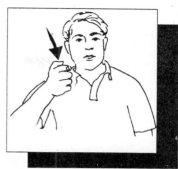

Eighteen

One Hundred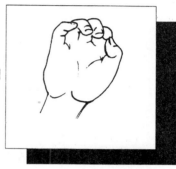

Nineteen

Thousand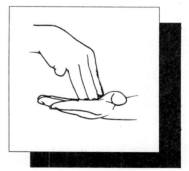

Twenty

Million

Notes

Appendix B

National Diversity Organizations

The following descriptions of the programs and services are derived from information provided by the organizations.

1. Human Diversity

**Resisting Defamation
2530 Berryessa Road, No. 616
San Jose, CA 95132
408-995-0570
408-995-5124 fax
This group works toward eliminating any slander, libel, or crimes against persons from different ethnic groups.

**Unity-and-Diversity World Council
5521 Grosvenor Boulevard, Suite 22
Los Angeles, CA 90066-6915
310-577-1968
213-748-0679 fax
This group provides worldwide coordinating body for cultural, scientific, educational, and religious nonprofit organizations, businesses, and individuals. It fosters "the emergence of a new universal person and civilization based on unity and diversity among all peoples and all life." The Council seeks to aid in establishing a new, worldwide civilization based upon the reality of the whole person by applying the methods and discoveries of modern science coupled with the insights of religion, philosophy, and the arts.

**People to People International
501 E. Armour Boulevard
Kansas City, MO 64109
816-531-4701
816-561-7502 fax

This is a multinational, nongovernmental, nonpolitical corporation of individuals communicating with each other through personal contact, letters and travel. The group promotes international friendship and understanding.

**The Friendship Force
57 Forsythe Street NW, Suite 900
575 S. Tower
Atlanta, GA 30303
404-522-9490
404-688-6148 fax

Regional groups: 250. Members in 42 countries promote understanding in the world through the "force of friendship." A group of citizens is flown to a city in another nation to stay in private homes for an exchange period of approximately two weeks. The goal is to exchange a cross-section from each community, representative of occupation, race, age, and sex.

**Worldwide Friendship International
PO Box 562
3749 Brice Run Road, Suite A
Randallstown, MD 21133
410-922-2795

This group bridges gap among people of all nations through correspondence, so that they can learn each other's culture, language, and values. Membership spans 115 countries and encompasses numerous traditions, creeds, colors, ages, and national origins.

2. The Culture of Diversity

**Institute for World Understanding of Peoples, Cultures and Languages
939 Coast Boulevard, 19DE
La Jolla, CA 92037
619-454-0705

The Institute conducts scientific research in establishing methodology for the comparative study of all populations, cultures, and languages. It also studies world organizations, especially in regard to the future of world civilization.

**American Community Cultural Center Association
19 Foothills Drive
Pompton Plains, NJ 07444
201-835-2661
The Association encourages people in all communities to develop cultural centers for the purpose of presenting cultural possibilities for everyone. regardless of economic status or geographic location.

**Federation of American Cultural and Language Communities
666 11th Street NW, Suite 800
Washington, DC 20001
202-387-0600
This is a coalition of ethnic organizations representing Americans of Armenian, French, German, Hispanic, Hungarian, Italian, Japanese, Sicilian, Ukrainian, and Vietnamese descent. Works to address areas of common interest to America's ethnic communities. The group seeks to further the rights of ethnic Americans, especially their cultural and linguistic rights.

3. The Rights of Diverse People

**American Civil Liberties Union
132 W. 43rd Street
New York, NY 10036
212-944-9800
State Groups: 50. Local Groups: 300. The ACLU champions the rights set forth in the Bill of Rights of the U.S. Constitution: freedom of speech, press, assembly, and religion; due process of law and fair trial; equality before the law regardless of race, color, sexual orientation, national origin, political opinion, or religious belief.

**Section of Individual Rights and Responsibilities
c/o American Bar Association
1800 M Street NW, South Lobby
Washington, DC 20036
202-331-2280
202-331-2220 fax
The Section concentrates on law and public policy as they relate to civil and constitutional rights, civil liberties, and human rights in the United States and internationally. Its projects include representation of the homeless, people with AIDS, and those facing capital sentences.

4. Racial and Ethnic Diversity

**International Committee Against Racism
231 W. 29th Street
Brooklyn, NY 10001
212-629-0003
Regional Groups: 4. State Groups: 30. Local Groups: 28. The Committee is dedicated to fighting all forms of racism and to building a multi-racial society. The group opposes racism in all its economic, social, institutional, and cultural forms and believes racism destroys not only those minorities that are its victims, but all people.

**American Society for Ethnohistory
Department of Sociology and Anthropology
Transylvania University
300 N. Broadway
Lexington, KY 40508
606-233-8147
email: fsbc@music.transy.edu
This Department promotes and encourages original research relating to the cultural history of ethnic groups worldwide.

**National Association for Ethnic Studies
Arizona State University
Department of English
PO Box 870302
Tempe, AZ 85287-0302
602-965-2197
602-965-3451 fax
email: naesi@asuvm.inre.asu.edu
This Association promotes research, study, and curriculum design in the field of ethnic studies, especially Native American, Black, Chicano, Puerto Rican, and Asian American.

5. Gender and Sexual Orientation

**National Organization for Men
11 Park Place
New York, NY 10007
212-686-MALE
212-766-4030
818-791-0578 fax
Regional Groups: 26. Local Groups: 30. The members of this group, men and women, are united in efforts to promote and advance the equal rights of men in matters such as affirmative action programs, alimony, child custody, men's health, child abuse, battered husbands, divorce, educational benefits, military conscription, and veterans' benefits.

**National Congress for Men and Children
851 Minnesota Avenue
PO Box 171675
Kansas City, KS 66117-0675
913-342-3860
913-342-1414 fax
State Groups: 50. Local Groups: 80. This is a coalition of organizations and individuals promoting fathers' rights, men's rights, and equality of the sexes. It advocates the validity of traditional male roles in the family and society.

**National Organization for Women
1000 16th Street NW, Suite 700
Washington, DC 20036
202-331-0066
202-331-9002 (TTY)
State Groups: 50. Local Groups: 800. This organization consists of men and women who support "full equality of women in truly equal partnership with men." The group seeks to end prejudice and discrimination against women in government, industry, the professions, churches, political parties, the judiciary, labor unions, education, science, medicine, law, religion, and other fields.

**National Council of Women of the United States
777 United Nations Plaza
New York, NY 10017
212-697-1278
The Council works for the education, participation, and advancement of women in all areas of society. It serves as an information center and clearinghouse for affiliated women's organizations.

**National Gay and Lesbian Task Force
1734 14th Street NW
Washington, DC 20009-4309
202-332-6483
The Task Force is dedicated to the elimination of prejudice against persons based on their sexual orientation. It assists other associations in working effectively with the homosexual community and engages in direct action for gay freedom and full civil rights.

**National Gay Youth Network
PO Box 846
San Francisco, CA 94101-0846
Regional Groups: 74. State Groups: 80. Local Groups: 94. With gay youth support groups, gay student unions, and other interested groups, this group serves as a networking resource for the exchange of information.

**Renaissance Education Association
PO Box 60552
King of Prussia, PA 19406
610-630-1437
215-630-1437
State chapters: 7. This association provides support and information about gender issues, including crossdressing, transvestism, transsexualism, and other transgender behavior.

**Equal Rights Advocates
1663 Mission Street, Suite 550
San Francisco, CA 94103
415-621-0672
415-621-6744 fax
This is a public interest law center specializing in sex discrimination cases.

6. Religious Diveristy

**National Legal Foundation
6477 College Park Square, Suite 306
Virginia Beach, VA 23464
800-424-4242
804-397-4242
804-420-0855 fax

The Foundation actively litigates in defense of First Amendment liberties, with special focus on religious freedom. It prepares briefs, educational materials, and other publications on church-state issues for lawyers, teachers, and interested individuals.

7. Socioeconomic Diversity

**Coalition for Economic Survival
1296 N. Fairfax Avenue
Los Angeles, CA 90046
213-656-4410

The Coalition addresses the economic concerns of senior citizens and low-income families, especially issues dealing with rent control, tenants' rights, and affordable housing.

**Center for Community Change
1000 Wisconsin Avenue, NW
Washington, DC 20007
202-342-0519
415-982-0346 (San Francisco office)
202-342-1132 fax

The center assists community groups of urban and rural poor in making positive changes in their communities. It focuses attention on national issues dealing with human poverty and works to make government more responsive to the needs of the poor.

8. Physical Diversity

**Council on Size and Weight Discrimination
PO Box 305
Mount Marion, NY 12456
914-679-1209
914-679-1209 fax
The goal of this council is to influence public policy and opinion in order to end oppression based on discriminatory standards of body weight, size, or shape.

**National Association to Advance Fat Acceptance
PO Box 188620
Sacramento, CA 95818
800-442-1214
Local chapters: 60. This association is dedicated to improving the quality of life for people who are fat by working to eliminate discrimination based on body size and provide people who are fat with the tools for self-empowerment through public education, advocacy, and member support. The group disseminates information about the sociological, psychological, legal, medical, and physiological aspects of being fat.

**Little People of America
7238 Piedmont Drive
Dallas, TX 75227-9324
800-24-DWARF
214-388-9576
Regional groups: 12. Local groups: 50. This group provides fellowship, interchange of ideas, moral support, and solutions to unique problems of little people. It aids in the exchange of information on medical treatment, employment, clothing, shoes, and education.

**National Information Center for Children and Youth with Handicaps
PO Box 1492
Washington, DC 22013
202-884-8200 (voice, TDD)
800-695-0285 (voice, TDD)
This center collects and shares information and ideas that are helpful to children and youth with disabilities and to people who care for and about them.

**National Association of the Physically Handicapped, Inc.
1151 N. Niagara
Saginaw, MI 48602
517-799-3060
517-792-4672
This association advances the social, economic, and physical welfare of persons who are physically handicapped in the U.S. and develops awareness of the needs of people who are physically disabled and supports legislation for their benefit.

**Access Unlimited
3535 Briarpark Drive, Suite 102
Houston, TX 77042
713-781-7441
This charitable non-profit special technology organization provides information on computer resources for children or adults with disabilities, their parents, or trainers.

**Administration on Developmental Disabilities
Office of Human Development Services
U.S. Department of Health and Human Services
200 Independence Avenue, SW
Washington, DC 20201
202-690-5504
202-245-2890
This office administers the Developmental Disabilities Assistance and Bill of Rights Act, whose programs and services assist persons with developmental disabilities to achieve independence, productivity, and integration into the community.

**Paralyzed Veterans of America
4330 East-West Highway, Suite 300
Washington, DC 20015
This organization has excellent materials for persons who are wheelchair users.

**Federation for Children with Special Needs
95 Berkeley Street, Suite 014
Boston, MA 02116
617-482-2915
413-562-5521
617-695-2939 fax
This is a coalition of eleven statewide parent organizations that act on behalf of children and adults with a variety of special needs.

**National Alliance of Senior Citizens
1700 18th Street NW, Suite 401
Washington, DC 20009
202-986-0117
The Alliance advocates the advancement of senior Americans. It seeks to inform the American public of the needs of senior citizens and of the programs and policies being carried out by the government.

**National Association of Child Advocates
1625 K Street NW, Suite 510
Washington, DC 20006
202-828-6950
202-828-6956 fax
State organizations: 40. This association works for the safety, security, health and education for all America's children by building and supporting state and community-based independent child advocacy organizations.

**United Nations Children's Fund
3 United Nations Plz.
New York, NY 10017
1-800-FOR-KIDS
212-326-7000
UNICEF works for sustainable human development to ensure the survival, protection, and development of children around the world.

9 - 10. Learning / Intellectual Diversity

**National Association for Gifted Children
1155 15th Street NW, No. 1002
Washington, DC 20005
202-785-4268
State Groups: 50. This association advances interest in programs for children who are gifted. It seeks to further educate those who are gifted and to enhance their potential creativity and Distributes information to teachers and parents on the development of the gifted child.

**American Mensa Limited
1701 W. 3Road Street 1-R
Brooklyn, NY 11223
This is a society for individuals who have established by score in a standard intelligence test that their intelligence is higher than that of 98% of the population.

**National Association for Creative Children and Adults
8080 Springvalley Drive
Cincinnati, OH 45236
513-631-1777
This association is a group of people that meet to share creative ideas and activities.

**American Association on Mental Retardation
1719 Kalorama Road NW
Washington, DC 20009
202-387-1968
800-424-3688
202-387-2193 fax
This is an interdisciplinary association of professionals and individuals concerned about the field of mental retardation. It promotes the well-being of individuals with mental retardation and supports those who work in the field.

**Council for Learning Disabilities
PO Box 40303
Overland Park, KS 66204
913-492-8755
913-492-2546 fax
This council works with individuals who have learning disabilities and aids all LD educators in the exchange of information through publications and conferences.

**Learning Disabilities Association of America
4156 Library Road
Pittsburgh, PA 15234
412-341-1515
412-344-0224 fax
State chapters: 50. Local chapters: 750. This is a national information center and referral services with hundreds of affiliates. It offers a free information packet and publishes a newsletter and journal.

**National Center for Learning Disabilities
99 Park Avenue
New York, NY 10016
This center provides financial support for research on learning disabilities.

11. Health Diversity

**ODPHP National Health Information Center
PO Box 1133
Washington, DC 20013-1133
301-565-4167
800-336-4797
This center aids consumers in locating health information. The group is funded by the Office of Disease Prevention and Health Promotion, Public Health Service, Department of Health and Human Services.

**National Organization for Rare Disorders
100 Rt. 37
PO Box 8923
New Fairfield, CT 06812
203-746-6518
203-746-6481 fax
203-746-6927 (TDD)
This is a clearinghouse for information on over 5,000 little-known disorders affecting some 20 million Americans. It is committed to the identification, treatment, and cure of rare disorders through programs of education, advocacy, research, and service.

**AIDS Hotline
Washington, DC
1-800-342-AIDS
Operated by the Center for Disease Control, this hotline provides current information about AIDS and HIV.

**National Easter Seal Society
2023 W. Ogden Avenue
Chicago, IL 60612
This organization has excellent materials regarding architectural barriers and transportation of persons with disabilities and sponsors camps for family respite care.

**Pathfinder Resources
Midtown Commons, Suite 105
2324 University Avenue West
Street Paul, MN 55114
612-647-6905
This group works to improve the health and well-being of children and adults with chronic health conditions. Pathfinder activities fall into four categories: networking, education, publications, and technical assistance.

**Association for the Care of Children's Health
7910 Woodmont Avenue, Suite 300
Bethesda, MD 20814
301-654-6549
301-986-4553 fax
This association advocates family-centered, psychosocially sound, and developmentally appropriate health care for children. It promotes meaningful collaboration among families and professionals across all disciplines to plan, coordinate, deliver, and evaluate children's health care systems.

**American Cancer Society
1599 Clifton Road NE
Atlanta, GA 30329
800-ACS-2345
This is a nationwide voluntary health organization dedicated to eliminating cancer as a major health problem and preventing cancer, saving the lives of persons with cancer, and diminishing suffering through research, education, and service.

**American Lung Association
1740 Broadway
New York, NY 10019
212-315-8700
800-LUNG-USA
This association is dedicated to the conquest of lung disease and the promotion of lung health.

**Epilepsy Foundation of America
4351 Garden City Drive
Landover, MD 20785
301-459-3700
800-332-1000 (information)
800-332-4050 (library)
301-577-2684 fax
This foundation is dedicated to the well-being of persons with epilepsy. It sponsors research and provides toll-free information to lay and professional inquirers. Local affiliates offer support groups, employment assistance, and other direct services.

**Immune Deficiency Foundation
25 W. Chesapeake Avenue, Suite 206
Towson, MD 21204
410-321-6647
800-296-4499
410-321-9165 fax
This foundation supports research and education for the primary immune deficiency diseases and offers various publications on these diseases.

**Juvenile Diabetes Foundation International
432 Park Avenue South
New York, NY 10016
212-889-7575
800-JDF-CURE
212-725-7259 fax
This is a voluntary health agency founded by parents of diabetic children who were convinced that, through research, diabetes could be cured.

**Muscular Dystrophy Association
810 Seventh Avenue
New York, NY 10019
212-586-0808 fax
This association provides comprehensive patient care throughout its nationwide network of 230 MDA clinics. It also supports an international research program to find the causes and treatments for muscular dystrophy and related neuromuscular diseases.

**National Multiple Sclerosis Society
733 3rd Ave, Sixth Floor
New York, NY 10017
212-986-3240
212-986-7981 fax
This group funds research into causes and cures for multiple sclerosis, provides a variety of publications, and has local chapters throughout the country.

**Tourette Syndrome Association
42-40 Bell Boulevard
Bayside, NY 11361-2861
718-224-2999
718-279-8596 fax
This association is dedicated to identifying the cause, finding the cure, and controlling the effects of TS, a neurological disorder. It provides information, referral, education, direct services, and medical research for people with TS.

12. Communication Diversity

**Voice Foundation
1721 Pine Street
Philadelphia, PA 19103
215-735-7999
215-735-9293 fax
This foundation supports programs of professional education, scientific research, and public information essential to solving vocal problems.

**American Speech-Language-Hearing Association
10801 Rockville Pike
Rockville, MD 20852
800-638-8255
301-897-5700 (Voice or TDD)
This association provides information and referral on a broad range of speech, language, and hearing disorders.

**National Center for Stuttering
200 East 33rd Street
New York, NY 10016
800-221-2483
212-532-1460
This center provides information to parents of children who stutter, offers treatment for children and adults who stutter, and provides training on the latest practices and theories for speech pathologists..

**National Council on Communicative Disorders
10801 Rockville Pike
Rockville, MD 20852
301-897-5700
This is a council of 28 national organizations concerned with speech and language disorders, deafness and hearing impairments.

**The Dyslexia Educational Foundation of America
4181 E. 96th, Suite 215
Indianapolis, IN 46240
317-571-2703
317-571-2704 fax
This foundation provides information about dyslexia, supports exemplary or innovative educational programs, educates the public about dyslexia, and supports efforts to enchance the self worth of persons with dyslexia.

**Orton Dyslexia Society, Inc.
8415 Bellona Ln., Suite 115
Towson, MD 21204
This organization honors Samuel T. Orton, a physician who studied children with language disorders. It combines the interests of both medical and educational professionals interested in dyslexia and language-learning disorders. It sponsors state and local units.

13. Behavior and Personality Diversity

**Autism Reseach Institute
4182 Adams Avenue
San Diego, CA 92116
619-563-6840 fax
The Institute conducts and fosters scientific research into causes and treatments for autism and other behavioral disabilities. It serves as a worldwide information and referral service.

**Autism Society of America
7910 Woodmont Avenue, Suite 650
Bethesda, MD 20814-3015
800-3-AUTISM
301-657-0881
301-657-0869 fax
Local chapters: 160. This is a national umbrella organization serving the needs of autistic citizens of all ages. It provides information and referrals to parents, professionals, and individuals.

**Children with Attention Deficit Disorders (CHADD)
1859 North Pine Island Road, Suite 185
Plantation, FL 33322
This is a national alliance of parent organizations which provides information to parents of children with attention deficit disorders.

14. Sensory Diversity

**Council of Organizations Serving the Deaf
4201 Connecticut Avenue NW
Washington, D.C. 20008
This is a central clearinghouse of materials for persons who are deaf.

**National Institute on Deafness and Other Communication Disorders
Building 31, Room 1B62
900 Rockville Pike
Bethesda, MD 20892
The Institute supports research and training on diseases and disorders affecting hearing and other communication processes, balance, smell, taste, voice, speech, and language.

**Alexander Graham Bell Association for the Deaf
3417 Volta Place NW
Washington, DC 20007
202-337-5220
This association encourages people with hearing impairments to communicate by developing maximal use of residual hearing, speech-writing, and speech and language skills. It also promotes better public understanding of hearing loss in children and adults, and helps oral deaf adults and parents of hearing impaired children.

**National Association of the Deaf
814 Thayer Avenue
Silver Spring, MD 20910-4500
301-587-1788 (voice)
301-587-1789 (TDD)
This is the largest consumer organization of disabled persons in the United States, with more than 22,000 members and 50 affiliated state associations. It serves as an advocate for the millions of deaf and hard-of-hearing people in America.

**American Council of the Blind
1155 15th Street NW, Suite 720
Washington, DC 20005
202-467-5081
The Council advocates legislation for persons who are blind. Priority areas of advocacy include civil rights, social security and supplemental income, national health insurance, rehabilitation, eye research, and technology.

**Association for the Education and Rehabilitation of the Blind and Visually Impaired
206 N. Washington Street, Suite 320
Alexandria, VA 22314
703-548-1884
Regional Groups: 7. State Groups: 44. This is the only professional membership organization dedicated to the advancement of education and rehabilitation of children and adults who are blind and visually impaired.

**International Guiding Eyes, Inc.
5431 Denny Avenue
North Hollywood, CA
This group provides guide dogs for sightless persons, 16 or older, at no coStreet It also provides room and board for training programs.

15. Family Perspectives

**National Council on Family Relations
3989 Central Avenue NE, Suite 550
Minneapolis, MN 55421
612-781-9331
612-781-9348 fax
Regional Groups: 3. State Groups: 41. This is a group of family life professionals, including clergy, counselors, educators, home economists, lawyers, nurses, librarians, physicians, psychologists, social workers, sociologists, and researchers. It seeks to advance marriage and family life through consultation, conferences, and the dissemination of information and research. The group specializes in family health issues, ethnic minorities, and religion and family life.

**Family and Corrections Network
PO Box 2103
Waynesboro, VA 22980
804-977-1028
This network provides information about programs serving families with a member in prison or involved in correctional systems.

**Institute of Marriage and Family Relations
6116 Rolling Road, Suite 306
Springfield, VA 22152
703-569-2400
703-569-7248 fax
Offering professionally staffed diagnostic, treatment, counseling, and education centers, this institute endeavors to assist individuals and families in coping with and working through problems in family life and relationships.

16. Educational Perspectives

**The Council for Exceptional Children
1920 Association Drive
Reston, VA 22091
703-620-3660
800-328-0272
This council advances the quality of education for all exceptional children and improves the conditions under which special educators work. The Council is divided into smaller divisions which address children with behavioral disorders, mental retardation, communication disorders, learning disabilities, physical disabilities, and visual impairments. It also addresses gifted children and culturally and linguistically diverse exceptional learners.

**American Federation of Teachers
555 New Jersey Avenue NW
Washington, DC 20001
800-238-1133
202-879-4400
202-879-4556 fax
Local Groups: 2,200. This federation assists teachers, educational organizations, and community organizations to work effectively with children.

**National Education Association
1201 16th Street NW
Washington, DC 20036
202-833-4000
202-822-7621 fax
State Groups: 53. Local Groups: 12,000. This is a professional organization and union of elementary, secondary, college and university teachers, as well as administrators, principals, counselors, and others concerned with education. Special committees address civil rights, minority affairs, international relations, and women's concerns.

**International Council for Learning Disabilities
PO Box 40303
Overland Park, KS 66204
913-492-8755
This is a professional organization dedicated solely to professionals working with those who are learning disabled and involved in remedial education.

17. Human Diversity in Society

**Unity-and-Diversity World Council
5521 Grosvenor Boulevard, Suite 22
Los Angeles, CA 90066-6915
310-577-1968
213-748-0679 fax

This is a worldwide coordinating body for cultural, scientific, educational, and religious nonprofit organizations, businesses, and individuals. It fosters "the emergence of a new universal person and civilization based on unity and diversity among all peoples and all life." The Council seeks to aid in establishing a new, worldwide civilization based upon the reality of the whole person by applying the methods and discoveries of modern science coupled with the insights of religion, philosophy, and the arts.

Notes

Human Diversity:
A Study Guide

by Craig Conley, B.S., M.A.

This study guide has been designed with three goals in mind:

- to review key points from each chapter and allow you to check your overall comprehension

- to prepare you for objective and subjective examinations by providing sample test questions

- to challenge you to consider some broader implications of your knowledge

Each chapter of this study guide corresponds to a chapter in the textbook. Five sections of exercises will help you to gain a fuller understanding of the concepts you just learned. The first section, entitled **"For Further Consideration,"** builds upon the knowledge you gained from the chapter by encouraging you to determine how the material relates to your life. The **"Terminology"** section will give you the opportunity to review the new terms which were presented in the chapter. Try to define them from memory before looking back to the text for definitions. The **"True/False"** and **"Multiple Choice"** sections examine some more specific concepts from the chapter. You can check your answers to these questions with the Key located at the end of the guide. The final section, **"Essay Practice,"** offers topics designed to prepare you for subjective test questions on the chapter's content.

Notes

Chapter One: Human Diversity

For Further Consideration:

> "No loss by flood and lightning, no destruction of cities and
> temples by hostile forces of nature, has deprived man of so
> many noble lives and impulses as those which his
> intolerance has destroyed."
> —Helen Keller.

Intolerance, Helen Keller suggests, can be the greatest destructive force on earth. Yet where does tolerance begin? Which is more important—the individual or society? The one or the many? Unity or diversity? Ultimately, we must embrace both the individual and the multitude. We must integrate unity and diversity. Diversity has to do with external qualities: human beings are diverse in that they are young and old; black, brown, red, yellow, and white; male and female; gay and straight; Christian, Jew, Buddhist, and Moslem; tall and short; large and small. Unity has to do with a more spiritual condition—the deeper nature of our thoughts and actions. Unity blossoms when we are peaceful, accepting, non-judgmental, and loving to ourselves and others. As we recognize and respect the diverse qualities within ourselves, doors will open to creative relationships that would not be possible otherwise.

Terminology:

Chapter One presents a number of important terms that you should know. Test your knowledge of the following concepts.

1. exceptionality:

2. labels:

3. culture:

4. disability:

5. diversity:

True/False:

Test your knowledge by determining whether these statements are true or false.

1. The expectations that a certain population has upon its members help to define exceptionality.

2. A disability is first and foremost a physical limitation.

3. Every person falls into some category of exceptionality.

4. Labeling may stigmatize a person and contribute to low self-esteem.

5. Labeling allows us to identify, distinguish, and describe people.

6. The expectations of influential people affect the success of exceptional people.

7. Even if you are in a bad mood, when you encounter someone who is different it is best to be pleasant, make eye contact, and smile.

8. When in the presence of a person who is different, you should substitute any possibly offensive vocabulary with less-offensive words.

9. Children should be discouraged from talking directly to people who are diverse about their differences.

Multiple Choice:

Choose the correct answer for each multiple choice question.

1. Why are labels important in our society?
    a. So we can identify people who are different.
    b. To compare the possible achievements of others with our own.
    c. So that professionals can communicate with each other about differences.
    d. Because people have an inherent need to classify and organize individuals within a societal group.

2. When dealing with a person who is different, you should
   a. alter your expectations so you won't embarrass the person.
   b. forget labels and concentrate on the person.
   c. alter your behavior, being careful not to offend.
   d. all of the above.

3. Whom should you not invite to go swimming with you?
   a. a person who is mentally retarded
   b. a person who is legally blind
   c. a person with epilepsy
   d. a person who can't swim

4. If you were the only person on earth not 8 feet tall, what would you prefer to be labeled?
   a. disabled
   b. handicapped
   c. exceptional
   d. vertically challenged

5. If someone has a negative reaction to your association with a person who is different, which of the following should you do?
   a. Say you were talking to a person, not a label.
   b. Say that you always try to be non-judgmental.
   c. Make it clear that you don't have anything in common with the exceptional person.
   d. both a and b.

Essay Practice:

Now examine the issues in more depth by attempting the following essay questions.

1. Why must we continually redefine what constitutes human difference?

2. In what ways does diversity enrich our culture?

3. Discuss the positive and negative effects of labels. Also, suggest reasons why some labels are necessary.

Notes

Chapter Two: The Culture of Diversity

For Further Consideration:

> "People are different. Expect it. Respect it."
> —from the "People Are People" program

While it is important for the diverse individuals of the world to unite, the diverse cultures of these people do not have to be lost in the process. There is an important distinction between cultural unity and cultural *harmony*. Cultural unity means homogenizing all cultures into a single cultural unit. Cultural harmony, on the other hand, means all categories of cultural diversity remain unique but exist in accord with one another. Clearly, it is cultural harmony that we want to achieve. If we expect and respect cultural diversity, cultural harmony will blossom spontaneously.

Terminology:

Chapter Two presents a number of important terms that you should know. Test your knowledge of the following concepts.

1. culture:

2. cultural pluralism:

3. melting pot:

4. ethnocentrism:

5. acculturation:

6. micro-culture:

7. subculture:

8. ideal culture:

9. implicit culture:

True/False:

Test your knowledge by determining whether these statements are true or false.

1. All cultures have a history, but not all have a heritage.

2. Group values are not technically part of a culture.

3. Rules of etiquette are social rather than cultural characteristics.

4. "Real" culture refers to what people say they believe.

5. "Ideal" culture refers to how people think they should behave.

6. Explicit culture can be described verbally.

7. Explicit culture includes religious beliefs.

8. "Acculturation" and "melting pot" refer to the same process.

9. Inter-cultural difficulties arise mainly from communication problems.

10. A micro culture may also be a subculture.

Multiple Choice:

Choose the correct answer for each multiple choice question.

1. Which of the following does implicit culture *not* include?
   a. fears
   b. values
   c. tools
   d. hidden elements

2. Which of the following are aspects of "real" culture?
   a. behaviors
   b. stories
   c. proverbs
   d. jokes

3. The micro-culture seeks to
   a. distinguish itself from the larger political society.
   b. mediate the ideas, values, and institutions of the larger culture.
   c. occupy a subordinate position in society.
   d. none of the above.

4. Every culture is made up of:
   a. emotions
   b. interests
   c. slang expressions
   d. all of the above

5. Explicit culture does *not* include:
   a. fashions of dress
   b. speech
   c. tools
   d. assumptions

Essay Practice:

Now examine the issues in more depth by attempting the following essay questions.

1. The idea of the melting pot is that many cultures can blend into one. Do you believe such a blending is possible? Is such a blending desirable?

2. This chapter has suggested that to destroy diversity is to destroy our own uniqueness. How can this be true?

3. Examine some concrete ways in which cultural diversity strengthens the human race.

Notes

Chapter Three: The Rights of People Who are Diverse

For Further Consideration:

> "The great law of culture is: Let each become all that he
> was created capable of being; expand, if possible, to his full
> growth; resisting all impediments . . . and show himself at
> length in his own shape and stature, be these what they
> may." —Thomas Carlyle, 1827.

We may enact any number of laws, but it is ultimately up to each person, as Thomas Carlyle suggests, to become all that he or she can be. It is individual ideas, expressions, and sharing that generate and fuel our culture. Without the contributions of every member of society, our culture is impoverished. We must continue to work toward securing the full participation in society for each person, regardless of exceptionality. Yet even as we envision a better tomorrow, we can begin changing the world today by improving our individual attitudes and dissolving our particular prejudices. It doesn't require legislation to treat our fellow human beings fairly. And once laws are passed, it takes individuals to see that they are carried out.

Terminology:

Chapter Three presents a number of important terms that you should know. Test your knowledge of the following concepts.

1. equal protection:

2. Job Training and Partnership Act:

3. Older Americans Act of 1965:

4. Rehabilitation Act of 1973:

5. Medicaid:

6. Brown v. Board of Education:

True/False:

Test your knowledge by determining whether these statements are true or false.

1. The Older Americans Act does not focus on employment of senior citizens.

2. No specific number of people is necessary to make up a legal family.

3. The struggle for equal opportunity is finally over.

4. State governments are prohibited from favoring certain groups of people over other groups.

5. Women are still fighting to claim equal rights under the law.

6. Speech impairment is the only category of disability *not* covered by the Rehabilitation Act of 1973.

Multiple Choice:

Choose the correct answer for each multiple choice question.

1. Title VII of the 1964 Civil Rights Act prohibits discrimination on the basis of:
    a. gender
    b. religion
    c. race, color, or national origin
    d. all of the above

2. The Rehabilitation Act of 1973 protects the rights of:
    a. homosexuals
    b. religious institutions
    c. people with health problems or physical impairments
    d. older Americans

3. A "civil rights bill" for individuals with disabilities is the:
    a. Rehabilitation Act of 1973
    b. Education of All Handicapped Children Act of 1975
    c. Americans with Disabilities Act of 1990
    d. Equal Pay Act of 1963

4. The Equal Protection Clause of the 14th Amendment guarantees equal protection under the law for:

    a. the poor

    b. non-citizens

    c. prisoners

    d. all of the above

5. The Equal Protection Clause of the 14th Amendment does *not* guarantee the rights of:

    a. children

    b. minorities

    c. older Americans

    d. none of the above

6. People of different racial and ethnic origins are protected by:

    a. The 14th Amendment

    b. Title VII of the 1964 Civil Rights Act

    c. both a and b

    d. none of the above

7. No well-defined body of law guarantees the rights of:

    a. older Americans

    b. homosexuals

    c. low-income families

    d. both b and c

8. Which of the following terms does not have a precise legal meaning?

    a. family

    b. minority

    c. citizen

    d. religion

Essay Practice:

Now examine the issues in more depth by attempting the following essay questions.

1. Explain how diverse people benefit from laws and legislation. Give examples of specific cases and laws in your response.

2. Why is it important to protect human and civil rights through legislation?

Chapter Four: Racial and Ethnic Diversity

For Further Consideration:

> "It's time for us to turn to each other, not on each other."
> —Jesse Jackson

It would be ideal to say that race doesn't matter, but we do not live in the best of all possible worlds. Realistically, race *does* matter to people and affects their feelings and actions in major ways, every day. There is only one solution to this situation: to redefine the importance we ourselves place on the concept of race. As we reformulate our own attitudes about race—one person at a time— society will start reflecting more enlightened perspectives.

Terminology:

Chapter Four presents a number of important terms that you should know. Test your knowledge of the following concepts.

1. ethnicity:

2. racism:

3. scapegoating:

4. prejudice:

5. minority:

6. discrimination:

7. nationality:

8. bias:

10. stereotyping:

True or False:

Test your knowledge by determining whether these statements are true or false.

1. "Americanization" and "melting pot" refer to the same phenomenon.

2. Ethnicity is primarily a product of perception.

3. Ethnicity and language are not related.

4. The genetic difference between two French women is greater than the difference between a French woman and a Spanish woman.

5. Human races are constantly changing and evolving.

6. There are only five genetically pure races in the world today.

7. There are as many as 2,000 completely distinct races.

8. Humans have always divided themselves into racial categories.

9. The concepts of race and culture are inseparable.

10. The gene that governs racial differences has been isolated by scientists.

Multiple Choice:

Choose the correct answer for each of the following questions.

1. We use racial categories to describe an individual's:
    a. personality
    b. intelligence
    c. character
    d. body build

2. A person's ethnicity has to do with his or her:
   a. race
   b. country of origin
   c. culture
   d. none of the above

3. A personal preference that prevents one from making a fair judgment is called a:
   a. prejudicial attitude
   b. bias
   c. discriminatory practice
   d. none of the above

4. The deliberate policy of blaming an individual or group when the fault actually lies elsewhere is known as:
   a. bigotry
   b. discrimination
   c. scapegoating
   d. bias

5. According to the Census Bureau, a person's race is determined according to his or her:
   a. personal preference
   b. country of origin
   c. parents' genetic stock
   d. parents' country of origin

6. The concept of a "minority" is derived from:
   a. anthropology
   b. sociology
   c. genetics
   d. none of the above

7. The concept of race is derived from:
   a. anthropology
   b. sociology
   c. genetics
   d. none of the above

Essay Practice:

Now examine the issues in more depth by attempting the following essay questions.

1. Some anthropologists suggest that the study of human differences merely serves to perpetuate prejudice. Do you agree or disagree? Why?

2. We pick up racial stereotypes from what we hear other people say, what we read, and what people around us believe. What are some of your own stereotypes, and how did you learn them?

3. When was the last time you heard a racist joke or remark? What was the context? What do you think led the person to make such a remark in the first place? What was your reaction, and why did you react the way you did? Will you react differently in the future? If so, how?

Chapter Five: Gender and Sexual Orientation

For Further Consideration:

> "Tolerance implies no lack of commitment to one's own
> beliefs. Rather it condemns the oppression or persecution
> of others."
> —John F. Kennedy

We might consider that we have conflict today *because* of the opportunity not to go on doing the same old things and thinking in the same old ways. Conflicts create the pressure to change. It is also important to note that good communication may not create agreement. Decide whether you want civility or true understanding of your viewpoint. How much damage to yourself are you willing to risk? You are entitled to respect, but you are not entitled to acceptance of your point of view, necessarily. Here are some pointers for conducting a civil discussion about gender and sexual orientation: Take responsibility for maintaining civil dialogue. Focus on commonalities. Don't tolerate degrading, demeaning, or hurtful attitudes. Don't squelch differences. Don't run away from emotions.

Terminology:

Chapter Five presents a number of important terms that you should know. Test your knowledge of the following concepts.

1. chauvinism:

2. sexism:

3. homosexuality:

4. transvestitism:

5. transsexuality:

6. bisexuality:

7. homophobia:

8. asexual:

9. gender gap:

10. lesbian:

True/False:

Test your knowledge by determining whether these statements are true or false.

1. All people suffer from gender stereotypes.

2. Scientists agree that people are born either heterosexual or homosexual.

3. A person's sexual orientation may change over the course of his or her life.

4. Many gay men and women are married to opposite sex partners and have children.

5. Women who drive trucks or work for the military are likely to be lesbians.

6. Any literature having to do with sexuality is pornography.

7. It is possible to determine someone's sexual orientation by the way he or she dresses, talks, and behaves.

8. Men as well as women are victims of gender inequality.

9. Some sexual orientations are more "normal" than others.

10. Sexual activity and sexual orientation mean the same thing.

Multiple Choice:

Choose the correct answer for each multiple choice question.

1. Which of the following occupations could be typical of a gay man?
    a. truck driver
    b. interior decorator
    c. athlete
    d. all of the above

2. Which of the following issues is a concern of the men's movement?
    a. child custody rights
    b. suicide prevention
    c. homelessness
    d. all of the above

3. The belief that one gender is superior to another is called:
    a. homophobia
    b. sexism
    c. chauvinism
    d. discrimination

4. Which of the following terms is *not* related to sexual orientation:
    a. homosexual
    b. transsexual
    c. transvestite
    d. none of the above

5. Which of the following statements is false?
    a. The majority of the population is strictly heterosexual.
    b. Reproductive rights are only one concern of the women's movement.
    c. It is best to call people what they prefer to be called.
    d. Labeling people promotes divisiveness.

6. Gender identity is formed by:
    a. parents
    b. peers
    c. society
    d. all of the above

Essay Practice:

Now examine the issues in more depth by attempting the following essay questions.

1. Our sexual orientation is invisible unless we choose to reveal it. In what ways do you reveal your sexuality to society? Where do you draw the line on public displays of affection?

2. Within every person, male and female, there exists both feminine and masculine traits. Which aspects of your personality are feminine and which are masculine, and how do both traits combine to make you a complete person?

3. Whether intentionally or not, our culture practices sexual discrimination all the time. Name three examples of discrimination that you have witnessed and propose solutions.

Chapter Six: Religious Diversity

For Further Consideration:

> "In Man, the positive content of religion is the instinctive
> sense–whether conscious or subconscious–of an inner unity
> and continuity with the world around. This is the stuff out
> of which religion is made." —Edward Carpenter

Mutual respect is the key to getting along with people who do not share your faith. Allow each other to express religious beliefs honestly, without fear of rejection. Accept what the other person says. You may not agree with him or her, but you can demonstrate that you accept that person's feelings. You show acceptance through the tone of voice and the words you use. Be a reflective listener. Make eye contact and concentrate on what the other says. Don't feel compelled to respond. Silently listen and make the person feel understood. Be a mirror for that person to see himself or herself more clearly.

Terminology:

Chapter Six presents a number of important terms that you should know. Test your knowledge of the following concepts.

1. Nirvana:

2. animism:

3. Karma:

4. Allah:

5. Yahweh:

6. meditation:

7. reincarnation:

8. Agnosticism:

9. Shamen:

10. Ecumenism:

True/False:

Test your knowledge by determining whether these statements are true or false.

1. All faiths share the same underlying religious impulse.

2. In order to understand another faith, you must believe its doctrines.

3. The *Talmud* collects the wisdom of Hinduism.

4. Judaism, Christianity, and Islam all worship the same God.

5. Judaism, Christianity, and Islam all acknowledge the same prophets.

6. Shinto is the dominant religion in Taiwan.

7. There is no such thing as a Confucian church.

8. An atheist is a skeptic.

9. New Religions are concerned primarily with social order.

10. Witchcraft is an ancient religion.

Multiple Choice:

Choose the correct answer for each multiple choice question.

1. A prophet is a:
    a. teacher
    b. visionary
    c. messenger
    d. all of the above

2. Tribal societies in Australia are typically:
   a. atheist
   b. animist
   c. adventist
   d. none of the above

3. Reincarnation is a belief of:
   a. Sikhism
   b. Buddhism
   c. Hinduism
   d. all of the above

4. Sikhism grew out of:
   a. Confucianism
   b. Jainism
   c. Islam and Hinduism
   d. Confucianism and Animism

5. Taoism teaches people to be:
   a. courageous
   b. inactive
   c. loyal
   d. passionate

6. All religions
   a. answer human questions.
   b. promote national loyalty.
   c. claim to be favored by God.
   d. stress self-discipline.

7. Studying other religions
   a. strengthens your own faith.
   b. helps you to see your faith in a universal context.
   c. improves human relations.
   d. all of the above

8. Which religion did *not* originate in the Middle East?
   a. Baha'i
   b. Sufism
   c. Jainism
   d. Zoroastrianism

Essay Practice:

Now examine the issues in more depth by attempting the following essay questions.

1. Look back at the discussion of major religions and look for similarities. Identify some concepts that most belief systems share.

2. Most world religions teach that we are all part of a larger design. Discuss some ways in which an understanding of this common point could lead to universal brotherhood.

3. Even Atheists are profoundly affected by the world's religions. Discuss how religious belief affects everyone's lives every day.

Chapter Seven: Socioeconomic Perspectives

For Further Consideration:

> When I was young I used to think that money is the most
> important thing in life. Now that I'm older I know that it
> is. –Oscar Wilde

What would you do if you had all the money in the world? When a young child was asked that question, the answer was, "Spend it." That seemed at first to be a childish and simplistic answer, but upon reflection it seems to be the only one. Money is just paper unless it circulates. It is natural to want all the money in the world. We are all entitled to the earth's bounty, and naturally we want to enjoy the freedom and the material comforts that money can buy.

Few of us would want to keep all the money in the world locked away in a safe. It would do nothing for us. It could not bring us pleasure nor could we use it as a tool for making more money. The question, then, becomes: Spend it on what? We can learn a lot about our real priorities by coming up with an honest answer. Will you travel? Give to a particular charity? Support a certain cause? Fund a scholarship in a field of study? Shower gifts on friends and family? Andrew Carnegie established libraries. Rockefeller endowed the arts. Thinking about how you would spend all the money in the world helps you to clarify your idea of money itself. Do you see it as a seed to be sown, a voucher for future security to be hoarded, or as one more element of the universal flow, to be channeled and used and passed along as you follow your life path?

Oscar Wilde was being facetious when he said the line above, but there is an element of truth to it. Try substituting the word "affluence" for money. Being affluent doesn't just mean being rich in dollars. It means being rich in generosity as well. As Dr. Deepak Chopra explains in his book *Creating Affluence,* a truly wealthy person never focuses his or her attention on money alone. Whatever the size of your bank account, if money is all you can think about then you are ultimately impoverished because you never feel satisfied. Allow your kindness, generosity, and good will to flow freely and you will increase affluence in your own life and in the people around you.

Terminology

Chapter Seven presents a number of important terms that you should know. Test your knowledge of the following concepts.

1. poverty:

2. Orshanksy's definition of poverty:

3. socioeconomic status:

4. multigenerational family:

True/False

Test your knowledge by determining whether these statements are true or false.

1. Children comprise most of the nation's poor.

2. Geographic location and income level are generally unrelated.

3. With massive numbers of women entering the workforce, median incomes for young families have increased over the last ten years.

4. The United States has a higher poverty rate than Canada.

5. The cost of living and the annual median income increase in direct proportion.

Multiple Choice:

Choose the correct answer for each multiple choice question.

1. A multigenerational family can help to combat poverty because
    a. multiple incomes pay the rent.
    b. children can care for elderly relatives.
    c. childcare services can be shared.
    d. all of the above

2. Which group is most likely to be plagued by poverty?
    a. Native Americans
    b. Hispanic Americans
    c. women of color
    d. children

3. Which of the following housing problems is most prevalent?
    a. overcrowded conditions
    b. substandard conditions
    c. homelessness
    d. both a and b

4. Which of the following statements about housing is *not* true?
    a. Millions of renters spend at least half of their income on housing.
    b. People of foreign birth generally have a higher unemployment rate than native-born citizens.
    c. People of foreign birth generally have lower per-capita income than native-born citizens.
    d. Employers are becoming more aware of the benefits of hiring workers with disabilities and are more willing to hire them.

5. The number of homeless people in America varies according to:
    a. how homelessness in defined
    b. the method of counting
    c. both a and b
    d. none of the above

Essay Practice:

Now examine the issues in more depth by attempting the following essay questions.

1. Children are the fastest growing segment of the population living under poverty. Identify some of the contributing factors to this situation. How can we ever hope to break out of this tragic cycle?

2. In what specific ways does the multigenerational (or extended) family help to combat some of the difficulties associated with poverty? What are some current societal trends that have contributed to the loss of the multigenerational family?

Chapter Eight: Physical Differences

For Further Consideration:

> "Example is not the main thing in influencing others. It is
> the only thing." —Albert Schweitzer

Most physical differences are quite visible to observers. In other words, you would be more likely to notice visible aspects of people with physical differences than you would be when observing individuals with learning, sensory, sexual orientation, health, religious, or intellectual differences. People with physical differences can, and do, make significant contributions to society. Most people with physical differences would like greater understanding from others and are willing to educate others about their physical differences. In order for this to occur, however, you have to display the desire to learn. Next, you need to interact directly with people with physical differences. You can learn a great deal from their example.

Terminology:

Test your knowledge of the following concepts. Provide a brief definition for each.

1. gigantism:

2. hydrocephalus:

3. Spina bifida:

4. Cerebral palsy:

5. spasticity:

6. dwarfism:

7. paraplegia:

8. dystrophy:

9. Traumatic Brain Injury

True/False:

Test your knowledge by determining whether these statements are true or false.

1. There has as yet been no successful treatment for dwarfism or gigantism.

2. Obesity is clearly caused by an eating disorder.

3. Multiple Sclerosis involves a hardening of the brain tissue.

4. Cerebral palsy does not necessarily affect an individual's intelligence.

5. Paralysis is a common feature of cerebral palsy.

6. Spina bifida literally means "curved spine."

Multiple Choice:

Choose the correct answer for each multiple choice question.

1. Traumatic Brain Injury does *not* apply to which of the following injuries?
   a. birth trauma
   b. external physical force
   c. closed head injuries
   d. none of the above

2. A degeneration of tissue, such as muscles and nerves, is known as:
   a. dystrophy
   b. atrophy
   c. mytonic dystrophy
   d. all of the above

3. Which of the following statements about Muscular Dystrophy is *not* true?
   a. there is no cure
   b. it is a progressive disorder
   c. the disease occurs primarily in females
   d. the outward physical appearance is one of health

4. Paralysis of the legs to a greater extent than the arms is called:
   a. monoplegia
   b. diplegia
   c. paraplegia
   d. hemiplegia

5. Cerebral palsy may include:
   a. spasticity
   b. ataxia
   c. tremors
   d. all of the above

6. Mixed cerebral palsy is a combination of:
   a. atonia and rigidity
   b. ataxia and spasticity
   c. spasticity and athetosis
   d. athetosis and ataxia

7. In addition to causing muscle weakness, spasticity, and balance difficulties, multiple sclerosis can also cause:
   a. visual impairments
   b. immune system deficiencies
   c. pulmonary difficulties
   d. dwarfism

Essay Practice:

Now examine the issues in more depth by attempting the following essay questions.

1. Some types of physical disabilities can be prevented. Identify at least two types and describe measures of prevention.

2. Our society's standards of physical beauty change over time. In the seventeenth century, for example, obesity was the ideal. Identify three ideal physical attributes of today. How are these ideals perpetuated by our society and taught to our children?

Notes

Chapter Nine: Learning Differences

For Further Consideration:

> "Learning is but an adjunct to ourself." —William
> Shakespeare

What we learn and how we learn it, Shakespeare suggests, does not affect or alter our true selves. Yet the area of learning disabilities has generated more controversy, confusion, and polarization among contemporary professions than any other area of exceptionality. Typically, children with learning disabilities have normal intelligence, but they experience academic difficulties, and perhaps social problems as well. Although discrepancies in prevalence estimates exist in all areas of exceptionality, the area of learning disabilities seems more variable than most, and it is one of the largest categories among exceptionalities. It is important to understand the varieties of learning difficulties, but at the same time we should remember Shakespeare's words and not confuse the disability with the person.

Terminology:

Chapter Nine presents a number of important terms that you should know. Test your knowledge of the following concepts.

1. dyslexia:

2. hyperactivity:

3. dyscalculia:

4. dysgraphia:

5. attention deficit disorder:

6. aphasia:

7. learning disability:

True/False:

Test your knowledge by determining whether these statements are true or false.

1. Because a learning disability is invisible, the problem is not as severe as a physical disability.

2. No two people learn in exactly the same way.

3. Most people use technology to augment their learning.

4. Nearly two million adults and children have been identified as having learning disabilities.

5. By definition, an individual with a learning disability has a lower than average I.Q.

6. Learning disabilities frequently inhibit scholastic achievement, but they rarely inhibit social development.

7. Poor motivation has been identified as a key problem with many people diagnosed with learning disabilities.

Multiple Choice:

Choose the correct answer for each multiple choice question.

1. Learning experts estimate that what percent of our population has a learning disability?
   a. 8%
   b. 18%
   c. 28%
   d. 38%

2. Which of the following terms is used by psychologists to describe a learning disability?
   a. perceptual disorder
   b. aphasia
   c. brain injury
   d. specific learning disability

3. Which of the following terms is used by educators to describe a learning disability?
   a. perceptual disorder
   b. dyslexia
   c. brain injury
   d. specific learning disability

4. Which of the following terms is used by speech and language specialists to describe a learning disability?
   a. hyperkinetic disability
   b. dyslexia
   c. brain injury
   d. specific learning disability

5. Which of the following terms is used by doctors to describe a learning disability?
   a. hyperkinetic disability
   b. brain injury
   c. aphasia
   d. specific learning disability

6. Which of the following may be considered a "specific learning disability"?
   a. dyscalculia
   b. dyslexia
   c. both a and b
   d. none of the above

Essay Practice:

Now examine the issues in more depth by attempting the following essay questions.

1. Learning disabilities have been called "invisible handicaps." Explain how the invisibility creates special difficulties and frustrations for both the individual with the disability and those around him or her.

2. Discuss five concrete things you can do to communicate more effectively with an individual with a learning disability.

3. How might you encourage a positive attitude toward the exceptionality of LD among your friends, family, and neighbors?

Chapter Ten: Intellectual Differences

For Further Consideration:

> "Almost all the joyful things of life are outside the measure
> of IQ tests." —Madeleine L'Engle

As with any category of human diversity, there is no one consistent type or profile of people with intellectual differences. The most gifted individuals to people with severe mental retardation span socioeconomic barriers, genders, races, and disabilities. People with either the highest or lowest intellects of any age benefit from special attention. Such attention may be provided in the home, the school, the workplace, and in leisure settings. Societal perceptions, stereotypes, expectations, and interactions affect the degree to which a person who is retarded or gifted may perceive his or her own abilities. As with any exceptionality, the important issue is that everyone is a person, deserving of the same respect and opportunities we would expect for ourselves.

Terminology:

Chapter Ten presents a number of important terms that you should know. Test your knowledge of the following concepts.

1. eugenics:

2. gifted:

3. mental retardation:

4. normalization:

5. amniocentesis:

6. Down syndrome:

7. phenylketonuria:

True/False:

Test your knowledge by determining whether these statements are true or false.

1. Gifted people by definition have advanced intellectual abilities.

2. Persistence is a prominent characteristic of gifted people.

3. People with mental retardation generally need to be institutionalized.

4. Eighty percent of mental retardation has an unknown etiology.

5. In Down syndrome, an accident in cell development results in 47 chromosomes instead of the usual 46.

6. PKU is a hereditary condition.

Multiple Choice:

Choose the correct answer for each multiple choice question.

1. Which of the following is *not* a known cause of mental retardation?
    a. PKU
    b. CVB
    c. toxic agents
    d. Down syndrome

2. Valid assessment of mental retardation considers:
    a. cultural diversity
    b. linguistic diversity
    c. communication differences
    d. all of the above

3. All but one of the following terms names a type of reform in how people treated people with mental retardation and other disabilities. Which term doesn't belong?
    a. Normalization
    b. Deinstitutionalization
    c. Generalization
    d. Mainstreaming

4. It is safe to say that most gifted and talented people
   a. make good judgments.
   b. do not have to work hard in order to succeed.
   c. excel in more than one area.
   d. none of the above

5. The two most commonly used intelligence tests are:
   a. Stanford Binet Intelligence Scale and Weschler Intelligence Scale for Children
   b. Kaufman Assessment Battery and Guilford Model
   c. System of Multicultural Pluralistic Assessment and Guilford Model
   d. Trial and Error Computerized Intelligence Scan and the SDGV Method

Essay Practice:

Now examine the issues in more depth by attempting the following essay questions.

1. What do you think makes an individual gifted? Is giftedness an inherited quality or does one come by it through experience and hard work?

2. There are many misconceptions concerning what people with mental retardation can and cannot do. From your experiences and knowledge, discuss three of these misconceptions and what the truth actually is.

Notes

Chapter Eleven: Challenges Related to Health

For Further Consideration:

> "If you don't have your health, you don't have anything."
> —Anonymous.

Imagine you acquired a serious disease and have only six months left to live. What will you do? How will you spend your time? Will your life have more authenticity for your acknowledging that it is limited? Perhaps you have devoted most of your time to your career. Will you now spend your time at home with your family? Or is your work so compelling and so important that you will continue it to the end? These questions help you to clarify your real priorities.

It is unlikely that most of us would give up our hobbies if our time were limited to six months. If we love painting, we would paint. If we enjoy sailing, we would sail. All those things which enrich our lives and give meaning to them would probably take priority. So why is it that we require a catalyst such as a death sentence to force us to commit to doing what we find most rewarding and enjoyable? We don't have to wait. We can choose to take the risk and embrace life.

Now that you have dealt with the news of your limited life span, consider another scenario. A wonder substance has been discovered. It is being added to water supplies all over the world. After today, the average lifespan is six hundred years. That calendar in your mind suddenly is more than seven times as long as you had previously constructed it. Six hundred years sounds like all the time in the world, doesn't it?

Continue the exercise your started earlier. How does knowing that you will live six hundred years affect your life choices? Where will you invest your energy, knowing that you have so much more than you'd imagined? Which endeavors seem relevant over this long term? Does your stake in the world seem different? Is your interest in the environment increased? What books do you now feel you have time to read? What good deeds do you have time to perform for your neighbor now that the pressures of time have been lifted? Will you do nothing, feeling that there's no hurry? Or will you soon adjust your mind so that six hundred years seems short?

Terminology:

Chapter Eleven presents a number of important terms that you should know. Test your knowledge of the following concepts.

1. AIDS:

2. epilepsy:

3. asthma:

4. diabetes:

5. leukemia:

6. HIV:

True/False:

Test your knowledge by determining whether these statements are true or false.

1. The percentage of men and women who smoke is steadily declining.

2. Slight to moderate alcohol consumption will not harm unborn babies.

3. Practicing safe sex prevents the spread of AIDS.

4. Practicing safe sex merely reduces the spread of AIDS.

5. By definition, diabetes involves an insulin dependency.

6. Tuberculosis is a communicable disease.

7. When a person has a seizure, it is important to call for medical assistance immediately.

Multiple Choice:

Choose the correct answer for each multiple choice question.

1. Which of the following diseases may be treated with a bone-marrow transplant?
   a. nephritis
   b. leukemia
   c. sickle-cell anemia
   d. hemophilia

2. AIDS is viral in nature and acts by attacking and weakening the body's:
   a. immune system
   b. reproductive system
   c. neurological system
   d. glandular system

3. Health impairments that are treatable but incurable are called:
   a. acute
   b. extended
   c. chronic
   d. orthopedic

4. "Petit mal" is related to:
   a. rheumatic fever
   b. tuberculosis
   c. epilepsy
   d. none of the above

5. Which of the following would be most typical of a psychomotor seizure?
   a. uncontrolled jumping
   b. a temporary loss of consciousness
   c. a blank stare
   d. dizziness

6. Which of the following is considered to be a safe sexual activity:
   a. oral sex
   b. vaginal intercourse
   c. anal intercourse
   d. masturbation

Essay Practice:

Now examine the issues in more depth by attempting the following essay questions.

1. Recall what you know about AIDS. Discuss prevention activities and myths.

2. What guidelines would you suggest for interacting with people who are health impaired? Use examples of different types of health problems in your response.

Chapter Twelve: Communication Diversity

For Further Consideration:

> "Though we cannot think alike, may we not love alike?
> May we not be of one heart though we are not of one
> opinion?" —John Wesley

We take our language and our customs for granted, and it's easy to unconsciously feel that ours is the "only way." But such an attitude is a hindrance to good communication amongpeople of different languages and cultures. When you encounter strangers who appear to offer a barrier to communication, such as a physical disability or an unfamiliar language, it often seems that there is an invisible wall around them. However, if your desire or need to communicate is great enough (e.g., if you are lost or need a phone or restroom and must ask for help) you will see that on some level you can and do connect. If you make this effort you will always be rewarded. You will learn something new about another or about yourself. You cannot fail to be richer when you connect with a fellow human being.

Terminology:

Chapter Twelve presents a number of important terms that you should know. Test your knowledge of the following concepts.

1. communication:

2. laryngectomy:

3. muteness:

4. illiteracy:

5. dyslexia:

6. aphasia:

7. articulation:

8. stuttering:

9. cleft palate:

10. body language:

True/False:

Test your knowledge by determining whether these statements are true or false.

1. Language and culture are inseparable.

2. Dance is a primary means of storytelling in many countries.

3. Primitive societies frequently have simple languages.

4. Aphasia is usually caused by brain damage.

5. Illiteracy is the result of a congenital abnormality.

6. More people speak Mandarin than speak English and Spanish combined.

7. Touching is an important form of communication in all countries.

8. Esperanto is accepted as the international language.

9. Hesitant speech indicates a slowness of thought.

10. Language is a major cause of failed communication.

Multiple Choice:

Choose the correct answer for each multiple choice question.

1. Language allows us to:
    a. share ideas
    b. transmit culture
    c. organize society
    d. all of the above

2. A system of body language which interprets sound through movement is:
    a. eurhythmy
    b. Esperanto
    c. aphasia
    d. none of the above

3. Stuttering is a disorder of:
    a. articulation
    b. fluency
    c. vocality
    d. none of the above

4. Speaking slowly is recommended for communicating with:
    a. speakers of foreign languages
    b. illiterates
    c. people with dyslexia
    d. all of the above

5. Nonverbal communication includes:
    a. folklore
    b. pantomime
    c. intonation
    d. all of the above

6. Facial expressions can communicate:
    a. feelings
    b. attitudes
    c. emotions
    d. all of the above

7. Studying other languages
    a. enriches your understanding of human nature.
    b. helps you to see your culture in a universal context.
    c. improves human relations.
    d. all of the above

8. Language disorders
    a. are usually due to physical abnormalities.
    b. prevent understanding.
    c. frequently draw attention to themselves.
    d. all of the above

Essay Practice:

Now examine the issues in more depth by attempting the following essay questions.

1. Assume that you are a foreigner in a country with a different alphabet. Trying to decipher road signs would be quite a challenge. What are some other frustrating situations in which you may find yourself?

2. It has been suggested that learning another language teaches you how other people think. How is this so? Explain this concept based upon either your own foreign language study or the experience of someone you know who is bilingual.

3. Consider the ways in which the ability to communicate means survival, both from a daily, personal perspective and from a worldwide, humanitarian perspective.

Chapter Thirteen: Behavior and Personality

For Further Consideration:

> "My son still does some bizarre things, but now that I know
> he has a behavior disorder, I don't go into a panic anymore.
> I simply address the problem behavior with him, and my
> family lives from crisis to crisis." –Anonymous.

Among the categories of human diversity, children and adults with behavior and personality disorders are perhaps the most misunderstood. Despite progress in many areas, the education, treatment, and integration of such persons into communities remain subject to debate among parents, community members, legislators, and educators. There is no denying that a small percentage of people who have behavior and personality disorders act in ways that are extremely offensive, even to the most tolerant among us. It is important to keep in mind, however, that this is true of a very small percentage of the population, and frequent interaction with such individuals is not likely. Proceed as naturally as possible.

Terminology:

Chapter Thirteen presents a number of important terms that you should know. Test your knowledge of the following concepts.

1. schizophrenia:

2. phobia:

3. bulimia:

4. ADD:

5. obsessive-compulsive disorder:

6. depression:

7. autism:

True/False:

Test your knowledge by determining whether these statements are true or false.

1. Everyone who has an emotional outburst or becomes hostile and aggressive at times has a behavior disorder.

2. The most disabling behavior disorder is considered to be psychosis.

3. A disturbance in thinking patterns is known as schizophrenia.

4. Bipolar depression involves mood swings.

5. Allergies or food intolerances may create symptoms similar to ADD.

6. Depressant medications are used to treat overactive people.

7. Anorexia and bulimia are two names for the same disorder.

8. Fear of heights is classified as an obsessive-compulsive disorder.

9. A compulsion is an intrusive thought.

Multiple Choice:

Choose the correct answer for each multiple choice question.

1. A psychotic breakdown is characterized by a radical change in:
    a. consciousness
    b. perception
    c. social behavior
    d. all of the above

2. People with schizophrenia typically experience:
    a. multiple personalities
    b. hallucinations
    c. phobic disorders
    d. significant weight loss

3. Obsessive-compulsive disorder is characterized by:
    a. repetitive acts
    b. impulsivity
    c. poor appetite
    d. all of the above

4. Behavior changes such as high-to-low mood swings may indicate:
    a. obsessive-compulsive disorder
    b. suicidal tendencies
    c. bipolar depression
    d. both b and c

5. Which of the following symptoms is most associated with anorexia?
    a. uncontrolled ingestion of food
    b. vigorous exercise
    c. weight loss to body weight 25% below average
    d. self-induced vomiting

6. Persons with emotional and behavioral problems may
    a. be severely antisocial and disruptive.
    b. show signs of severe anxiety or depression.
    c. vacillate between extremes of withdrawal and aggression.
    d. all of the above

7. Approximately what percent of children and adolescents exhibit emotional or behavioral problems?
    a. 10
    b. 8
    c. 6
    d. 4

Essay Practice:

Now examine the issues in more depth by attempting the following essay questions.

1. Define some common characteristics of behavior disorders.

2. What are the warning signs of suicide and how can one help a person who is considering suicide?

Chapter Fourteen: Sensory Differences

For Further Consideration:

> "The responsibility for tolerance lies in those who have the
> wider vision." —George Eliot

George Eliot uses the word *vision* to mean *insight, foresight,* and *perspective.* When we have a broad perspective, we are equipped to incorporate tolerance into our daily lives. People who do not have hearing or visual disorders often have misconceptions about those who do, including beliefs that deafness and blindness lead to a life of deprived socioeconomic and cultural existence. Granted, deafness and blindness sometimes create social isolation. However, people with hearing and vision loss are generally capable of learning basic skills and enjoying leisure time and recreational activities. In reality, deafness and blindness do not hinder one from leading a successful and independent life.

Terminology:

Chapter Fourteen presents a number of important terms that you should know. Test your knowledge of the following concepts. Some of the terms may be similar, but each has a particular definition.

1. deafness:

2. tinnitus:

3. TDD:

4. legal blindness:

5. tunnel vision:

6. hard of hearing:

7. low vision:

8. hearing impaired:

9. visually impaired:

10. partially sighted:

True/False:

Test your knowledge by determining whether these statements are true or false.

1. What hearing entails depends upon the context, the listener, and the tools he or she uses.

2. Much of what we call vision is totally subjective.

3. No one can escape the world of sound.

4. Blindness is usually correctable.

5. A radio telescope is a hearing aid.

6. A light bulb does not qualify as a visual aid.

7. Vision is the most important sense for social interactions.

8. Of all the senses, hearing is the most flexible.

9. Vision allows us to assimilate knowledge.

10. Blindness by definition limits what information an individual can obtain.

Multiple Choice:

Choose the correct answer for each multiple choice question.

1. We may extend our field of vision using:
    a. radio telescopes
    b. TDDs
    c. X-rays
    d. electronic cochlear implants

2. What percent of the population is considered legally blind?
   a. .1%
   b. 1%
   c. 10%
   d. 20%

3. A person with profound hearing loss may be able to hear:
   a. loud environmental sounds
   b. loud voices
   c. both a and b
   d. none of the above

4. Sound waves are collected by the:
   a. auditory canal
   b. eardrum
   c. outer ear
   d. cochlea

5. Light is initially captured by the:
   a. retina
   b. optic nerve
   c. cornea
   d. pupil

6. The term *visually impaired* may include individuals with:
   a. partial sight
   b. complete loss of sight
   c. prenatal blindness
   d. all of the above

7. The term *hearing impairment* may include:
   a. mild to moderate loss
   b. moderate to severe loss
   c. severe to profound loss
   d. all of the above

8. If a totally blind person is exposed to bright light, it will affect his or her:
   a. moods
   b. hormones
   c. both a and b
   d. none of the above

9. Which of the following is *not* an element of blind culture?
   a. getting someone's attention
   b. leave-taking
   c. introducing oneself
   d. none of the above

Essay Practice:

Now examine the issues in more depth by attempting the following essay questions.

1. Why are prevalence figures for people who are visually impaired hard to determine?

2. Discuss proper actions and behaviors when interacting with a person with a hearing disability.

3. Discuss proper actions and behaviors when interacting with a person with a visual disability.

Chapter Fifteen: Family Perspectives

For Further Consideration:

> "The family only represents one aspect, however important
> an aspect, of a human being's functions and activities... A
> life is beautiful and ideal, or the reverse, only when we
> have taken into our consideration the social as well as the
> family relationship." —Havelock Ellis

The vital functions that families provide for their members are complex. They aren't things that one can summarize into a tidy list and post on the refrigerator door. Intricate and subtle connections, interactions, involvements, and interrelations take place which help all the members to develop and thrive. Just as it is important for parents to support their children, it is equally important for parents to receive assistance, encouragement, admiration, respect, and affection from other adults in the home or from nearby relatives, friends, or neighbors. As Havelock Ellis suggests in the quotation above, the quality of an individual's life is equally tied to family dynamics and to social interactions beyond the family.

Terminology:

Chapter Fifteen presents a number of important terms that you should know. Test your knowledge of the following concepts.

1. nuclear family:

2. circle of friends:

3. extended family:

4. blended family:

5. latchkey children:

6. physical abuse:

7. emotional abuse:

True/False:

Test your knowledge by determining whether these statements are true or false.

1. Reports of child abuse indicate physical injury and neglect in about equal proportion.

2. Emotional abuse may include abandonment.

3. Emotional abuse may involve malnourishment.

4. Verbal degradation is classified under physical abuse.

5. The number of step families today is a new phenomenon in American history, linked to high divorce rates.

6. No family can escape having members who fit some category of exceptionality.

Multiple Choice:

Choose the correct answer for each multiple choice question.

1. Which of the following does not qualify as a "normal" family?
     a. single-parent household
     b. reconstituted family
     c. blended family
     d. none of the above

2. Which of the following families is most likely to be happy and successful?
     a. nuclear family
     b. extended family
     c. step family
     d. none of the above

3. Which of the following constitutes an "ideal" family?
     a. father, mother, two children
     b. grandparents and other relatives living at home
     c. support system of friends and neighbors
     d. opinions vary according to individual beliefs, societal trends, and cultural traditions

4. The process of accepting an exceptional family member may involve:
   a. denial, guilt, anger
   b. adjustment, education, acceptance
   c. both a and b
   d. none of the above

5. Which circumstance is most likely to lead to child abuse?
   a. single parent household
   b. low income
   c. marital discord
   d. all of the above

Essay Practice:

Now examine the issues in more depth by attempting the following essay questions.

1. Do you consider the "latchkey" phenomenon to be a form of child abuse? Discuss both the reasons it might qualify as abuse and the reasons it might not quality. Suggest possible solutions to the latchkey phenomenon.

2. "The experience of diversity among those whom we love best motivates us to give up our fear and to move forward." Do you agree with this statement? Why or why not?

3. The number of single-parent families has soared in recent years. Since this is a trend that isn't likely to go away overnight, what are some specific things society can do to help ease the difficulties of single-family life?

Notes

Chapter Sixteen: Educational Perspectives

For Further Consideration:

"Education is not just another consumer item. It is the bedrock of our democracy." —Mary Hatwood Futrell

Human beings have an innate thirst for knowledge. It is through education that we cultivate our minds to enable us to accomplish all we would like to accomplish in life. Education enables us to make full use of our potential. All around the world, educational systems and curricula are being reformed to accommodate new trends in society. Whether one is entirely self-taught or attends public, private, or parochial schools, the goal of education should be to fully develop an individual into a responsible citizen of the world. Such a citizen understands and appreciates the full range of human thought, recognizing that truth and knowledge may take many different forms and may be approached from a multiplicity of perspectives.

Terminology:

Chapter Sixteen presents a number of important terms that you should know. Test your knowledge of the following concepts.

1. risk factors:

2. public schooling:

3. home schooling:

4. parochial schooling:

5. special education:

6. handicapped:

7. assistive technology:

8. Individualized Education Plan:

9. zero reject:

10. mainstreaming:

11. integration:

12. inclusion:

True/False:

Test your knowledge by determining whether these statements are true or false.

1. Students with two or more risk factors are six times as likely to drop out of high school.

2. A private school offers an environment which is likely to be culturally and racially diverse.

3. Children taught at home by their parents are likely to score below average on achievement tests.

4. Special education is designed to help students achieve personal self-sufficiency and academic success.

5. Persons with severe allergies do not qualify for "handicapped" status.

6. According to Public Law 94-142, children and youth with disabilities should rarely be placed in general education classes so that their special needs may be fully addressed.

7. Students have more needs in common than they have differences.

Multiple Choice:

Choose the correct answer for each multiple choice question.

1. A child's individualized education plan is designed by:
    a. the child
    b. the parent or guardian
    c. the teacher
    d. all of the above

2. The concept that children and youth with disabilities should be educated alongside nondisabled students to the maximum extend possible is known as:
    a. nondiscriminatory evaluation
    b. least restrictive environment
    c. due process
    d. zero reject

3. Which type of schooling specializes in offering social interaction with a broad range of students?
    a. public
    b. private
    c. parochial
    d. alternative

4. Which type of schooling specializes in offering flexible schedules and intensive studies?
    a. public
    b. private
    c. parochial
    d. alternative

5. Which type of schooling is based upon an individual or traditional learning philosophy?
    a. public
    b. private/parochial
    c. special
    d. alternative

6. Which type of schooling is best?
   a. public
   b. private/parochial
   c. alternative
   d. depends upon the individual

Essay Practice:

Now examine the issues in more depth by attempting the following essay questions.

1. Identify some modern risk factors in students' lives. How do the daily problems that children are confronted with outside of school directly affect their academic performance? What hope, if any, is there of significantly reducing such problems?

2. Choose a current controversial issue in education and suggest reasons it has come under fire.

3. Special accommodations allow students with disabilities the same access to their educational activities as nondisabled students. Identify five such accommodations and their uses.

4. How is a child initially assessed for special education? Outline and discuss the steps educators follow to determine a child's placement.

Chapter Seventeen: Human Diversity in Society

For Further Consideration:

> "How wonderful it is that nobody need wait a single moment
> before starting to improve the world." —Anne Frank

As you end your study of exceptional people, here is a final challenge. You are now educated about the varieties of human diversity, and you will notice that many of your friends, family members, and fellow members of society are still uninformed about diversity. Your challenge is to avoid letting your ego rule your actions. It is easy to feel superior to people whose comfort level differs from yours, or whose attitudes seem less enlightened than yours. Show *everyone* the same compassion and understanding. Remember that we are *all* exceptional people. We are all at different stages of development, yet everyone is learning every day. Teach others by your own example, and always be aware of practicing respect.

Essay Practice:

Since the material in the final chapter encourages you to look at broader issues, there will only be essay practice questions here.

1. Assume that your best friend has a negative attitude toward diverse individuals. What specific guidelines can you practice to assist your friend in improving his or her attitude?

2. Imagine that all of humanity is a giant diamond. In order to see the whole diamond, you must look at each individual facet. Each facet shines in its own unique way, and all contribute to the sparkle of the whole. Any discussion of human diversity is by definition complicated because in order to explain the underlying human similarity we must use potentially divisive terms. In other words, we must look at the individual facets to examine the whole. Do you think this textbook has successfully examined the whole diamond, or does it focus too much on the individual facets? Discuss your thoughts.

3. The phrase "your comfort level" has come up frequently throughout this textbook. Describe your comfort level at the beginning of this course and compare it to your current comfort level. How have you changed? What prejudices, if any, have you dispelled?

Notes

Study Guide Answer Key

Chapter 1:
Human Diversity

1. T	1. c
2. F	2. b
3. T	3. d
4. T	4. any
5. T	5. d
6. T	
7. F	
8. F	
9. F	

Chapter 2:
The Culture of Diversity

1. F	1. c
2. F	2. a
3. F	3. b
4. F	4. d
5. T	5. d
6. T	
7. F	
8. F	
9. T	
10. T	

Chapter 3:
The Rights of People who are Diverse

1. F	1. d
2. T	2. c
3. F	3. c
4. T	4. d
5. T	5. d
6. F	6. c
	7. b
	8. a

Chapter 4:
Racial and Ethnic Diversity

1. T	1. d
2. T	2. c
3. F	3. b
4. T	4. c
5. T	5. a
6. F	6. b
7. F	7. a
8. F	
9. F	
10. F	

Chapter 5:
Gender and Sexual Orientation

1. T	1. d
2. F	2. d
3. T	3. c
4. T	4. b
5. F	5. a
6. F	6. d
7. F	
8. T	
9. F	
10. F	

Chapter 6:
Religious Diversity

1. T	1. d
2. F	2. b
3. F	3. d
4. T	4. c
5. F	5. b
6. F	6. a
7. T	7. d
8. F	8. c
9. T	
10. T	

Chapter 7:
Socioeconomic Perspectives

1. T	1. d
2. F	2. d
3. F	3. d
4. F	4. c
5. F	5. c

Chapter 8:
Physical Differences

1. F	1. a
2. F	2. d
4. T	3. c
5. T	4. b
6. F	5. d
7. F	6. c
	7. a

Chapter 9:
Learning Differences

1. F	1. c
2. T	2. a
3. T	3. d
4. F	4. b
5. F	5. b
6. F	6. c
7. T	

Chapter 10:
Intellectual Differences

1. F	1. b
2. T	2. d
3. F	3. c
4. T	4. d
5. T	5. a
6. T	

Chapter 11:
Challenges Related to Health

1. F	1. b
2. F	2. a
3. F	3. c
4. T	4. c
5. F	5. a
6. T	6. d
7. F	

Chapter 12:
Communication Diversity

1. T	1. d
2. T	2. a
3. F	3. b
4. T	4. a
5. F	5. b
6. T	6. d
7. F	7. d
8. F	8. c
9. F	
10. T	

Chapter 13:
Behavior and Personality

1. F	1. d
2. T	2. b
3. T	3. a
4. T	4. d
5. T	5. c
6. F	6. d
7. F	7. a
8. F	
9. F	

Chapter 14:
Sensory Differences

1. T	1. c
2. T	2. a
3. T	3. a
4. F	4. c
5. T	5. a
6. F	6. d
7. F	7. d
8. T	8. c
9. T	9. d
10. F	

Chapter 15:
Family Perspectives

1. T	1. d
2. T	2. d
3. F	3. d
4. F	4. c
5. F	5. c
6. T	

Chapter 16:
Educational Perspectives

1. T	1. d
2. F	2. b
3. F	3. a
4. T	4. d
5. F	5. b
6. F	6. d
7. T	

Notes

<u>Our Policy</u>

We respect human diversity and provide equal opportunity
and treatment regardless of race, sex, disability, religion,
sexual orientation, age, size, or other irrelevant criteria.

S.S., B.K., C.C.